INDONESIA
AFTER SUKARNO

INDONESIA AFTER SUKARNO

Justus M. van der Kroef

UNIVERSITY OF BRITISH COLUMBIA PRESS
Vancouver

published 1971
by University of British Columbia Press
Vancouver 8, Canada
available in North America only
ISBN 0-7748-0011-9
published in Singapore
by Asia Pacific Press Pte Ltd as
"Indonesia Since Sukarno"

printed in Singapore

Contents

Preface

THE ABORTIVE COUP of 30 September 1965 in various parts of
Java, and the subsequently accelerating fall from power of President Sukarno, form a major turning point in the modern history
of Southeast Asia. Indonesia's seemingly steady drift toward
Communist ascendancy at home, and toward ever closer partnership with People's China abroad, were halted and then reversed.
Political parties were enabled to break with the confining practices
of Sukarno's "guided democracy", and a new and meaningful
effort at rehabilitating the nation's badly neglected economy got
underway. At the same time the intractable problem of finding
an acceptable constitutional structure remained, as did the difficulties in defining the place of the military and of Islam, in
integrating the Chinese minority, in maintaining the rule of law
in the face of the continuing threat of Communist subversion,
and in legitimizing the permanent acquisition of West New
Guinea — to name but a few areas of tension and concern. And
over all there hovered the demands of a new Asian regional
security system, characterized by diminished British and American
involvement and interest, and predicated upon the necessity of
arriving at new forms of accommodation with Indonesia's neighbours.

The following pages offer a brief survey of some of the major
Indonesian developments and policies in these first few years of the
post-Sukarno era. Though this volume is intended primarily for
the general reader, it is hoped that the specialist may also here
and there find matter of interest. The author has preferred, however, to stand as little as possible in front of the data presented,
not least because of a conviction that much of the theorizing and
conceptualizing in the field of Indonesian studies in recent years
has had the tendency to obscure the rich and enduring diversity
of the Indonesian experience.

For some of the material in this book the author has drawn
on previously published articles, specifically on "Indonesian Communism since the 1965 coup", *Pacific Affairs*, vol. 43, Spring

1970, pp. 34-60; "West New Guinea: The Uncertain Future", *Asian Survey*, Institute of International Studies, University of California at Berkeley, vol. 8, August 1968, pp. 691-707; and *"Gestapu* in Indonesia" and "Sukarno's Fall", both in *Orbis,* The Foreign Policy Research Institute of the University of Pennsylvania, vol. 10, Summer 1966, pp. 458-87, and vol. 11, Summer 1967, pp. 491-531, respectively. For permission to reprint, the author is grateful to the editors and institutes concerned.

This book is for M.F.E., *sahabat setia.*

JUSTUS M. VAN DER KROEF
University of Bridgeport, Connecticut

July 1971

CHAPTER ONE

Gestapu and its Origins

IN DJAKARTA, on the evening of 27 March 1968, General Suharto, aged 46, was formally sworn in as President of Indonesia by decision of the Provisional People's Consultative Assembly (*Madjelis Permusjawaratan Rakjat Sementara*—MPRS) which under Indonesia's Constitution is the country's highest policy-setting body and which elects the chief executive. Southeast Asia's largest and most populous nation thus set the seal upon a drastic change in domestic and foreign policy which had begun two and a half years before with the abortive *coup d'etat* of 30 September 1965 in Djakarta and in portions of Central Java. This change had culminated in the accelerating slide from power of Indonesia's first President and the man who, more than any other, had virtually dominated it during most of the first two decades of its national independence—Sukarno. As Suharto was being sworn in, the 66-year-old Sukarno, a virtual prisoner, was some forty miles south of Djakarta in the hill town of Bogor. Rumoured to be suffering from a variety of nervous and other disorders, and held in utter disrepute among most of the country's students and intellectuals, Sukarno yet had a potent, lingering charismatic appeal in the Javanese countryside, and remained a force to be reckoned with until his death more than two years later.

No outburst of popular elation greeted Suharto's formal presidential investiture. This was partly, perhaps, because he had already held *de facto* presidential authority for two years and had been officially named Acting President by the MPRS on 12 March 1967, while Sukarno presumably retained the shadow of his original title. But it was probably also due to growing political tensions between Suharto and major political and social groupings in Indonesia (see chapter II), and, perhaps, to a relative sense of "let-down" over the necessary but unspectacular stabilization efforts of Suharto, after the more flamboyant and diverting political gestures of Sukarno.

It was Sukarno who, to most of his fellow Indonesians and others abroad, had become the symbol of his country's independence aspirations, its emergent national unity, and its struggle against Dutch colonial rule. Anciently Indonesia had known little of such national unity. To be sure, before the coming of the Dutch merchants to the Indonesian islands late in the sixteenth century, there had flourished important empires and principalities based mainly on Java and Sumatra. These states had a highly developed, Hinduized (usually with some Buddhist influence) and later, Islamic cultural life. But it was not until Dutch colonial rule — exercised first by the Dutch East India Company, and later, as of the beginning of the nineteenth century, by the Dutch State Government—that the many scattered islands of Indonesia and their greatly diverse population groups had very gradually been welded together into a single, overcapping administrative and political entity. It was through this Dutch colonial system too that the Indonesian people, however inadequately, were launched into the world of modern education, public health services, jurisprudence, and a developed agricultural and minerological export economy. Even so, the early Indonesian nationalism, as it emerged during the first two decades of the present century, tended to reflect the persisting variety of regional, religious and class interests in the country. Though he had his critics and competitors in the nationalist movement, Sukarno was unquestionably the most tireless articulator of the idea of a united Indonesia, a nation which culturally and politically would synthesize this historic diversity of its peoples and their devement.

Born in Blitar, East Java, on 6 June 1901, of a Balinese mother and a Javanese school teacher of aristocratic family, Sukarno (like many Indonesians he had but one name) in 1926 became a graduate in architecture at the Dutch Government's College of Engineering in Bandung, West Java, but he had little interest in practising his profession. These were the years when the Dutch colonial system, though it had, just after World War I, made a modest beginning by granting Indonesia some measure of autonomy, was under increasing strain to accommodate the political and economic demands of a growing number of educated and nationally conscious younger Indonesians. Sukarno threw himself into the rapidly developing nationalist movement and suffered imprisonment and exile at the hands of the Dutch authorities. When early in 1942, during the Second World War, the Dutch East Indian colonial empire ended with the Japanese Occupation of Indonesia, Sukarno, while collaborating with the Japanese, nevertheless continued to scheme toward an *Indonesia Merdeka*

(Free Indonesia). Neither during the closing decades of Dutch colonial rule, nor during the subsequent years of Japanese Occupation (1942-5) had Sukarno been the only nationalist leader of prominence. Indonesian nationalism, with its taproots in traditional and Reform Islam, in ethnic and regional subcultures, in Marxism, in the peasant as well as in urban middle class and modern secularist aspirations, has always had a more broadly varied character and, also historically, a longer process of elite formation than many accounts of its history and development have tended to take note of. But when on 17 August 1945, with the somewhat reluctant consent of the Japanese, and in the closing hours of World War II, Sukarno proclaimed the independence of the Indonesian Republic, most of the leading nationalists, at least on Java, rallied to his cause.

For more than four years Sukarno, as President of the revolutionary Republic, led the struggle against the returning Dutch and their Indonesian allies, the latter particularly to be found on the islands beyond Java. Sukarno's authority was repeatedly threatened: for example, in September 1948, in Madiun, East Java, the Indonesian Communist Party (*Partai Komunis Indonesia* — PKI) briefly mounted an unsuccessful coup against his regime. But when at last, after United Nations intervention, the Dutch, at the so-called Round Table Conference in The Hague at the end of December 1949, formally transferred their sovereignty over Indonesia to a new federal Indonesian Republic (with the exception of West New Guinea, which remained under Dutch authority), it seemed natural that Sukarno would become its President also.

During the first fifteen years of Indonesia's post-revolutionary existence as a nation, and as partisan political opinion and activity became more and more sharply divisive, Sukarno seemed to find it increasingly necessary to resort to authoritarian procedures. These included the abolition of parliamentary democracy, an ever-tightening press censorship, and, eventually, political arrests, to stabilize his position. Provincial dissatisfaction, especially in Sumatra, with the heavy hand of Djakarta-based bureaucracy, and with the inadequate returns to the provinces of exchange earned by major exports like rubber, soon evolved into a string of Army-backed regional rebellions in 1956-7. The President's seemingly increasing co-operation with the resurgent PKI also aroused mounting concern. The discontent exploded in February 1958, in a near civil war, as important leaders of the *Masjumi* (Muslim Federation) and Socialist (PSI) parties joined Army dissidents in the proclamation of a new Revolutionary Government of the Republic of Indonesia (*Pemerintah Revolusioner Republik Indonesia*

3

— PRRI) based in west Sumatra and northern Sulawesi (Celebes). With the aid of loyal Army commanders and the major political parties, including the PKI, Sukarno weathered the storm, and shortly Indonesia embarked upon a high-pitched campaign of national "confrontation" against the Dutch in order to acquire West New Guinea, or Irian Barat as Indonesians call it. When, by the middle of 1962, the Dutch, under strong pressure from the Kennedy administration in the United States, gave in to the Indonesian demand, Sukarno (all the while ceaselessly purveying new verbal symbols of the nation's political direction and greatness to which obedience was exacted from all political groupings) had gone far indeed in establishing a quasi-totalitarian regime, precariously balanced on the mutual antagonism between the top commanders of the Army and the ever more influential PKI. Before the end of 1962 the confrontation campaign resumed, this time against the impending creation of the Malaysian Federation (composed of Malaya, Sarawak, Sabah or North Borneo, and initially Singapore) and against which the PKI had already been fulminating on the grounds that it was a "neo-colonialist project" of the British.

With little doubt these "external" ventures of confrontation and the crisis atmosphere they created, helped in the short-run stabilization of the Sukarno regime, although virtually all meaningful economic development seemed to be grinding to a halt. Perhaps even more important was that during 1963-5 and in the context of the anti-Malaysian confrontation — as in the case of the earlier confrontation of Dutch-held West New Guinea, characterized by an international press war scare, a psychological pressure campaign, infiltration by paratroopers, and Indonesian guerilla and terrorist attacks — Peking and Djakarta established an ever warmer pattern of international political co-operation. It was then too that the PKI, under its chairman Dipa Nusantara Aidit, rose to the position of its greatest influence since its founding in May 1920. Already in March 1962, Aidit, along with leaders of other major parties, had become a cabinet minister without portfolio, and in the following months overt and covert Communist representation in the Cabinet widened. Meanwhile Sukarno, in December 1964, ordered the abolition of the belatedly formed anti-PKI organizations like the *Badan Pendukung Sukarnoisme* or Body for the Support of Sukarnoism, just as four years earlier he had banned the anti-Communist *Masjumi* and PSI parties on the grounds that some of their leaders had been involved in the PRRI rebellion. And as in public addresses he urged the PKI to "go ahead" and to "grow, grow further", the PKI accelerated its militant confrontation of "landlords", "capitalist bureaucrats", "CIA agents" and "imperialist culture", seizing foreign, especially British-owned estates and attacking United States Information Service libraries.

With a membership which by early 1965 approached two million, and with additional tens of thousands in its labour, peasants', women's and youth fronts, the PKI had in fact become the largest political party in Indonesia. Its power radiated to all areas of government, from village officials to provincial governors and from managers of major government enterprises to the armed forces. While most Army officers remained anti-Communist, PKI influence increasingly extended itself to lower naval and Marine Corps (*Korps Komando Operasi* — KKO) personnel, and even to the top command of the Indonesian Air Force. Indeed, even in the Army itself PKI cadres were making special efforts to win over individual officers who, for various reasons, were discontented with top Army policies, or were gripped by promotion or service speciality jealousies. This process was undoubtedly facilitated by the fact that PKI cadres, with official approval, lectured to the armed forces on the nature of the Indonesian Revolution and the party's place in it.

By the middle of January 1965, the PKI, in the teeth of bitter Army opposition, also began a campaign to arm "workers and peasants" in an independent, so-called Fifth Force (so named to distinguish it from the already existing four "forces", the army, navy, air force and police), ultimately winning Sukarno over to the idea. PKI-directed demonstrations culminated in various parts of Java in seizures by Communist peasant front groups of "landlords' lands" and during the ensuing violence scores were injured or killed. Elsewhere, meanwhile, rising tensions between Muslim villagers and PKI militants erupted in other bloody clashes. Despite the unmistakable, if covert, rising popular opposition to all these PKI pressures the party seemed increasingly to have its way. One incident is illustrative. On 3 August 1965, it was announced that the High Court of North Sumatra province would shortly meet, not in its usual location in Medan, but in Djakarta. There it was expected to reach a "more suitable" verdict than the fifteen- to twenty-year prison sentences it had just meted out to twenty-three cadres of the PKI peasant front who had been convicted previously of beating to death an Army officer. The officer in question, sent to clear squatters from government land, had, according to the Communist press, "provoked" the "people's leaders" (that is the peasant front cadres). The PKI raised such an outcry over the original verdict that the Government deemed it wiser to order the court to reconsider the case — but this time in (for the Communists) the more sympathetic atmosphere of Djakarta, a precedent in Indonesia's judicial history and a portent of the PKI's power hardly to be minimized.

Already, toward the close of December 1964, reports had appeared in the Malaysian (though not in the censor-ridden Indonesian) press about a recently exposed PKI Central Committee document describing stepped-up agitation planned for 1965, in preparation for an eventual *coup d'etat*. Whatever the accuracy of these reports, it is likely that any PKI plan for a *coup d'etat* were — at least until August 1965 — greatly modified by the consideration that the party was ascending so steadily in power that a coup might not at all be necessary. What ultimately prompted the formation of the conspiracy of the so-called 30 September Movement (*Gerakan September Tiga Puluh*, usually abbreviated to *Gestapu* by acronym-minded Indonesians) is still shrouded in a good deal of controversy and uncertainty. But it now seems likely that PKI leaders, alarmed in August 1965 over reports of Sukarno's rapidly declining health, allied themselves with a number of dissident Army officers, some of them in the Central Java-based Diponegoro division, others in the East Java-based Brawidjaja division. So began the preparations for a pre-emptive strike against top Army commanders designed to nullify an expected Army move against the Communists in the event of Sukarno's sudden death or total incapacity. Members of *Gerwani* (*Gerakan Wanita Indonesia* — Indonesian Women's Movement), the PKI's women's front, and of *Pemuda Rakjat* (People's Youth), the Communist youth organization, were mobilized both in Central and West Java during the latter half of August 1965. Some 2,000 members of these organizations, with the connivance of Air Force officers, were eventually given military training in small rotating groups in an isolated and marshy spot called Lubang Buaja (crocodile hole), within the perimeter of Halim Air Force base near Djakarta.

The Government of People's China, from the start, was aware of and materially assisted the *Gestapu* conspirators. At least two weeks *before* the coup, for example, Bangkok and Hong Kong sources reported on the extensive supplies of arms and explosives being sent to Indonesian Communists by Communist China via small East and West Java ports and fishing villages. This military hardware was packed in crates supposedly containing building materials being sent by Peking to assist in constructing facilities in Djakarta for the forthcoming August 1966 Conference of the New Emerging Forces, the Sino-Indonesian rival organization to the United Nations (indicative of the growing political *rapprochement* between Djakarta and Peking had been Indonesia's decision to leave the United Nations, in January 1965). The importation of these crates containing weapons occurred without customs inspection because of an earlier agreement between Indonesia's Foreign Minister Subandrio and Chinese Foreign Minister Chen Yi. It was not least because of his behind-the-scenes assistance to the *Gestapu* plotters that after the coup Subandrio came widely and popularly to be branded as Durno, the nefarious scheming adviser figure in the Javanese *wayang* (shadow play) repertoire. In fact, during his trial in October 1966, Subandrio declared that through his intelligence organization he had heard rumours of the impending *Gestapu* plot. However, he had not informed Sukarno, said Subandrio, because he believed that the President himself was already well familiar with the planned coup!

There can be, indeed, little question that Sukarno was aware of the preparations for *Gestapu*. Also, apart from the uncertainties for his future posed by his health, Indonesia's President evidently believed that even after the establishment of the plotters' "Revolutionary Council", as announced in the first rebel broadcast in Djakarta early in the morning of 1 October 1965, he would in effect retain his position. There is the testimony of the later-executed Air Force Major Sujono, commander of the Halim base security force, who directly supervised the training of the Communist assassin squads at Lubang Buaja, and who, reportedly, was delegated by the PKI to indoctrinate Lieutenant-Colonel Untung, the nominal leader of the *Gestapu* conspirators, in the Communist ideology. Sujono testified during the trial of captured PKI Politburo member Njono, in the middle of February 1966, that Sukarno was apprised well in advance of the coming coup. Moreover, Sukarno's behaviour during the critical first hours of the coup period can only deepen suspicion. For example, in the early morning hours Sukarno went voluntarily to — of all places — Halim Air Force base, which he almost certainly knew to be the headquarters of the *Gestapu* plotters. Sukarno's own explanation is that he went to Halim so that he would have been able to fly away "should an unwanted eventuality have risen" At Halim, he was seen to pat the shoulder of Brigadier-General Supardjo, one of the chief conspirators, after Supardjo reportedly told him of the murder of six Army generals by the Lubang Buaja assassin squads just a few hours before. This presidential pat, of which subsequently much was made by Sukarno's critics, may have been a congratulatory or a restraining gesture. But it should be noted that well after the coup Sukarno had contact with and attempted to protect Supardjo and even exchanged letters with him while Supardjo was in hiding.

7

Perhaps the most careful assessment of Sukarno's alleged place in the *Gestapu* affair was made by General Suharto himself in a report to the MPRS on 7 March 1967. In this report Suharto apparently also used, in part, the findings of a somewhat earlier investigation of Sukarno's relationship to the *Gestapu* affair made by the Attorney-General's office. Sukarno, declared Suharto, could not be marked down "as a direct instigator, or the master-mind, or even an important figure of *Gestapu*/PKI", unless new facts became available. Rather, Sukarno had helped create the recent political climate in Indonesia which so greatly encouraged the PKI. When shortly before the coup Sukarno had been warned by Army Brigadier-General R. H. Sugandhi that a subversive plot was about to be hatched (reportedly Sugandhi's participation in the *Gestapu* affair had been solicited by PKI chairman D. N. Aidit) Sukarno, according to Suharto, turned Sugandhi aside with a warning not to give in to "this Communist phobia". Also, Sukarno, upon hearing reports (presumably given him by Supardjo at Halim) of the killings by *Gestapu* terrorists of leading Army generals, had dismissed the matter with the remark that "such things will happen in a revolution". And on 2 October 1965, at a time when the coup had to all intents and purposes already failed, Sukarno — according to Suharto — continued to deal with Supardjo, even though he was known by then as one of the chief *Gestapu* plotters. Yet Sukarno also knew that the day before, Suharto and the "provisional leadership of the Army" had already branded those involved in the coup as traitors and declared them dishonourably dismissed. Later, after the coup, Suharto noted, Sukarno in various speeches and public exhortations had tried to protect the role of Communism in Indonesia's national development and though he denounced the coup itself he had all along failed to take legal steps against known *Gestapu* leaders.

Even so, it is probable that the extent of Sukarno's fore-knowledge of and the propriety of his conduct during and after the coup will be debated for a long time to come. The same is likely to be true also for the PKI's role in it, even though leading party figures unquestionably prepared for and collaborated closely with Army dissidents in the whole *Gestapu* affair. Pre-meditation and planning speak readily from the establishment on the morning of 1 October 1965 in the Central Java city of Surakarta (nearly simultaneously, it might be added, with the first radio announcement of Untung's Revolutionary Council in Djakarta) of a local Revolutionary Council. This council's guiding force was Utomo Ramelan, Surakarta's mayor and prominent PKI member. PKI planning speaks equally from "Operation Naming Names", that is the practice before the coup

8

of PKI cadres in a number of areas in Java and Kalimantan (Borneo) of compiling lists of prominent local party opponents, and from the earlier-mentioned training of Communist assassin squads at Lubang Buaja. There is also the evidence given after the coup by exiled or captured PKI spokesmen. In its July-August 1968 issue, the magazine *Tricontinental,* which is published in Havana as the mouthpiece of the Castro-sponsored Solidarity Organization of the Peoples of Africa, Asia and Latin America, carried long excerpts of the testimony at the trial of Sudisman, a top PKI leader and Politburo member. The testimony record, which *Tricontinental's* editors claim came to them from "honourable people" present at Sudisman's trial, shows Sudisman stating that he "made decrees and drew up the plan for the Council of Revolution" (that is Untung's Council) and that he, Sudisman, was present at Halim and Lubang Buaja at the time the *Gestapu* affair began. This trial testimony also shows Sudisman saying with reference to the coup that "all actions were executed by individuals who happened to be members of the PKI". Nevertheless, Sudisman asserted, the PKI as such was not involved in the plot. (*Inter alia* it might be noted that the excerpts of Sudisman's trial testimony printed in *Tricontinental* wholly conform to the unpublished Indonesian transcript of Sudisman's trial by the *Mahmillub* or special military court which the present writer was privileged to see.)

Underground and exiled PKI members in their evaluations of the coup have also been quite candid about Communist involvement and intent. The purpose of the coup, according to one Indonesian evaluation in the October 1967 issue of the *World Marxist Review,* the Prague-published voice of Moscow-orientated Communist parties in the world today, was not only to frustrate a "conspiracy" of Indonesian generals. It was also to establish a revolutionary government, with the participation of the Communists and other groups, "as a preliminary to People's Democracy" A similar statement appears in the evaluation attributed to a Moscow-orientated group of Indonesian Communists in exile somewhere in Southeast Asia. Considering the meaning which Communists attach to the term "People's Democracy", it is difficult to interpret these assertions other than that the coup was intended by PKI leaders themselves as a step toward the creation of a Communist state in Indonesia. It seems equally evident, however, that the statements of Sudisman and other Indonesian Communists, that the PKI as such was not involved in the coup, have some substance of truth also, although wittingly or not many party and front members were obviously engaged in preparations for it. Available evidence thus far strongly suggests that, either because of caution or because of poor co-ordination, only a few Politburo members and party provincial and district leaders appear to have been aware that a coup was being planned. And even fewer were familiar with tactical details, including the date and the manner of the strike. Poor co-ordination in overblown party and front organizations was, indeed, a major reason why the party's destruction could occur with such astonishing speed in the first weeks after the failure of the coup.

Finally, there is the role of the Army in the *Gestapu* affair. Official Army sources identify two main evil geniuses. One was Lieutenant-Colonel Untung, a veteran officer and Sukarno protege, who, during the earlier-mentioned PKI uprising in Madiun in 1948, had for a while fought on the side of the Communists. Untung nevertheless appears not to have been greatly held back in his career because of this, and on the day of the coup he was a battalion commander of the presidential palace guard. The other was Army Brigadier-General M. S. Supardjo, long known for his pro-Communist sympathies, who at the time of *Gestapu* was commander of the Army Strategic Reserve's Fourth Combat Command stationed in Menggaian, West Kalimantan. Supardjo, concerned with carrying on Indonesia's anti-Malaysia confrontation along the Sarawak border, was well placed at this post. For not least because of his political sympathies he had little difficulty in assisting in the development of joint guerilla operations with dissident Communist-orientated Chinese in Sarawak.

Still other military, for example a number of field-grade officers of the Diponegoro division in Central Java, also played not insignificant roles in the coup attempt in their area. But since they were far from the Djakarta scene they tended to remain outside the spotlight. And certainly principal allies of Supardjo and the plotters were Air Marshal Omar Dhani, Indonesia's Air Force chief, who knew all about what was happening at his Halim base and with whom Supardjo conferred directly upon his arrival in Djakarta from Kalimantan forty-eight hours before the coup, and Colonel A. Latief, brigade commander of the Djakarta garrison. Moreover, in the latter half of 1968, when for months scores of military from all major services branches were being arrested for alleged complicity in the *Gestapu* affair, Indonesian Army spokesmen gave the strong impression that the number of conspirators in the Army was far greater than was originally supposed. One cannot be sure, however, that some of the Army's arrests during and since 1968 were not actuated by keeping alive a "Red scare" in order to justify the Army's emergency powers.

Apparently, throughout all of August and September 1955, secret meetings took place in Djakarta, attended by Untung, Sujono, a representative of the PKI Central Committee (usually Tjugito, known as Sjam or as Sjam Kamaruzaman), and occasionally emissaries of Supardjo and Latief. Sometimes the plotters met in Latief's home. It was during these meetings that the principal tactical decision of the coup was taken — to kill Defence Minister General Nasution, Army commander Lieutenant-General Ahmad Yani and other top Army leaders, in order to immobilize and demoralize any potential resistance to the coup. Also in those discussions the deployment of the forces at the disposal of the plotters was agreed upon. In addition to the 2,000 Communists trained at Lubang Buaja, Untung's own palace guard battalion (most of the junior officers of which had been persuaded by Untung with promises of rapid promotion to join the plot), and a few elements of Sujono's Halim base security force and of Latief's Djakarta garrison troops, the *Gestapu* conspirators also counted on the support of a paratroop battalion of the Army's Diponegoro division and on one battalion from the Army's Brawidjaja division. These latter had recently arrived in the capital in connection with the parade to be held on Armed Forces Day, on 5 October. Top officers of these battalions had been subverted by the PKI, but their rank and file appeared to have had but small idea as to what end they were being used. As a matter of fact, by the afternoon of the first day of the coup, the rebellious Brawidjaja battalion had been talked into surrendering by General Suharto, and later even participated in crushing the rebel remnant. Untung and Supardjo also appeared to have believed that they had backing from a Siliwangi division armoured unit in West Java, from other Diponegoro companies in Central Java, and that they had naval and KKO support at the Surabaya naval base. These expectations were, with the exception of the Siliwangi elements, not without some foundation. But in the event, only units of the Diponegoro division were to give the conspirators any significant support in Central Java.

Why the *Gestapu* plotters decided to strike on the night of 30 September to 1 October 1965 is still not clear. A principal reason may have been that by this time there was considerable danger of a leak and that the planned attacking force could not be kept in high alert much longer. For example, Major-General S. Parman, the Army's chief of Intelligence Services, in one of the tragic ironies of the *Gestapu* affair, appeared to have been informed several hours before the coup that the Communists were planning some sort of surprise attack. Before he could find

11

out more or act on this information Parman was struck down by Lubang Buaja assassins on the night of 30 September.

And so, shortly after midnight, several hundred youthful Communist assassins, augmented by palace guards, went to their bloody task. Within a couple of hours General Yani, Harjono and Pandjaitan had been killed in their homes and their bodies taken to Lubang Buaja. Shortly, three other generals, Parman, Surprapto and Sutojo, who had been taken alive to Lubang Buaja, were there clubbed and hacked to pieces and their remains were thrown, together with the bodies of the three generals killed earlier, in a well. But miraculously, Nasution escaped the assassins, even as the *Gestapu* main force, consisting of the Brawidjaja and Diponegoro battalions, was moving on to Merdeka Square in the heart of the capital. There the rebel battalions swiftly surrounded the President's palace (Sukarno was away, spending most of the night at the town residence of one of his wives and in the early morning hours, apparently having been informed of the coup, was driven to Halim air base), and occupied the government radio and telecommunications facilities on the other sides of the square.

A little after 7 a.m. on the morning of 1 October, startled Djakartanese were informed for the first time in a broadcast over the government radio that power had been seized by a "30 September Movement", headed by Lieutenant-Colonel Untung. The movement was said to have acted to prevent a planned coup by an Army "Council of Generals", aided by the American CIA. This Council of Generals, according to the rebel broadcast, had been expecting the allegedly ill President Sukarno to die. It had therefore planned to seize power by means of the troops being brought to the capital for the celebrations of the 5 October Armed Forces Day. The broadcast announced the impending formation of a "Revolutionary Council", in the capital as well as the provinces, which would include both civilians and military who supported the 30 September Movement.

Shortly, Air Marshal Dhani, in an order of the day from Halim, in effect committed the Air Force to the rebels. And a second rebel broadcast at 2 p.m. on 1 October, announced a forty-five-man Revolutionary Council. This was a strange body that included the chief plotters like Supardjo, Untung and Latief, a few PKI and pro-Communist figures, but also a number of top military, like General Basuki Rahmat, and naval and police chiefs. The latter, as well as Deputy Premier Johannes Leimena, could hardly be said to be coup supporters and they were, like most members of the council, probably included without their knowledge or consent. But the tide had already decisively begun to turn against the rebels. The commander of the Army's Strategic Reserve Forces (*Kostrad*), General Suharto, aided by the escaped Nasution and loyal senior Army commanders, energetically rallied counter-coup forces in the early morning hours of 1 October. Suharto had not been on the list of the Lubang Buaja assassins. Indeed he was not at his Djakarta home on the night of the coup, according to some accounts because he had taken his son hunting and fishing; in fact. however, Suharto had been visiting one of his children, ill in a Djakarta hospital. Suharto soon neutralized the rebel East Java Brawidjaja battalion and before his assembled forces, late in the afternoon of 1 October, needed to attack the remaining and increasingly demoralized rebel units at Merdeka Square, the latter withdrew towards Halim base. Contrary to rebel expectations, most Djakarta garrison troops and a loyal *Kostrad* brigade had at once rallied to Suharto's banner. It was also soon clear that the Army Siliwangi division was remaining loyal. Shortly, the government radio broadcast an official condemnation of the "counter-revolutionary" *Gestapu* movement, as, meanwhile, roaming groups of Lubang Buaja terrorists, bereft of direction, were rounded up or disbanded and went underground.

When it became apparent that Suharto, who had skilfully continued to rally and co-ordinate his forces in Djakarta and West Java, would shortly be able to strike at Halim the rebel command collapsed. Before midnight 1 October, Sukarno had left Halim for his Bogor residence. Supardjo and Untung also disappeared, leading small groups of followers. They were soon captured. Dhani flew to Madiun, East Java, vainly attempting to rally supporters by radio from the air. And PKI chairman D. N. Aidit, perhaps the coup's mastermind, who sometime in the morning of 1 October had joined the coup leaders at Halim (according to later testimony of Mrs Aidit her husband had been "kidnapped" by rebels and brought to the air base), after having kept wholly out of the limelight during the dramatic events of the night, was flown by an Air Force plane to Djokjakarta. Here a number of officers of the Diponegoro division had staged their version of the *Gestapu* coup. By dawn of 2 October Suharto's troops had occupied Halim however, and with very little difficulty began rounding up Sujono's fleeing Air Force security guards and elements of the mutinous Diponegoro battalion that had briefly occupied Merdeka Square.

Still, for nearly a week following there was hard though intermittent fighting in and around Djokjakarta and Surakarta, as *Pemuda Rakjat* and mutinous Diponegoro soldiers reassembled in the Merapi-Merbabu area for guerilla resistance. In Semarang, where *Gestapu* insurgents had briefly seized control, there were clashes also. On 24 November 1965, Aidit, captured by the Army days previously (reportedly with the aid of an informer), was shot. Gradually, an accelerating anti-*Gestapu* movement was getting underway which would shortly topple Sukarno from power.

There are three and, to an extent, inter-related developments that require primary attention in a consideration of the immediate post-*Gestapu* period. The first of these is the bloody purge of Communists and *Gestapu* conspirators, suspects, and — it is to be feared — innocents, which continued for months on end after Suharto restored control. Secondly, there is Sukarno's vain attempt to preserve the domestic political *status quo* that existed before the coup. And finally, there is the emergence of the post-Sukarno *Orba* (from *Orde Baru* or New Order) with the appearance of new influential groups, like the students and intellectual action fronts, and the realignment of older political forces. (The last two developments will be dealt with in the next chapter.)

There is still no accurate estimate of the number of those who fell victims to the post-*Gestapu* massacre. Estimates have ranged from the 78,000 figure supplied by a group of nine government investigators at the close of 1965, to a high of one million, the figure suggested six months later by a team of University of Indonesia graduates especially commissioned by the Army to inquire into the extent of the killings. Nor does the massacre necessarily appear to be over. On 30 November 1968, more than three years after the coup, the London *Economist* reported, for example, that in the context of new recent operations against suspected underground Communist activity in East Java, "hundreds and perhaps thousands of Communist suspects are being shot in political prisons on the island of Java. Indonesia's newspapers have not reported the shooting ... but senior Army generals admit in private that mass executions, reminiscent of the holocaust of 1965-6 have been taking place for the past six or eight months." In a press conference on 3 February 1969, President Suharto denied that in recent months thousands of political prisoners had been killed. However, there were still an estimated 110,000 political prisoners at the end of 1969, and their condition had led to several and repeated protests from abroad.

Aided almost everywhere by the Army, gangs of youths (usually, though not always, belonging to Muslim youth groups like *Ansor,* an affiliate of the *Nahdatul Ulama* party) led the mass killings, particularly in Central and East Java. In Bali, where some 35,000 alone are estimated to have died by the beginning of 1966, it was the Tamins, the storm-troopers of the PNI, (Indonesian Nationalist Party) who did the slaughter. And

14

throughout Java and Sumatra, night after night, for months, local Army commanders loaded trucks with captured PKI members —their names checked off against hastily drawn lists—or suspected Diponegoro division rebels, and alleged *Gestapu* sympathizers who had been denounced by neighbours or informers, and drove them to an isolated spot nearby for execution, usually by bullet or knife. The bodies of the victims were sometimes thrown into hastily dug mass graves. Often too, they were thrown into rivers, and in November 1966, there were reports that at certain points the Brantas River, near Surabaya, was "choked with corpses". Another report has it that near the hill town of Batu, in East Java, so many were executed within the narrow confines of a small police courtyard that it was decided that it would be simpler to just cover the piled-up bodies with layers of cement. Whether this tale is true or not, popular folklore today knows of the grisly but unmarked mound, which is only spoken of in whispers. There was occasional resistance. From the Klaten-Bojolali area in Central Java in late November 1965, a few bands of hunted *Gestapu* military and PKI members swarmed out to pillage and terrorize. But this only whipped the counter-terrorists to greater fury.

Under the cover of the anti-*Gestapu* and anti-Communist pogrom long-standing personal and ethnic animosities were given free rein. Almost everywhere in the major cities there were attacks on Chinese, for example, particularly those believed to be members or sympathizers of *Baperki*. This organization was originally founded in 1954 to advance the interests of Indonesian residents or citizens of Chinese origin. There is little question that by 1965 the PKI had considerable influence in *Baperki* (for example, one *Baperki* chairman had been an editor of the PKI's daily). But by no means were all its members pro-Communist. In the overheated atmosphere of the anti-Communist pogrom numerous business, personal and political jealousies were "settled" by means of denunciations to the authorities of alleged Communist sympathy or complicity in *Gestapu*.

Within the Army itself there were eventually to be waves of arrests for alleged complicity in *Gestapu*. These have continued to this day. Already on 15 October 1965, Sukarno, pressed by outraged Army commanders, had appointed Suharto as Army chief. Suharto replaced Major-General Pranoto Reksosamudra, who had been given the post by Sukarno, at the height of *Gestapu*, on 1 October 1965. Pranoto had succeeded the slain General Yani and was widely considered to have been sympathetic to the *Gestapu* plotters (at the close of May 1968, Pranoto was ordered confined, preparatory to standing trial for presumed involvement in the 30 September coup). Almost immediately

15

upon assuming office as Army chief, Suharto began intensive investigations of Army personnel suspected of disloyalty. Intra-service jealousies soon unfortunately obtruded into this purge. It was not until 1968, however, that arrests in the Army began to reach sizeable proportions.

To its perpetrators the anti-PKI pogrom seemed to acquire the character of a self-justifying crusade, which, indeed, was believed to be necessary as an instrument of policy for years to come. Through the length and breadth of Java the pogrom poisoned the atmosphere with fear and suspicion, as month after month reports and rumours of new massacres spread. This could not but render suspect — also abroad — the bona fides of those who sincerely believed that the quelling of the coup provided a legitimate opportunity for much needed constitutional and policy changes. It was in this melancholy context that the struggle to divest Sukarno of his powers began.

CHAPTER TWO

The End of the Sukarno Era

IN THE VERY midst of the post-coup blood-bath and the heightened tensions aroused by it, Sukarno sought to preserve his particular conception of Indonesia's national development and his own position with it. He only succeeded in becoming a target of the growing anti-*Gestapu* furor and so hastened his own political demise.

There are three fairly well-defined stages in Sukarno's accelerating slide into ignominy. The first is the period from 30 September 1965 to 11 March 1966, when Sukarno ordered Suharto to "take all steps" to re-establish domestic tranquillity and to safeguard Sukarno's "personal safety and authority". The second phase begins with Suharto's assumption of this special security mandate and ends with Sukarno's statement of 10 January 1967 to the MPRS, in reply to recent criticism of him. The final phase dates from the issuance of this January statement to the MPRS decision of 12 March 1967 revoking Sukarno's presidential powers and making Suharto Acting President. The period from this 12 March 1967 MPRS decision to the formal investiture of Suharto as "full" President a year later, mentioned at the beginning of this book and treated more fully in the next chapter, seems but an epilogue to this story of Sukarno's fall. As one reviews the decline of Sukarno one is tempted to suggest that the whole process was by no means inevitable and that, for example, as late as the beginning of 1967 Sukarno could probably still have weathered the mounting political storm had he really chosen to do so. That a master politician like Sukarno declined to act differently, thus provoking an open, head-on collision between himself and his opponents, has seemed most "un-Indonesian" to many observers. Nevertheless, Sukarno's tactics were not altogether out of keeping with his known political style.

The chief feature of the first phase in Sukarno's fall was his persistent effort to protect the pivotal role of the radical Left in general, and of the Communist ideology in particular, in Indonesian domestic and foreign policies. In the first few days after *Gestapu*, as details of the coup were only slowly becoming known to a wider public, Sukarno had, with fair success, reasserted his authority, counting on the confusion still surrounding many aspects of *Gestapu* and on his prestige to see him through any unpleasant aftermath. No one at this point, whether in the press or Parliament, seemed ready to call him personally and publicly to account. In the Army leadership there was a similar reluctance and uncertainty, bred of concern over the consequences which any determined action against Sukarno would bring. Only in the rapidly rising student movement did open criticism begin to be voiced of Sukarno.

But then, as days lengthened into weeks and months, and as his own conduct during the coup — particularly his presence at Halim and his easy consorting with known plotters like Supardjo — was increasingly becoming better known and subjected to attack, Sukarno in various speeches and impromptu exhortations kept on warning Indonesia not to swerve "to the Right", insisting that Indonesia's revolution was a "Left revolution", and repeating again and again the necessity of preserving *nasakom* (a Sukarno acronym, referring to the unity of Indonesia's main political forces: *nasionalisme*, *agama* or religion, and *komunisme*). Sukarno also accused anti-Communist groups of making the Left "victims of slander", and he chastised Muslims for allegedly violating Muslim law by not burying the bodies of slain Communists. At one point Sukarno even threatened that he would order the Army to "shoot to kill" in order to stop further demonstrations and violence against the Communists. He accused the United States of trying to bribe him in order to spread "Western ideas" in Indonesia, and he urged a restoration of friendly relations with People's China. As late as 14 February 1966, Sukarno publicly praised the PKI as "the only party which made considerable contribution and sacrifice for the independence of the country".

These utterances greatly infuriated important segments of Indonesian society and polarized relations between the President on the one hand, and on the other such intransigent anti-Sukarno student organizations as the approximately 10,000-member Indonesian University Student Action Front (KAMI), the *Ansor* organization, anti-Communist and Army-dominated trade unions, Muslims, a number of military commanders, academicians, intellectuals, and so on. In these circles and especially in KAMI, which had been founded on 25 October 1965 with Army encouragement, Sukarno's own treasonous association with the *Gestapu* affair was held to be an incontestible fact, even before the subsequent trials of prominent former officials, like Subandrio and Dhani, and of *Gestapu* conspirators, like Sujono and Untung, gave ample ground for such belief. According to many in these circles it was Sukarno's own guilty conscience that led him into such an imprudent defence of the Leftward course of the Indonesian Revolution and of the PKI in the months after *Gestapu*. This may or may not have been the case. But it should be remembered that Sukarno's typical political role, particularly in the half-a-dozen years or so before *Gestapu,* had been that of the balancer of contending power factions, the principal ones among which were the Army and the PKI. The anti-*Gestapu* and anti-Communist pogrom, by threatening the destruction of the PKI, would leave Sukarno politically at the mercy of the Army. In the tense post-*Gestapu* months Sukarno also counted too much on his prestige as the father of Indonesian independence. His expectation that his admonitions, as in the past, would be heeded was unrealistic, not only because of his evident foreknowledge of and suspicious conduct during the coup period, but also because already several years before the coup his reputation had begun to slide, especially among the young. Sukarno's bombastic sloganizing, international diplomatic prancing, and nigh ceaseless womanizing had for many, long since, rendered him a figure of ridicule.

Yet he was by no means wholly without support, especially in the Central and East Java countryside where much of the village population venerated him almost as they would traditional Javanese rulers, and in such parties as the PNI with which his personal political fortunes had long been identified. By the end of 1965, and throughout much of 1966, there were street fighting and other minor altercations in many Javanese cities between anti-Sukarno and pro-Sukarno student groups, the latter frequently tied to the PNI. The PNI's Left wing, which, like Sukarno, had stood for accommodation of and political collaboration with the PKI, and which was led by former Premier Ali Sastroamidjojo and one-time Irrigation Minister Surachman, in the weeks after the coup adopted the first letters in the names of its leaders, ASU, as its informal slogan, but made the resulting acronym stand for *Anak Sukarno* (Children of Sukarno). There had been a serious rift within PNI ranks well before the *Gestapu* affair over the party's co-operation with the Communists, and now anti-Communist PNI leaders, supported by the Army, demanded that the party purge itself. This only solidified the ASU wing, however, which openly turned to Sukarno for leadership. Left-wing PNI students (soon reported to be infiltrated by the scattered Communist *Pemuda Rakjat*) and ASU activists, undoubtedly with

Sukarno's covert encouragement, formed new mass pressure organizations like the Sukarno Front (*Barisan Sukarno*), the I-am-a-Sukarno-Supporter organization (*Aku Pendukung Sukarno*), and similar "people's action front" groups.

It was also apparent that Sukarno had a following among the armed forces, particularly among the restive KKO (Marine Corps), members of which fought with anti-Sukarno student groups in the streets. Finally, numbers of political party leaders, not just in the PNI, and officials in the government bureaucracy, alarmed over the probable threat to their own positions coming from anti-Sukarno *Orba* enthusiasts generally, and from demonstrating KAMI intransigents particularly, tended to gravitate politically toward the beleaguered Sukarno whatever their reservations about his conduct during the *Gestapu* affair. Like Sukarno, they too felt that their positions depended on a continuation of the checks and balance system of contending political forces in the country.

Under the circumstances, those committed to the total political demise of the President — from KAMI's street commandos and leading intellectuals, like the later Education Minister Mashuri, to leaders of the proscribed *Masjumi* and Socialist parties waiting for a political come-back, and strong anti-Sukarno Army commanders like Major-General Dharsono (subsequently commander of the West Java-based Siliwangi division) backed behind the scenes by Defence Minister Nasution — had to proceed cautiously, taking care not to drive their differences with the President to the point of an immediate and complete rupture. They could not afford to have arrayed against them men like Suharto who, though privately highly critical of the President, would not have lent themselves to, or tacitly approved, at least at this point, of a flagrantly unconstitutional manoeuvre or a known anti-Sukarno cabal. They also had to make sure that Sukarno would be unable to project himself in the public mind as a "Left progressive" alternative to threatening "Right-wing" Army rule. Thus, on 30 November 1965, in a ceremony marking the KKO's twentieth anniversary, Nasution managed to sound almost like Sukarno, declaring that the Indonesian Revolution remained "Leftist", "anti-feudal" and "anti-*nekolim*" (*nekolim*, one of Sukarno's many acronyms, stands for *neo-kolonialisme, kolonialisme* and *imperialisme*). Nasution, also on this occasion, excoriated the "neo-colonialists" and "neo-imperialists" who, after the Army had crushed the *Gestapu* coup, had made "slanderous and insulting statements" to the effect that the Indonesian armed forces were "planning to deviate the national revolution to the Right".

In the months before the *Gestapu* affair, the PKI-initiated and, subsequently, officially endorsed Indonesian confrontation against the Malaysian Federation had perhaps been the most concrete expression of Sukarno's "Left progressive" and "anti-*nekolim*" course for his nation. For months after *Gestapu*, and as the anti-Sukarno forces cautiously solidified their own position for the impending struggle to bring the President down, Nasution, Suharto and other Army commanders again sounded like nothing less than Sukarno himself when it came to public exhortations to *ganjang Malaysia* (crush Malaysia). Already in October 1965, a "spokesman" for Nasution had stated that the confrontation against the *nekolim*, including Malaysia, was being stepped up, and that "there will be no compromise with neo-colonialist Malaysia". As late as April 1966, when Sukarno had already lost some of his *de facto* powers to Suharto, the chief of the Indonesian Naval Information Section declared that recent "fierce fighting" in the Indonesian-Sarawak border area was "proof that our confrontation against the *nekolim* project of Malaysia is not an empty slogan", and at about the same time Suharto, by then emerging as Indonesia's strong man, also reiterated that Indonesia was "compelled" to continue the confrontation.

Within a few weeks of these pronouncements, however, when Suharto had largely succeeded in solidifying his position, official and well-publicized Indonesian gestures began to be made to end the confrontation. Until then the confrontation demand of the anti-Sukarno forces, particularly among the military, was probably best understood as part of a carefully thought out "Fabian" tactic, designed to break Sukarno's power without plunging the country into civil war. By formally asserting their continuing adhesion to the "Leftist" course of the Indonesian Revolution, and by backing the anti-Malaysia campaign (a manoeuvre which had the added advantage that it justified the Army's retention of emergency powers), Army commanders could continue quietly to purge their ranks and, not to be forgotten, also give encouragement to the bloody anti-Communist pogrom generally. Army leaders did little to discourage the radical anti-*Gestapu* reaction — indeed, during the closing weeks of 1965 and through much of 1966 the steady stream of revelations by the Army information services, concerning the planned machinations of Communist and *Gestapu* plotters, only tended to whip up the frenzy even further. Although, for good measure, the Army also periodically broke up the more exuberant anti-Sukarno student demonstrations in major cities in Java.

It hardly seems possible that Sukarno was not aware of his enemies' tactics. Certainly by early February 1966, it had become clear to him that unless he wished to see his position steadily erode he would have to dramatically reassert his authority, counting on his lingering charismatic attraction, especially in Java, and on the support of his own student fighters, the ASU, the remnant of the radical Left in the trade unions, the KKO and much of the Air Force officers corps, and others. Sukarno may also have been influenced by a reported new secret agreement concluded between Indonesian Foreign Minister Subandrio and Communist Chinese Foreign Minister Chen Yi, either in December 1965 or January 1966. The document of this agreement, which was discovered by student demonstrators as they were sacking the Foreign Ministry early in March 1966, and which was turned over to the Army, allegedly disclosed Peking's support for Sukarno's proposed Conference of the New Emerging Forces (this conference, it may be recalled, was the Djakarta-Peking axis's answer to the United Nations), in return for the assassination of anti-Communist Army generals (among them Nasution) who had not been massacred by the *Gestapu* terrorists. Sukarno may have read into Peking's continuing support for his New Emerging Forces concept an expression of sympathy and confidence' that might be translated into more tangible assistance in the event of his position being really endangered by an Army coup against him. The latter contingency, to be sure, Sukarno could consider as relatively remote, since the Army would be unlikely to carry its opposition to him to the extent of provoking or tolerating a possible civil war. Even so, the purported Subandrio-Chen Yi agreement may well have emboldened him further.

And so, on 21 February 1966, after a minimum of consultations with party leaders or even with his close advisers and supporters, and despite the continuing unrest and student demonstrations in major cities, especially in West Java, Sukarno asserted himself and announced a reshuffling of his Cabinet (under the prevailing Constitution the President is, in effect, concurrently Premier). Minister of Defence Nasution was dropped, as were, *pro forma*, three major PKI leaders, among them the slain D. N. Aidit. But major PKI sympathizers and some widely suspected of complicity in the *Gestapu* affair returned to ministerial office. Among these were Foreign Minister Subandrio, Central Bank Affairs Minister Jusuf Muda Dalam, Aircraft Industry Minister Air Vice-Marshal Omar Dhani, Minister of State Oei Tjoe Tat (of Chinese descent and generally considered as "Peking's man" in the Cabinet). Included in the new Cabinet also were unsavoury figures like Lieutenant-Colonel Mohammad Sjafei ("Minister for Security Affairs seconded to the President"), said to be closely involved in the operations of major vice rings in the capital.

As he installed the new Cabinet on 24 February, Sukarno freely used the Communist jargon of phased revolutionary development. The Indonesian Revolution, Sukarno said, was at the stage of "national democracy", during which the task was to "exterminate" imperialism and feudalism. The second stage, for which the nation was presently heading, would be that of "socialism". The present job of the Cabinet was therefore to intensify the anti-imperialist struggle especially against Malaysia. Sukarno also noted at the cabinet installation that there had already been public criticism that the new Cabinet was a "*Gestapu* Cabinet". But, Sukarno said, he had asked each new minister: "Are you a Communist?" and had only obtained negative replies. Truculently, the President concluded his cabinet installation speech with a warning to his attackers: "Do not try to push me." He added, "I am not a leader who can be pushed. I know my job and I know what I have to do."

Sukarno's defiance only aroused his opponents still further. Even before the cabinet installation, agitated students and youths had penetrated deep into the security perimeter of the presidential palace in Djakarta, engaging in fights with the guards and sacking the State Secretariat building on palace grounds. Now the student action command in Bandung and Djakarta, with the covert support of some (by no means all) local Army commanders, seemed determined to intensify its demonstrations. However, on 26 February, Sukarno abruptly banned KAMI, after the student group had led a mass funeral procession through Djakarta in memory of three students killed in previous demonstrations. At the same time Sukarno banned gatherings of more than five students throughout the country. It soon became evident that with these measures Sukarno was merely compounding his mistakes. The KAMI ban was all but ignored by students confident of Army backing. But now a number of party leaders particularly in the PNI Right wing, and in the NU, were becoming alarmed that their own organizations or their youth ancillaries might suffer a similar ban if Sukarno proclaimed an "emergency" in the wake of the continuing student agitation. There was also the rising fury in Army and anti-Sukarno circles over the removal of Nasution from the Cabinet and over the ministerial appointment of figures like Omar Dhani and Oei Tjoe Tat.

But perhaps most disquieting to Sukarno must have been the new tactics of the student demonstrators. For anti-Sukarno agitation now increasingly took on the character of a children's crusade, which had a way of negating the security measures in the capital for which General Suharto, who had been named Minister and Commander of the Army in the new Cabinet, was to a great extent responsible. On 3 March 1966, for example, thousands of high school teenagers stormed the entrance of the Ministry of Basic Education because it was a "nest of *Gestapu/ PKI*". Two days later some 3,000 school children, some not even in their teens, attempted to invade the offices of Foreign Minister Subandrio and simultaneously thousands of students barricaded themselves inside the University of Indonesia in open defiance of Sukarno's ban against student congregations. All over the capital, and in other major West Java cities as well, the wall scribbling, the pamphlet war, and the impromptu student demonstrations and mass meetings against Sukarno were reaching a new crescendo. Though the Army was ordered to disperse the demonstrators without inflicting casualties, "chasing children is not my job", one irate top Army commander was quoted by a British journalist as saying, and in some cases KAMI activists continued their marches and agitation with the tolerant connivance of the police and Army. Only occasionally were demonstrations effectively dispersed and the leaders arrested.

The lesson was not lost on the chief political parties which, pressured by their own youth organizations, now began urging Sukarno to rescind the ban on KAMI, even as the President himself was attempting to provide greater co-ordination to his own followers, including the pro-Sukarno students. But the latter, kept under surveillance by the police and Army, were clearly out-manoeuvred, and Sukarno simply seemed unable to exert sufficient political leverage in the capital or get any significant purchase on public opinion in the city. On 10 March, Sukarno summoned the leaders of the principal parties to the palace for what was described as a heart-to-heart talk but which, according to participants, soon turned into an angry presidential harangue. Although party heads were persuaded at this meeting to issue a statement condemning the student demonstrations, within hours most of them had repudiated the statement.

By now Sukarno must have been deemed to have come to the end of his tether, and his opponents riding the crest of the wave of student agitation lost no time. On 11 March as Sukarno was addressing his Cabinet, an *aide* approached and reportedly told him that "soldiers of an unidentified unit" were nearing the palace. Whether the report was true is still uncertain. But pleading the demands of an "important development" Sukarno at once left the cabinet meeting, flying by helicopter to his Bogor Hill resort palace. There, a few hours later, three top Army commanders closely associated with Suharto (among them the Djakarta garrison commander, Major-General Amir Mahmud) apparently informed Sukarno that there seemed no way to effectively quiet the student agitation and that in the Army leaders' opinion the President's position and safety could no longer be guaranteed unless the Army was given special security powers. Sukarno can hardly have been under any illusion as to the real meaning of this proposal. For in point of fact the Army already had all the power it needed to quell student and other unrest if it really wanted to use that power; what the Army desired was a formal alteration in the structure of executive authority. But under the circumstances Sukarno had little choice and in any event he probably counted on the always mercurial course of Indonesian politics to bring a reversal of his then sagging fortunes.

Assured that he would keep his titles and formal Head of State position, Sukarno agreed to the three Army commanders' demands, as well as to yet another cabinet revision and to an official ban on the PKI. Demand for such a formal proscription of the Communist party had been rising steadily in the months after *Gestapu*. However Sukarno, in keeping with his general efforts to preserve the "Leftist course of the Indonesian Revolution", had dallied and equivocated. At one point, in mid-February 1966, Sukarno was even reported to have "confirmed" a public remark attributed to Subandrio that the PKI had already been "dissolved" within the "framework" of an "integral" post-*Gestapu* solution. But skeptics stressed that no official decree to this effect had ever been issued. Late in the afternoon of 11 March, Sukarno signed a decree formalizing his agreement with the Army: General Suharto as Minister and Commander of the Army was given power "to take all steps" to guarantee domestic tranquillity and to "safeguard the personal safety and authority" of the President and "Great Leader of the Revolution". Among Suharto's very first acts as security head was to sign a decree, dated 12 March 1966, banning and dissolving the PKI throughout the country, on the grounds that the nation had, of late, been subjected to "subversive activity" by alleged "remnants" of the "counter-revolutionary forces" of the *Gestapu*/PKI.

For Sukarno, meanwhile, it was plainly evident that his slide from power was being spear-headed by a relatively new force in Indonesian politics. As he observed to a meeting of territorial military commanders and cabinet officials shortly after the 11 March transfer of power to Suharto, "there are four hundred ways to topple a government, among them the employment of children to block streets and roads — as stated in a CIA handbook". Such an alleged CIA handbook, Sukarno said, he had recently been studying. Youth groups had existed in Indonesia since the dawn of the nationalist awakening in the first decades of the present century. But this was the first time in Indonesian history that pressure from a youthful action front had largely been responsible for bringing about a significant alteration in the national power structure. This is all the more remarkable because the anti-Sukarno student movement, particularly KAMI, and its loosely allied action fronts among high school students, scholars and intellectuals, women, and so on, was a relatively spontaneous affair, emerging within days of *Gestapu* in the major cities of Java.

To be sure, throughout its existence, KAMI's claimed 10,000 membership and scattered "co-ordinating executives" have always wanted for organization. And such parties as NU, the PKI, and the small but influential Christian confessional parties (the *Partai Katolik* and the Protestant *Parkindo*) competed from the start for influence on KAMI's leadership, frequently producing debilitating trends. It remains remarkable nevertheless how quickly and decisively KAMI could on occasion mobilize and pinpoint its forces on tactical objectives. Without the covert, and sometimes not-so-covert, backing of the Army, it is true, KAMI demonstrations would have had much less effect. Still KAMI leaders sometimes showed considerable insight into the mechanics of winning mass support. Early in January 1966, for example, KAMI announced a boycott of all university lectures until the Government retracted recent price rises in petrol, kerosene (widely used as fuel for cooking and for lighting), postal rates and train fares. The campaign had little practical result. But it certainly aided the students' "image" in that it identified the little man's problems with the KAMI demonstrators at a time when Djakarta's grandiose, costly, Sukarno-inspired monuments were increasingly being viewed as symbols not of national greatness but of Government waste and incompetence.

As Sukarno no doubt had anticipated, the 11 March 1966 transfer of powers to Suharto only whetted the student demonstrators' appetite: students now took to occupying government buildings and to "arresting" ministers, among them the Lenin Prize winner and Co-ordinating Education Minister Prijono and Central Banking Minister Jusuf Muda Dalam. The students' new action prompted Suharto to take a number of ministers formally into "protective custody" (in fact arrest), including Prijono, Dalam, Basic Education Minister Sumardjo and Foreign Minister Subandrio (both Dalam and Subandrio shortly found themselves on trial). Suharto let it be known that he had acted upon receiving reports that KAMI had threatened to behead some ministers and impale their heads on the spiked wall of Merdeka Palace. In the midst of this confusion, Sukarno, on 16 March,

26

took to the radio to assert that he was still in full control of the Government, and predictably the next day KAMI staged a new demonstration, "sitting-in" at two government ministries. Cries for a new cabinet "free from Communists" now were beginning to be mixed with another set of slogans demanding the ouster of Sukarno as President altogether.

Then, on 23 March, Djakarta garrison troops reportedly discovered caches of arms and ammunition within the compound of the Central Intelligence Office (*Badan Pusat Intellidjen* — BPI) This civil agency had, until his recent arrest, been headed by Subandrio. It was through his BPI contacts, it may be recalled, that Subandrio, according to his own testimony, had heard of the impending *Gestapu* coup well before it occurred but had done and said nothing about it because he believed the President also knew all about it. An Army announcement charged that the BPI had in fact been used as a distributing centre of arms for underground Communists and "pro-Communist" (read also pro-Sukarno) students. Whether the accusation was true or not, it greatly inflamed opinion against Subandrio. This, along with the fact that a number of other ministers were now also being detained, forced Sukarno to promulgate a new cabinet, a decision which, despite his earlier agreement to do so, he had tried to postpone for as long as possible.

After a brief consultation with Suharto, Sukarno on 27 March 1966 announced formation of a new and considerably smaller Cabinet, headed by a six-man presidium. Sukarno retained his customary Premiership but Suharto (keeping his special 11 March emergency powers) became Fifth Deputy Premier in charge of defence and security. Nasution returned as Minister and Deputy Supreme Commander of the Crush Malaysia Command (KOGAM), a loosely constructed official body of mass mobilization designed to continue the confrontation. It was a relatively minor post and Sukarno, knowing the Army's real feelings about continuing the anti-Malaysia confrontation behind its facade of support for it, may well have wished to embarrass Nasution with such an appointment. Two close associates of Sukarno, Johannes Leimena and Ruslan Abdulgani also were retained as Deputy Premiers. Inevitably, dissatisfaction with the new Cabinet was voiced by anti-Sukarno and anti-*Gestapu* organizations like the Pantja Sila Front, while among student groups there was criticism that the Cabinet still had "Communists" in it. To meet at least some of this criticism Suharto, on 31 March, ordered all government departments and services to "immediately intensify" the "cleansing" of their personnel of any lingering PKI or pro-*Gestapu* elements. And in the following months Army commanders, amidst considerable publicity, announced new efforts to wipe out so-called underground "PKI nests".

Reports of recently discovered plots against the lives of Nasution and Suharto alternated with Army revelations of new Communist terrorist groups bearing such code names as Iceberg and Black Cat, and with accusations against unnamed politicians who were supposedly joining the *Gestapu* remnant's *gerpol* (from *gerilja politik* or political guerilla warfare) against the Army and the new Government. Shortly, additional announcements of waves of arrests in Java and Sumatra of suspected underground Communists and of the discovery of Communist literature further heightened the tension. There were also intermittent clashes, particularly in West and Central Java, between groups of Muslims and anti-Sukarno youths on the one hand, and the PNI student Left, occasionally supported — as in Surabaya — by KKO members, on the other.

By the middle of 1966 Sukarno's enemies apparently were counting to a considerable degree on this deepening crisis atmosphere in order to accelerate the President's fall. Hopes focused now on the speedy reconvening of the MPRS, the body which under the Constitution elects the President and the Vice-President and sets forth the major State policies. Under the slogan "The President must be constitutionalized", some anti-Sukarno forces planned to have the MPRS either formally nullify the extraordinary and extra-constitutional authority which Sukarno had acquired in the era of guided democracy, or else accomplish the election of a new Vice-President (an office that had been vacant since 1957 when Mohammad Hatta resigned, after falling out with Sukarno's policies), and then vote Sukarno out of office so that the new Vice-President could succeed him. Within the Army and such parties as the NU and in the PNI Left there was considerable uncertainty about, if not outright opposition to, such a strategy, however, not least because of partisan rivalry over Sukarno's potential successor and fear that voting the President out of office might yet plunge the country into civil war.

The uncertainty as well as the time needed for a replacement of "purged" Communist members of the MPRS, led to a postponement of the MPRS meeting originally planned on 12 May 1966. KAMI immediately took to the streets again. On 23 May 1966, some 5,000 students marched on Parliament in Djakarta, presenting a demand that the MPRS be convened not later than 1 June. During the demonstration one student was bayoneted and troops were forced to fire warning shots. Meanwhile Suharto was working quietly behind the scenes, warning students

28

not to create a "rift" between the Army and themselves. He also promised alarmed party leaders and Sukarno supporters (also some in the Army itself) that no attempt would be made to oust Sukarno. On 20 June the 546-member MPRS finally met. It elected Nasution chairman, and its decisions confirmed Suharto's special security powers given him on 11 March by Sukarno. It also determined (MPRS decision no. 15/1966) that in the event of the President being unable to carry out his duties Suharto would become Acting President (it declined, however, to elect a new Vice-President). The MPRS also ordered a review of all of Sukarno's presidential decrees and, for good measure, undoubtedly mindful of the cry to "constitutionalize" the President, revoked its 1963 decision naming Sukarno "President for Life". The latter decision, the MPRS was careful to note, did not affect the President's present Head of State position. Other MPRS decisions provided that general elections for a new parliament and MPRS be held by 5 July 1968, approved the ban on the PKI, outlawed Marxist-Leninist doctrine except for purposes of academic study, and recommended that steps be taken to end the anti-Malaysia confrontation.

The MPRS had also asked Sukarno to give it a "progress report" on the state of the nation. Once again Sukarno, who so often in the past had shown himself to be a past master in sensing and utilizing the public temper, was given an opportunity to stabilize his position. Instead, the President's 22 June address, called *Nawaksara* (Nine Points), was one of the shortest policy speeches he ever delivered and also one of his most truculent, as if he was intent on deliberately arousing the MPRS's hostility and frustration. The MPRS had elected him the nation's leader, said Sukarno, and that meant not only that he had an obligation, but also that the MPRS and the nation had a responsibility to to follow him. Moreover, he argued, the MPRS had accepted earlier presidential policy directives as laid down in his speeches as the State's future guide-lines, and these had to be implemented. He stressed that the present MPRS membership was only provisional, and that, hence, as a provisional body, it had better not make decisions from which later the duly elected MPRS might have to deviate.

The angry MPRS reaction was predictable: in another resolution on 5 July, the MPRS demanded that Sukarno give a "full and detailed report on national issues" since becoming President, and in particular that he provide a full account of the causes of *Gestapu,* and of the "economic and moral deterioration of the country". The resolution noted that the President's *Nawaksara* speech had "failed to meet the expectation of the people", because it did not detail his policies surrounding the *Gestapu* affair. The day after this resolution Suharto publicly praised the MPRS's work, and warned that whoever opposed the MPRS's decisions was placing himself outside the law.

Here was as unequivocal a threat to Sukarno supporters (and indeed to the President) as Suharto had made thus far. And it paved the way for the acceptance, without disturbance, of yet another cabinet change, announced by Sukarno on 25 July.

This new Ampera Cabinet which, Sukarno said, he had formed "together" with Suharto, was almost certainly forced on the President by the Army, and in principle may have been agreed on even before the MPRS met. It may also well have been the agreed price the President and his supporters had to pay to ward off a formal MPRS decision to depose Sukarno or to restrict his powers still further. Greatly reduced in size, compared to its predecessors, it featured Suharto as Chief Minister (Sukarno still technically retained the Premier's title), and Adam Malik and the Sultan of Djokjakarta, Hamengku Buwono, as Foreign Affairs and Economics Ministers respectively. Such was the new triumvirate of power, which, with Nasution (not in the Cabinet but as MPRS chairman) in the Olympian position of being its confidant and arbiter, would now begin to dominate New Order policies. Sukarno had little liking for the Cabinet (some of his favourites, like Ruslan Abdulgani and Leimena were gone), and during the new Cabinet's installation on 28 July, the President made a highly petulant and emotional speech, declaring, "I am still Premier because I have been appointed President of the Republic of Indonesia." Then, to Suharto's surprise, Sukarno proceeded to announce two additional cabinet appointments (Abdulgani as chairman of State corporations and Leimena as vice-chairman of the Supreme Advisory Council). This display of presidential wilfulness did little to bolster Sukarno's prestige, however.

Indeed, through the remainder of 1966 it became increasingly clear that Sukarno had lost the political initiative, and that every passing day was accustoming Indonesians to the steady erosion of the President's position. Already at the end of May 1966, Indonesian and Malaysian officials held successful talks in Bangkok looking toward the "beginning of the end" of the Indonesian confrontation. Now, with the MPRS resolution to sustain the Indonesian negotiators, the two countries, on 11 August 1966, reached a formal agreement on ending all hostilities and on a future exchange of diplomatic representation. Malaysia, in a face-saving gesture to Indonesia, also agreed to hold "free and democratic" elections in the near future in Sabah and Sarawak so that the population in these areas would have an opportunity to "reaffirm" its previous decision about their adhesion to Malaysia. During his 17 August 1966 Independence Day speech Sukarno claimed that it had been at his insistence that the Malaysians had agreed to hold these future Sabah and Sarawak elections. But there were few who, by this time, did not realize that the end of the campaign against Malaysia was yet another blow to the President's crumbling authority.

Through the remainder of 1966 the Army also stepped up its purges and arrests of alleged Communist and *Gestapu* suspects (and there is little doubt that many known Sukarno supporters were also among the principal targets of the continuing pogrom). On 20 September 1966, Attorney-General Soegih Arto announced in Djakarta that the number of civilian prisoners detained "because of their involvement in the *Gestapu*/PKI attempted coup" was 120,000. In late August and early September, during the trial of former Central Bank Affairs Minister Jusuf Muda Dalam, and again in October during the trial of former Foreign Minister Subandrio, testimony linking Sukarno to financial malversations and questionable conduct with women, as well as alleging an attempt by the President to protect Aidit from the Army's wrath after the coup, gravely compromised Sukarno further. During the trial of Omar Dhani in December, testimony was presented showing that Sukarno had approved of the training of PKI terrorist squads, that he had concurred in the secret supply of small arms from Communist China to the *Gestapu* plotters and in Dhani's earlier-mentioned "order of the day of 1 October 1965", committing the Air Force to the *Gestapu* cause, and so on. Some of this trial testimony had little corroboration, and it is obvious that the prosecution during the court proceedings (which were Army controlled) never lost sight of the political implications of such testimony. Whether, indeed, the very staging of the trials of Muda Dalam, Subandrio and Dhani shortly after the MPRS session was another well-calculated step in the campaign of Sukarno's enemies in the Army to bring the President down gradually, cannot now be proven. But there is no question that the trials greatly undermined the remaining vestiges of Sukarno's prestige.

Sensing this, Sukarno, in the last few months of 1966 began a kind of oratorical counter attack, raising once again — as he had done so often in the past — the spectre of a foreign conspiracy, and publicly charging that "CIA snipers" had orders to kill him. He reaffirmed that he was still Head of State, that his ideology was still the official guide of the nation, and he ridiculed attempts (such as the recent MPRS decision) to ban Marxism-Leninism. But Sukarno only succeeded in polarizing

31

tensions. Expressions of support for the President in the PNI paper *Suluh Marhaen,* and reports during the middle of October 1966 that restive pro-Sukarno student groups in Central and East Java were getting ready for a dramatic "march on Djakarta" in order to "save the President/Great Leader of the Revolution", were countered by new anti-Sukarno student agitation in Djakarta, and by increasing public demands that Sukarno be put on trial. On 1 October 1966, the first anniversary of the *Gestapu* affair, some 6,000 students led by KAMI converged on the presidential palace in the capital shouting that Sukarno be tried for leading the *Gestapu* coup. Academicians and sections of the Djakarta press now also began to demand that the President resign, while local and provincial legislative councils in Sumatra and Sulawesi (Celebes) passed resolutions demanding that the President explain his "involvement" in the 30 September events. Pro-Sukarno and covert pro-PKI groups like *Germindo* (from *Gerakan Maha-siswa Indonesia*— Indonesian Students Movement), and the Bung Karno University Students Association, also continued their demonstrations in the capital, however, and on 19 December 1966 at a rally of his supporters in Djakarta, Sukarno felt emboldened enough to call for a restoration of guided democracy in the country. Such demands readily infuriated his opponents and provoked more demands for drastic action against Sukarno.

But, as the slogan *"Mahmillubkan Sukarno!"* ("Try Sukarno by a special military court!") found an ever bigger following, Suharto and his associates, as well as Sukarno's own friends in the PNI, began quietly to put pressure on Sukarno to mitigate his tactics and to suggest that in his own interest he occasionally make a conciliatory gesture. Evidently the Army feared that aroused public sentiment was running ahead of its own careful Fabian tactic, and that a bloody explosion might yet occur. What advantage Sukarno may have seen in acquiescing to such suggestions is unclear. Perhaps he hoped to cut some of the ground from under his opponents' charges, or win over some of the doubtful. At any rate, already on 5 October 1966, at a parade in Djakarta in celebration of Indonesian Armed Forces Day, Sukarno condemned the *Gestapu* coup as treasonous (the first time he had publicly done so). In an emotional scene he also paid his respect at the graves of the six Army generals slain by the *Gestapu* terrorists. Considering the mounting furor over Sukarno's alleged conduct during the coup, however, such gestures made at this late date probably appeared to not a few to be hypocritical.

By the middle of December 1966, Suharto apparently became even more concerned over the continuing popular pressure for the President's removal and the provocative conduct of Sukarno supporters. On 21 December, with tensions running at a new high over Sukarno's demand for the restoration of guided democracy, Suharto and principal armed forces commanders issued a joint statement declaring that "after attentively studying the recent internal political developments" the Indonesian armed forces would "consistently" defend the Constitution and the decisions of the MPRS, and would oppose "any group" violating the Constitution or obstructing the work of the Cabinet. The warning seemed as much directed to their own militant followers as to the pro-Sukarno elements. In discussions with the President, armed forces chiefs also persuaded a reluctant Sukarno to issue a "supplement" to his *Nawaksara* address to the MPRS, in conformity with the MPRS resolution the previous July that he give an accounting of the *Gestapu* affair and of the country's "economic and moral deterioration". To lend weight to the Army's 21 December statement, eleven battalions from various units of the armed forces staged what was billed as a "show of force" parade in Djakarta on 28 December.

It was late — probably too late — for a *mea culpa;* yet, if he had been willing even now to pronounce one, and been able to link himself successfully, as so often in the past, with the nation's hopes, errors and tribulations, Sukarno might yet have had a chance to neutralize the stratagems of his enemies and salvage all or most of his constitutional position. But Sukarno declined to take that chance. With his *Nawaksara* supplement, issued on the evening of 10 January 1967, and read in an angry voice to reporters shortly after a copy had been sent to the MPRS executive, Sukarno sealed his political doom. In the supplement Sukarno declared that MPRS had no constitutional right to demand from him an account of specific political decisions except in so far as they touched broad lines of State policy. (Sukarno was technically correct. Under the Constitution the MPRS is to be concerned only with laying down broad policy lines, leaving their implementation to the President and Parliament. But Sukarno chose to ignore the question of what specific political decision could really be considered wholly apart from the policy line laid down by the MPRS.) He went on to say that he had already condemned the *Gestapu* coup, the occurrence of which had been a "complete surprise to me". The coup had three causes, Sukarno said: blundering PKI leaders, the cunning of the *nekolim* and the activities of persons who were "crazy", If he was to be held solely responsible for the *Gestapu* affair, then he would ask that "truth and justice" be served and that it also be determined who was responsible "for the series of

33

attempts on my life in the past". As for the deterioration of the Indonesian economy, it was not the responsibility of one person, but was the result of "objective factors" and of decisions taken by government and society as a whole; the same principle of collective responsibility, Sukarno said, and the "process of consciousness" in the entire nation, underlay any moral deterioration. Defiantly Sukarno asked why he only was asked for an accounting in connection with the *Gestapu* affair: "Is not, for instance, the then Co-ordinating Minister for Defence and Security (namely Nasution) responsible too?"

After this statement yet another acceleration in Sukarno's slide from power began. The general chorus of criticism and calumny of the *Nawaksara* supplement, now coming from virtually all political groups (with the notable exception of the PNI executive) and all levels of society, soon turned to a demand for Sukarno's replacement as President. On 20 January 1967, it was announced that the MPRS would shortly meet to discuss Sukarno's further tenure in office. A week later MPRS leaders were quoted as saying that most people now held the view that Sukarno had been involved in *Gestapu,* that there was public unanimity that the *Nawaksara* supplement was unacceptable, and that the President had in effect "neglected" his constitutional duties (presumably by having given an inadequate accounting to the MPRS). Foreign Minister Malik was to declare later that in this period he had repeatedly counselled Sukarno ("my old comrade in arms") to step down voluntarily, but that Sukarno remained "stubborn". After the *Badan Pekerdja* (Executive Standing Committee) of the MPRS had by mid-February formally rejected the *Nawaksara* supplement and resolved to demand the ouster of Sukarno, Suharto, according to Malik, also began to persuade the President to resign voluntarily. Malik thought it "illogical" by this time that Sukarno's resignation would plunge the country into civil war.

It is still uncertain whether Sukarno, faced with an imminent MPRS decision to revoke his authority altogether, might have already reached a compromise with Suharto and the Army, or whether he now hastily sought such a compromise himself after earlier suggestions that he resign voluntarily had come to nought. As late as 10 February he was reported to have spent a lonely night under a banyan tree in his Merdeka Palace garden, trying to make up his mind, and subsequently — as he wept — to have told unnamed emissaries from the Army and police that he would not step down. Whatever the ultimate precipitating factors, on 22 February 1967, Information Minister Diah announced to the press, after a plenary cabinet meeting, that as of 20 February Sukarno had surrendered all his governing powers to General Suharto in accordance with "the spirit of MPRS decision no. 15/1966". This decision, which was one of a raft promulgated by the MPRS the previous July, it may be recalled, had provided that in the event of the President being unable to carry out his duties, Suharto would become Acting President. This transfer of governing authority would still leave Sukarno with the formal title of President, and it was stipulated that Suharto would regularly report to Sukarno "on the implementation of the task transferred to him". The Diah statement stressed that the transfer of authority had taken place "without diminishing the aim and spirit" of the Constitution, under which Sukarno remained the official "mandatory" (that is chief executive) of the MPRS.

Thus, almost a year after he had granted Suharto authority "to take all steps" to guarantee domestic peace, Sukarno relinquished the rest of his *de facto* constitutional powers. By this time most of his vocal support, such as the PNI Left wing, the KKO rank and file, and the Sukarnoist student fronts had, at least for the moment, been cowed into an uneasy silence. All during January 1967 thousands of anti-Sukarno students had kept up the pressure, staging New Order rallies in Java and Sumatra. Among the principal political parties, too, a momentum was now developing to settle what was euphemistically referred to as the "dualism in the State leadership" (that is the problem of the divided executive authority of Sukarno and Suharto). The antagonism between Suharto and the President could not last indefinitely, it was now being argued. If Sukarno was not removed from power, and soon, the political pendulum might eventually begin to swing back toward him again, particularly as problems of economic stabilization continued to press.

The Army meanwhile, despite its protestations that constitutional procedures needed to be observed, had pushed forward with its own anti-Sukarno campaign, and local commanders kept up a steady drum-fire of allegations against and veiled warnings to the President's followers. On 13 February 1967, in a radio broadcast, Nasution, in effect, laid sole responsibility for the *Gestapu* affair on Sukarno. The MPRS chairman was replying to Sukarno's demands, made in his *Nawaksara* supplementary statement, that Nasution explain his own conduct in relation to the *Gestapu* affair. Nasution implied that Sukarno disliked him because he, Nasution, was anti-Communist.

Three days later Nasution presented a document to the MPRS executive committee purporting to show Sukarno's full support of the coup. According to this document Sukarno allegedly threatened to strike an officer who refused to join the *Gestapu* plot, after telling the officer that "in a revolution a father may devour his own children". The veracity of these and similar charges is hard to substantiate. It may be noted that Suharto, in his earlier-mentioned 7 March 1967 report to the MPRS on Sukarno's involvement in the *Gestapu* affair, makes no explicit reference to these allegations. But the effect of such charges — and of such additional revelations that Sukarno had provided one of the chief *Gestapu* plotters, former Brigadier-General Supardjo, with a "letter of protection" — might well have convinced Sukarno and his friends that, under the circumstances the President would be lucky to retain his titular authority and escape a humiliating public trial. In his March report to the MPRS on Sukarno's conduct during *Gestapu*, Suharto himself appealed to the MPRS not to dismiss Sukarno formally; rumour had it that permitting Sukarno formally to retain the presidential title had been Suharto's end of the bargain making the 20 February transfer of authority possible.

And so, during the first half of March 1967, a reconvened MPRS put its stamp of approval on what was described as a "typically Indonesian" compromise. In its decision no. 33 of 12 March 1967, the MPRS formally legitimized the 20 February transfer of power to Suharto, by declaring him Acting President and by formally revoking its "mandate" to Sukarno. Sukarno was in effect replaced, but the MPRS refused to formally declare him "dismissed" (the demand of anti-Sukarno students). The MPRS said that Sukarno had failed in his "constitutional responsibility" toward the MPRS and in the execution of directions and decisions it had given him. It also noted that Sukarno had not given "a clear account" of his policy that had led to Indonesia's economic and moral decline, and indeed, that Sukarno had carried out a policy which "indirectly benefited" the abortive 30 September 1965 coup. The same MPRS decision barred Sukarno from engaging in "political activities" until after the forthcoming general elections and ominously stipulated that "further legal procedures" with regard to "the person" of Sukarno be conducted with regard for the due process of law but "at the discretion of the Acting President".

Additional MPRS decrees at this time also revoked Sukarno's title of Great Leader of the Revolution and demanded a reorientation of the country away from the Sukarnoist ideology. For weeks afterwards uncertainty about the President's exact constitutional status and rights prevailed, although prominent Indonesian leaders in effect endorsed the verbal ambiguity of MPRS decision no. 33. Referring to Sukarno, Suharto reportedly told students, "If it is dismissal I will be unable to cope with the security situation," and on the night of 12 March, MPRS chairman Nasution also refused to clarify for foreign reporters whether Sukarno was still — if only titularly — the President of Indonesia, pleading, "You must understand the Indonesian way of thinking".

Under virtual house arrest, and barred for the time being from further "political activities", Sukarno's political teeth now seemed to have been effectively drawn, although, as will become apparent in subsequent chapters, his residual influence continued to make itself felt on the Indonesian scene. That he would retain some such influence, and that in the mercurial course of Indonesian politics and amidst the staggering problems of national reconstruction, his chance of a come-back to power could even now not be wholly discounted, may — along with the evident strength of his opponents — well have been among the main considerations that led Sukarno eventually to accept the events of 20 February and following. His tactics of calculated defiance, followed by reluctant retreat, of relying on his charisma and appealing over the heads of Army and party leaders to the masses, and of attempting to polarize political and ideological patterns by making himself the spokesman of the Left "progressive" course of the Indonesian Revolution, had all failed. The Army had *not* been provoked into precipitate action ahead of public opinion. It had *not* allowed itself, in the crucial early months after *Gestapu,* to become generally identified as the Right wing "reactionary" target of Sukarno's followers and the Left remnant. And, above all, it had succeeded in carefully, if ruthlessly, eliminating or neutralizing many of its principal PKI enemies and their allies. Throughout its confrontation with Sukarno the Army's tactic was to allow, and even to encourage, an accelerating public reaction to the President and his provocative conduct and that of his followers, while at the same time seeming to limit and, in fact, occasionally to repress that reaction. But at all times the Army demonstrated that it was, and intended to stay, in control of the rising public agitation (for example the warning by Suharto and other Army commanders on 21 December 1966 that they would not tolerate a "deviation" from constitutional procedures).

There has been much speculation that already in the closing weeks of 1965 Nasution, Suharto, General Dharsono, and a bevy of anti-Sukarno intellectuals in close touch with the student movement, devised the basic Fabian tactic of forcing the President from power, a tactic code-named *Operasi Lembing Mas* (Operation Golden Spear). It may well have been so.

Certainly the evidence points to frequently careful co-ordination between Army commanders and student leaders in various demonstrations and to occasionally equally disciplined resistance by the same New Order activists to any tendency toward a precipitate response to Sukarno's provocations.

But whether or not there was a *Lembing Mas* operation, it must always be remembered that as late as his *Nawaksara* supplementary statement of 10 January 1967, Sukarno retained some chance of saving his political position had he been willing to play, if only for a while, the contrite role which most of the MPRS, the Army, and much, though by no means all, of the parties' leaders were demanding of him. To be sure, for KAMI and its other academic allies, any political rehabilitation of Sukarno in whatever form would have been unacceptable — they wanted him gone, once and for all. But others, particularly many in the PNI and NU rank and file, and in the civil bureaucracy, calculating the strength of the President's residual popularity, and anxious not to allow the Army to dictate the new pattern of Indonesian politics, were (if only in the interests of preventing a bloody chaos) quite prepared to have Sukarno remain on the political scene. He would have to be divested of his superhuman and extra-constitutional aura, of course. But as a power centre and political balance in his own right he would be both needed and wanted in post-coup Indonesia.

Sukarno was not prepared to play this role, however. A few conciliatory gestures, as for example in October 1966, when he participated in a brief commemorative ceremony at the graves of the six generals killed by *Gestapu* terrorists, were the limit of his willingness to accommodate his enemies. He calculated — and who could say at the time that he was altogether wrong — that delivery of a *mea culpa* would only weaken his position further, without placating in any way those seeking his downfall, and that, in any case, whatever he might then salvage of his position, he would become too heavily dependent on the Army. His, after all, was a highly personalized conception of government, a mixture of messianic ardour, sometimes bordering on megalomania, and impulsive intransigence — a less theatrical, less Olympian, more legalistic and more carefully circumscribed type of leadership was not his political style. Above all — and again who can confidently predict here that he was unrealistic — Sukarno counted on the fluidity, the institutional instability of Indonesian government and politics. Might the continuing deadlock of "dualism" in the national leadership, for example, not eventually have produced a prematurely rash action on the part of the Army, the students or, for that matter, even of Sukarno's own supporters, a development providing the President with, possibly, new leverage? And, finally, even if Sukarno for the moment had lost his contest with the students and the Army, who could confidently foretell — again considering the volatile course of past Indonesian political developments — that a future political come-back had then become wholly out of the question?

For the Army, therefore, not to be provoked — indeed, seemingly not to move at all except when pushed from behind by a wave of popular indignation — was the essential tactic. There was, moreover, the concern of Suharto, Nasution, and many of their followers, for the preservation of at least a semblance of constitutional procedures as the erosion of Sukarno's powers progressed. Hence, each transfer of authority by the President to Suharto, whether in March 1966, or in February 1967, was retroactively legitimized by the only body constitutionally able to tamper with the chief executive's authority, namely the MPRS. Even so, Suharto and his friends could hardly hope to escape the charge of their critics that such *ex post facto* legitimizations, following the pressures of street mobs which the Army itself had helped to arouse, had only spurious constitutional value. Sensitivity on this point may account for the description by Suharto in a radio broadcast on 13 March 1967 of Sukarno as "for the time being" a "president without powers", thus deliberately obscuring his own constitutional position.

Above all, the Army's anxiety to prevent a civil war should be stressed. As noted earlier, as late as March 1967, when the MPRS revoked Sukarno's presidential powers, Suharto feared that domestic security might not be maintained if, in fact, the President were declared "dismissed". Deposing Sukarno thus had to occur gradually, if it was to occur at all. And Suharto's Fabianism — indeed, the Army's appearance of periodically even acting as if it were the President's defender — probably outraged Suharto's supporters as often as it puzzled his enemies.

The year-and-a-half-long duel between Sukarno and his opponents unquestionably aggravated Indonesia's domestic economic problems. It is probably correct to say that the postponement of meaningful reforms during this constitutional contest (as all the while living conditions in the country further deteriorated) eventually began to act as an added popular impetus for a change in leadership. Already by the end of 1965 the Indonesian economy seemed to be plunging into new and dangerous depths. A retrospective survey of the state of the Indonesian economy, published in the 13 February 1969 issue of the *Far Eastern Economic Review* noted:

At the end of 1965 the consumer price index (1958=100) had stood at 36,347, with prices seven times the level of the previous January. Inflation spiralled in 1965 at a rate of 594% as against 135% in 1964 and 128% in 1963. The index of real income for labourers in Djakarta (1958=100) stood at less than 40; the money supply rose over 1965 from Rps 675,107 million to Rps 2,582,014 million.

During 1966, the same source indicates — although the MPRS at its meeting in June had ordered the Government to halt the inflation and begin rehabilitating the economy — that little could be accomplished besides implementation of new regulations, announced on 3 October, liberalizing the position of foreign investment and introducing much needed changes in budget policies. The consumer price index toward the end of the year rose to 267,276, "well over seven times the level at the beginning of 1966". The 1966 inflation rate was 635 per cent (more than four times the 1964 rate), while the money supply rose more than eight times to Rp.21,024,000 million. The official exchange rate of the rupiah, which had been 39 to the US dollar in January 1966, plunged to 122 to the dollar by December of that year. Throughout the months' long constitutional crisis, as Sukarno and Suharto and their followers were jockeying for power, one thing became ever clearer and that was that the plight of the average Indonesian was steadily worsening. In a number of cities, as has been indicated, KAMI demonstrators successfully linked their anti-Sukarno agitation with a demand for lower prices. A climate was developing in which a change — almost *any* change — in national leadership seemed called for, if complete disaster was not to engulf the country.

This dangerous retrogression was in many respects but an acceleration of the decline that had already become particularly apparent in virtually all phases of economic life since Indonesia undertook its confrontation against Malaysia. At that time government officials, from Sukarno down, announced a deliberate disregard of economic problems and development for the sake of concentrating on Indonesia's "revolutionary spirit". Among many deleterious consequences of such a policy one feature, the return of the malaria problem, may be briefly noted here by way of illustration.

In 1960 the Indonesian Government, with the help of the World Health Organization, began a ten-year programme to eradicate the scourge of malaria from Indonesia, which up to that time was causing an estimated 120,000 deaths per annum, and which was believed to be responsible for from ten to fifteen per cent of Indonesia's infant mortality rate. Already by 1964, after an intensive campaign, virtually the whole of Java was free from malaria, and the eradication programme was rapidly being extended to the other Indonesian islands. Then, suddenly, foreign exchange and aid funds for the programme were cut off, and neither insecticides nor spare parts for spraying equipment and vehicles could be obtained; Sukarno meanwhile told the United States to "go to hell" with its aid. Shortly malaria returned to Java. Today, the disease rate again runs at about 15,000 cases a year. "Politics is the reason malaria has come back," Dr Sulianto Saroso, director of the communicable diseases centre of the Indonesian Health Ministry, remarked in early March 1969, adding that "malaria is once again our most serious health problem".

Despite the seemingly enormous capacity of Indonesians for adjusting to new drops in their already low living standards, including chronic malnutrition and even periodic incidences of famine, it is evident that the steady running down of the economy and the chaos in so much of the civil administration and in the transportation, communication and other phases of public life, significantly sharpened demands, especially among the young and the intellectual community, for a drastic break with the *Orla* or *Orde Lama* (Old Order). Fairly or not, Sukarno, more than anyone else in the nation, was the symbol of *Orla*. His removal came to be seen by many as indispensable to the initiation of the long overdue process of national rehabilitation.

It is well to stress also that the whole constitutional struggle between Sukarno and Suharto was virtually a Java-centred, indeed, in critical respects, a Djakarta-centred affair. Diffused over scores of islands large and small, the Central Indonesian Government's authority has a tendency to weaken with the distance from the capital and, for example, neither in the western part of the country in strongly Muslim Acheh, North Sumatra (where Sukarno had never been popular), nor more than 2,000 miles away to the east in the Moluccas, with their sizeable concentrations of Christians (among whom there had generally also been little sympathy for Sukarno), did the tumultuous events in the capital produce more than a slight echo. The regional Indonesian press beyond Java, heavily dependent on wire service reports of the Government's own news agency or on bulletins over the government radio, provided little more than a belated and bare outline of the major political changes, and often not even that much. Radios still are not in general use, and the wholly inadequate inter-island transport and communications system and utter isolation of even sizeable coastal centres throughout the Indonesian archipelago, helped to virtually insulate the contending factions in Djakarta from any significant provincial reaction. Such reaction as might have come in due time was generally undercut with considerable efficiency. During most of 1966, for example, Suharto, Nasution, and their Army supporters, had moved swiftly in transferring or administratively quarantining those officers and units in the areas beyond Java of whose loyalties they were not altogether sure. At other times, as during the Dhani and Subandrio trials, in a clear effort to discredit the President, anti-Sukarno Army commanders arranged for the periodic supply of quantities of Djakarta newspapers to regions beyond Java.

In a few areas, for example in North Sumatra, Bali, and Western Kalimantan (Borneo), local Army commanders, aided by secondary school students' action fronts and/or religious groups, were responsible for local pogroms of Communists and suspected sympathizers (which, except for Bali, did not reach the bloody dimensions of similar campaigns in Java), and for arrests and purges among civil servants and a few PKI party leaders. But these came generally after the main wave of killings and incarcerations on Java. In most of the Indonesian islands beyond Java, and, indeed, in the more remote southern sections of Java itself, the daily round went on much as before, with the Army, the police, and local bureaucracy largely undisturbed, exercising routine authority as they had usually done.

But now Indonesia had a new *de facto* President, and even in Java and among significant sections of the Djakarta intelligentsia, let alone abroad, little was really known about him. Who was the successor to the legendary Sukarno, and who were the people arrayed for and against him?

Even today, after a spate of Ministry of Information releases and lively popular biographies about "Pak Harto", Indonesia's new strong man seems rather colourless compared to his flamboyant predecessor. Born on 8 June 1921, in the village of Kemusu, in Central Java, Suharto later attended schools in Wurjantoro, a small community near Djokjakarta, and Wonogiri. Some sources report that his grandfather had served in the bodyguard of the Sultan of Djokjakarta; but in any event young Suharto seems, since his early youth, to have been steeped in the traditions of feudal-aristocratic Javanese culture and its mystical dimensions. Through one of his father's friends, in whose house he lived in Wonogiri, young Suharto came under the influence of one Raden Mas Darjatmo, a religious teacher and soothsayer, who deepened the boy's interest in traditional Javanese lore. By 1940, when Suharto matriculated at a military academy at Gombong, he had in manners and beliefs become the typically marginal individual which colonial systems tend to produce: westernized,

42

indeed, "dutchified" to a degree, but Javanese underneath (he is said to continue to set great store by the advice of a *dukun* or *kebatinan* — soothsayer or medium).

During the Japanese Occupation of Indonesia (1942-5) Suharto entered the quasi-military Japanese PETA organization as a second lieutenant and subsequently, throughout the Indonesian Revolution against the Dutch (1945-9), he served with distinction, rising to lieutenant-colonel. It was eight years before a full colonelcy came his way, however, and during Indonesia's early years of independence, when military service rivalries and generation conflicts and competition between Army officers were particularly intense, Suharto was usually in the background. Quietly competent, relatively unknown and unpretentious, he must frequently have struck his more politically minded Army superiors as an ideal compromise appointment for controversial or difficult positions. Thus Suharto was eventually to find himself administrative head of such dubious bodies as the Army's Ad Hoc Retooling Office, a Sukarno-inspired investigatory agency charged with purging military, as well as civil personnel in Army service believed to be "disloyal" or at any rate less than enthusiastic toward Sukarno's guided democracy and its policies. It was especially the Indonesian Communist Party which in the early sixties pressed the Retooling Office to remove party enemies from important posts, and Suharto, though never known to be publicly critical of the President or of the PKI at this time, can hardly have relished his job. His family life, then as now, probably provided him solace. Since 1947 he has been married to the daughter of an aristocratic family in Surakarta, Central Java. Monogamous and family centred — he has five children — Suharto's private life, in its sobriety, has been in marked contrast to that of Sukarno.

In 1960 Suharto was promoted to brigadier and in 1962 to major-general, after which he assumed a broad military supervisory position as commander of the campaign to "liberate" West New Guinea. None of his commands offered him an opportunity for particular distinction and his appointment to the command of *Kostrad* (the Army's Strategic Reserve), the post he held at the time of *Gestapu*, was a routine affair, dictated by seniority and proven, if unspectacular, abilities. There is no doubt, however, that he acted with unusual skill and initiative during the 30 September coup (though one might wonder what would have happened if Nasution too had fallen under the assassins' hands). Still, the fact remains that he was not considered important enough by the Lubang Buaja terrorists to be on their list of the top commanders of the Army marked for death.

Gestapu and its aftermath catapulted him into a prominence which he neither particularly wanted nor, indeed, was believed to be suited for in the opinion of many observers familiar with the pattern of contending political forces developing in the coup's aftermath. Despite his decisive crushing of the *Gestapu* coup, Suharto never personally emerged as a fanatic anti-Sukarnoist. Indeed, if Sukarno had been able to make the conciliatory gestures of the *mea culpa* that might well have saved his position, Suharto would not have stood in his way. To some in the capital, therefore, General Nasution seemed a more logical choice to lead the anti-Sukarno New Order struggle. To others, a still-respected elder statesman, who had publicly disagreed with many of Sukarno's policies without becoming involved in anti-national cabals, for example former Vice-President Mohammad Hatta, seemed the man for such a job. It was Suharto, however, who was to become, more and more, *Orba's* new symbol, not least, one suspects, because of his comparative colourlessness. Then again he was the ideal compromise candidate for a controversial role, a role which always would have to reckon with the inflamed sentiments of pro- and anti-Sukarno partisans. Neither a heavy thinker, nor an Army militant (like Dharsono), nor a party leader, nor a grand old man of the revolution, Suharto was first and foremost expected to project his natural image: a quiet, good man in a difficult job. He was to be *Pak* (father) Harto, an appellation that suits him as well as the designation *Bung* (an idiomatic Indonesian expression of fraternal common man-nishness, perhaps best translated by the Australian term "mate") fitted the Jacobin authoritarianism of Karno, that is Sukarno, although on occasion *Pak* has also been applied — if much less appropriately — to the latter. In these predicates *Pak* and *Bung* there lie, for the Indonesian, important if subtle differences in personal ways of life and public images, critical to a public acceptance of the post-Sukarno *Orde Baru* and its leaders, at least initially.

Even before the 20 February 1967 transfer of executive authority to Suharto, a new mosaic of contending political forces had begun to emerge. Within the branches of the armed forces, the political parties, the pressure groups like the students action fronts and their other academic allies, the trade unions, the civil bureaucracy, and other power structures and organizations, the end of the Sukarno era was bringing about new alignments of interests and loyalties. The pattern of these competing interests, and the efficacy of the political system in expressing and dealing with them, will engage our attention in chapter III.

CHAPTER THREE

The Politics of the New Order:
Parties and Parliament

"WE HAVE a presidential system of government. But the political party system was a left-over from our parliamentary system of government," the distinguished Indonesian journalist Mochtar Lubis wrote recently. And, in fact, two often mutually antagonistic trends have run through Indonesia's national political life. One trend views the country essentially from the vantage point of modern Western constitutional democracy, in which the parliamentary process, based on a competitive political party system, and on ministerial responsibility, generally prevails. The nation's chief executive tends to be relatively weak and largely ornamental in such a system. Already in the nineteen-twenties and thirties, the closing decades of the Dutch colonial period, this view found expression in Indonesian nationalist circles in the proud slogan and demand, *"Indonesia berparlemen!"* ("A parliament for Indonesia!") But the other trend too has roots in the early nationalist period. It aspires to a more autochthonous Indonesia and, in stressing the ethnic diversity as well as the dispersed geographical structure of the country, it favours a strong, national executive leadership in the form of a so-called presidential system of central government. Parliament or other representative bodies would by no means be wholly insignificant. But, typically, formal ministerial responsibility would not exist, and the burdens of policy development and implementation would fall far more heavily on the national executive than in the other system.

Already in Indonesia's revolutionary period (1945-9) adherents of these two trends had clashed sharply. In the early fifties, however, Indonesia began its national constitutional history with, essentially, a concept of parliamentary supremacy, cabinet responsibility and a relatively weak national executive. As, increasingly, regional discontent with the centre and the tendency of dissident military to assume political power became more and more apparent, Sukarno (whose own political style had always been based on a strong presidential system) succeeded in progressively emasculating parliamentary powers.

Sukarno's semi-dictatorial system of guided democracy, as it developed in the late nineteen-fifties and early sixties was made possible by several factors. Pivotal was the so-called Constitution of 1945 (imposed by Sukarno's decree in July 1959, after an elected Constituent Assembly seemed to have reached a complete deadlock in its formulation of a proposed new fundamental law for the nation). The new Constitution, replacing the one of 1949-51, sanctifies wide presidential powers. There was also the mutual antagonism and hence resulting weakness of diverse political parties which in many respects had been deeply aggravated since the 1955 general parliamentary elections, the only poll of this kind held in the country thus far. It was the PKI which, making a virtue out of Parliament's weakness, identified itself closely with Sukarno and his verbal symbols and thus proved perhaps most adept in exploiting the presidential system to its own advantage. Finally, it should be stressed that the Indonesian Army benefited from the drift toward authoritarian government. Loyal Army and other armed forces elements, operating first against regional rebels, and later mobilized in the West New Guinea and Malaysia confrontation campaigns, saw their prestige and political powers steadily enhanced. In the prevailing state of emergency local Army commanders increasingly exercised pro-consular authority. Nor could there be any thought of a retrenchment of the overblown size of the armed forces establishment or of a halt to costly purchases of weapons in such circumstances.

Throughout the later Sukarno era emphasis was placed on the truly "Indonesian" character of the guided democracy system. For example, *mufakat* and *musjawarah* — mutual deliberation and concensus — were seen as the proper methods of parliamentary deliberations, not the juxtaposition of contending views in debate and a resulting division of the House in voting procedure. *Gotong rojong* — a term referring to traditional patterns of mutual co-operation in the village sphere — supposedly expressed the spirit of the Sukarno system. Yet *gotong rojong* practices had long since eroded (or, indeed, never existed) in many rural areas and the term, in practice, often came to mask an enforced ideological conformism and a steady undermining of individual political rights.

The end of the Sukarno era unleashed sharply divergent demands for constitutional reform. In the first instance demands for change went in the direction of a restoration of Parliament's authority, but in this field some wished to go much farther than others. For leading *Orba* intellectuals — for example later Education Minister Mashuri, the Government's radio and television director Dr Umar Khayam, the historian and later ambassador to the United States Sudjatmoko, and the journalist Mochtar Lubis — as well as for many student front activists (among them KAMI leaders Rahman Tolleng and Y. Anwar) and prominent anti-Sukarno military (for example Major-General Dharsono, then commander of the West Java-based Siliwangi division), it was not just a matter of returning to a parliamentary system. Some of the members of this group, either formally or informally, had been identified with the small but influential *Partai Sosialis Indonesia* (PSI) before it, along with *Masjumi,* had been banned in 1960. This group envisaged a complete transformation of Parliament *and* the party system together. Parties in the past, according to this view, had been ineffective or worse because they were mainly articulators of specific elite or ideological interests with little in the way of distinctive or practical work programmes. Hence, it was argued, existing parties should be "encouraged" to form into two "blocs", one with a more "progressive", the other with a more "conservative" programme as a kind of prelude to the eventual development of a two-party system.

But others in this group who had reflected on the resistance to past attempts to "simplify" the Indonesian party system, instead favoured the creation of a new "party" or bloc. This new bloc would consist of capable persons, unaffiliated with any of the major parties, who, acting as an "Independent Group", could co-operate with the armed forces and perhaps also lead the other parties in the planned constitutional transformation. All such notions of reform, however, were greeted with much less enthusiasm, if not with open hostility, by most of the existing parties themselves. Opposition was apparent not only among the two biggest groups, the *Nahdatul Ulama,* the conservative and largely Java-based Muslim party, and among the badly divided PNI, but also among the much smaller but quite influential Christian confessional parties (the *Partai Katolik* and the Protestant *Parkindo*) and the United Indonesian Islamic Party (*Partai Sharikat Islam Indonesia* — PSII). None of these parties relished the idea of a merger or a dual-party system, and virtually all of them looked distrustfully at the Independent Group. For the parties the end of the Sukarno era essentially meant a return to a parliamentary and constitutional system in which their influence would once again be decisive; some in the parties even toyed with the idea of restoring some modified version of the

47

"parliamentary" Constitution of 1949-51.

But scrapping the presidential system and the 1945 Constitution that legitimizes it was anathema to a number of so-called "functional groups", including a number of Army-dominated labour organizations which had always looked to a strong executive for protection. It was also anathema to the small IPKI party (Independence Upholders Party) strong among the military, and, eventually, to not a few intellectuals who feared most a return to the free-wheeling and often debilitating system of parliamentary and party politics of the early nineteen-fifties before Sukarno imposed his guided democracy. Above all, the notion of a fundamental constitutional change came to be repugnant to Nasution, Suharto and other top armed forces leaders, mostly because they were not inclined to have the arduous struggle of clipping Sukarno's political wings complicated by or culminate in the return of an uncertain parliamentary system. Indeed, some of the most vociferous anti-Sukarno Army officers held — and continue to hold — a very low opinion of party politics and, by implication, of Parliament as well. As indicated earlier, the Army had by and large benefited from the authoritarian dimensions of Sukarno's guided democracy and the reimposition of the 1945 Constitution. Now, in the difficult post-Sukarno era, the Army hardly felt ready to divest itself of its vast political powers. In the view of many Army leaders it was Sukarno personally, Sukarno's incessant ideological abacadabra, his ruinous anti-Malaysia confrontation and his policy of deliberately ignoring economic problems that had to go. But as for Sukarno's constitutional *system* — that was another matter, and though considered to be in need of modification that system, on the whole, was believed to be quite serviceable still.

These divergent constitutional aspirations and demands had already by the end of 1968 largely resolved themselves in a new alignment of political forces which to a degree tended to polarize military and civilian interests. Certainly by that time the PSI-Independent Group and the advocates of parliamentary reform and of a two-party system had demonstrated their lack of significant mass support though, individually, the group's members remained highly influential in the upper echelons of the Government. Reluctantly many in this group were beginning to consider affiliating with the party system but were encountering difficulty, in some cases, in finding a congenial party "home". The Constitution of 1945 seemed likely to remain for the time being. The political authority of the armed forces, though somewhat clipped and increasingly subject to public criticism, appeared relatively secure, at least until after the general elections (now to be held by the middle of 1971). And Parliament and the parties, though likely to be divested of some of the procedural and operational restrictions of the guided democracy era — for example the *musjawarah* concept of unanimity in parliamentary decisions was undergoing attack — for the moment appeared more intent on consolidating their position and electoral following rather than in pressing for immediate fundamental constitutional reforms.

Even so, on several occasions parties had collided heavily with the post-Sukarno regime. One of these parties was the PNI which, even before the *Gestapu* affair, had been rent by factional disputes over collaboration with the PKI. After *Gestapu* the PNI came under increasingly heavy Army pressure, supported by *Orba*-orientated military and civil officials in the provinces, to purge itself of its Left and PKI collaborationist wing led by former Premier Ali Sastroamidjojo and former Irrigation Minister Surachman. PNI branches in Central and East Java resisted the purge, however, and as indicated in the previous chapter there were frequent clashes between PNI youth groups and anti-Sukarno student action fronts throughout 1966-7. The efforts of anti-Communist PNI executives, like Osa Maliki and party secretary-general Usep Ranawidjaja, to project a new image for their organization seemed at first unsuccessful. Among local Army commanders, aided — as in the case of the bloody pogrom of Communists — by Muslim youths (many of them affiliated with the NU, whose leaders were not displeased to see one of their principal political competitors in difficulty), the PNI retained its image of being a party of PKI collaborators. There is every indication that Suharto by and large shared this view. In October 1967, Army authorities declared the PNI suspended throughout Sumatra. But now even Usep and other PNI leaders in basic sympathy with the post-coup New Order became increasingly defiant. Other parties, including the Christian confessional groups, also expressed concern over the PNI ban, their leaders probably realizing that the entire party system was in jeopardy and that — who knows — the time might come when their own groups could be subjected to a similar action.

Mounting pressure on Suharto to "constitutionalize" the PNI ultimately resulted in a decision by the Acting President on 21 December 1967, instructing all local government authorities (including local Army commanders) to cease interfering with the PNI and to assist the latter in "crystallization and New Order consolidation within itself". This decision was announced only hours after PNI leaders formally declared that their party had dissociated itself from Sukarno and his teachings, which had been the official PNI "philosophy". The suspension of PNI activities

49

in Sumatra was eventually lifted after a personal visit of Army Chief of Staff General Panggabean to Sumatran commanders. Nevertheless, in Sumatra throughout 1968, student groups protested against the PNI's legitimization, local Army commanders kept up harassment of branch activity, and in June 1968, the Governor of South Sumatra, Asnawi Mangku Alam, barred former members of the ASU (Ali-Surachman) wing of the PNI from holding local office in the rural areas. Elsewhere too the PNI continued to experience difficulties. However, in the new Indonesian Parliament, announced by Suharto in February 1968, the PNI was awarded seventy-eight seats, a slight drop from its previous representation but still making it the largest single parliamentary delegation. By this time Suharto had undoubtedly come to the full realization of the simple political truth that had so often infused Sukarno's domestic tactics, that is that executive stability in Indonesia in no small measure depends on preserving diverse and contending power centres and factions, however much one might personally dislike one or the other among them. Still it was not until early January 1969 that the East Java military commander, Major-General M. Jasin, declared that the "crystallization and consolidation" of the PNI had been completed in his province, permitting the party to be once again legally active. And even so, Jasin asserted that he was still not entirely satisfied with the party's structure and cautioned it against permitting "Communist" influence to appear within its ranks.

PNI leaders were not long in learning their lesson. Throughout much of 1969 PNI provincial leaders from East and Central Java began to seek a *rapprochement* with some top Army commanders. The latter had become particularly alarmed over rising Islamic political power and the new pressures of Muslim orthodoxy for recognition. For the forthcoming elections the Army needed friends among the parties, and for Javanese military leaders the PNI, if properly adjusted to the New Order, seemed an ideal new partner. The test came during the PNI party congress in April 1970. Opposition to the prominent PNI leader and former Deputy Premier Hardi coming from military figures, like Generals S. Humardani and Ali Murtopo, was enough to cost the former the party's chairmanship. Instead, Hadisubeno, the party's leader from Central Java, was elected to the chair to the evident satisfaction of the Army. Ironically (and perhaps as part of an informal agreement with Army leaders) some of the PNI Left stalwarts appear now to be making a come-back in second-echelon party leadership positions. They are unlikely to give the Army trouble in the elections, however.

50

Even harder was the problem of establishing a new Muslim political party, as a kind of informal successor to the banned *Masjumi* party. Before dealing with this question it is necessary first to stress the divisions within the Indonesian Muslim community. Though the overwhelming majority (some eighty-five per cent) of the 115 million or so Indonesians consider themselves Muslims, there are significant differences in degrees of orthodoxy, religio-cultural eclecticism and adaptation to modern scientific values among them. For example, more orthodox and "fundamentalist" Indonesian Muslims (by no means necessarily better or modern educated ones) have always looked askance at their more syncretic and less rigid fellow-believers — as common in the cities as in the rural sections — who readily mix the tenets of the Prophet with pre-Islamic Hindu-Javanese or with animistic religious beliefs and practices. The antithesis between these two groups, particularly in political and sociological terms, has frequently been overdrawn by non-Indonesian observers. Differences between the two groups are often (by no means always) a matter of shadings and degrees. But certainly one distinctive and important Muslim segment has consisted of followers of modern Reform Islam, sympathetic to modern scientific advances and often mildly Socialist, though generally anti-Communist, in outlook. Politically, this part of the Muslim community tended to focus on the *Masjumi* party until Sukarno banned it in 1960 along with the PSI because some of its principal members had led the earlier-mentioned regional revolt of the PRRI in Sumatra and Sulawesi in 1958. Politically "homeless" since then (at least until February 1968, when the new Muslim party was finally permitted to come into existence) former *Masjumi* members on the whole were warm supporters of the general "de-Sukarnoization" process since the coup of 30 September 1965. Even so, relations between them and the Suharto Government have occasionally been strained for reasons to be noted presently.

Between the modern Reform Islamic community in Indonesia and a more traditionalist Muslim element centring especially, though not exclusively, in the rural areas and provincial towns of Central and East Java, there has often been little love lost. The latter's chief political vehicle has been the *Nahdatul Ulama* (Muslim Scholars — NU) party. NU, despite some occasional internal dissension through the period of guided democracy and Sukarno's close collaboration with the PKI, readily adapted itself and, indeed, even flourished. This was partly because NU's more nativistic outlook and its opportunistic muting of usual Muslim anti-Communist sentiment suited Sukarno's own brand of anti-Western "new nationalism", and partly because Sukarno, in his own role of political balancer, needed a strong Muslim party. Particularly in the post-*Gestapu* era it became apparent that NU's quiescence in the policies of the Sukarno regime had sometimes divided the party leadership and that even before the coup, when PKI activists and peasant front cadres had repeatedly clashed with Muslims in villages in East and Central Java, there had been strong pressure from NU's youth organization, *Ansor*, on the central party executive to adopt a more militantly anti-Communist stance. One former *Ansor* chairman, Imron Rosjadi, even went to prison for his attacks on Sukarno's guided democracy and on Muslim collaboration with the PKI. It was *Ansor*, it will be remembered, which played a major role in the bloody anti-PKI pogrom in the months after the *Gestapu* affair.

In the turbulent post-*Gestapu* era, however, NU's internal divisions did not prove very durable. A noted erstwhile guided democracy collaborator, Idham Chalid, remained NU chairman. The party was able to present a virtually solid front when it became apparent, already early in 1966, that efforts were being made to revive the *Masjumi*, at first in its original form and later, after Army opposition became more pronounced, as a new organization. These efforts to revive *Masjumi* came at first mainly from former *Masjumi* executives, including Prawoto Mangkusasmito and former Premiers Muhammad Natsir and Sjafruddin Prawiranegara, as well as from leaders of the influential educational and social service organization, *Muhammadiyah*. By the middle of December 1965, a Muslim Co-ordinating Body representing sixteen former *Masjumi* affiliated groups, began to spear-head the drive to rehabilitate the *Masjumi*. It must also be noted that Prawoto and his friends had from the start the indirect support of a few non-*Masjumi* intellectuals associated loosely with the earlier-named Independent Group. Throughout 1966-7 the Independent Group's gradual realization that it required an organized power base of its own gave the movement to establish a new *Masjumi*-type party a measure of encouragement at a time when it was running into considerable opposition.

This opposition came from several sources, all of which Suharto could not easily ignore. There was the NU, which for perhaps tactically sound partisan reasons did not care to see its dominant political role in the Indonesian Muslim community undercut by the reappearance of its old competitor, the *Masjumi*, or by a similar organization. To the more ardent anti-Sukarnoists, however, particularly in the secular intellectual community, the NU was hardly in a position to frame the political structure of *Orba*, tainted as NU's leaders themselves were with guided democracy collaboration. Perhaps more significant was the opposition coming from Army circles. These had not objected to the restoration of the individual political rights of *Masjumi* members involved in the PRRI regional rebellion. But the restoration of *Masjumi* as a party, they believed, could not but set a precedent that might well lead to the rehabilitation of the PKI. If the *Masjumi,* after its leaders' involvement in anti-Government activity, could be made legitimate once again, then why not the PKI, whose leaders similarly had plotted against the State? It should be noted that Army leaders were by no means of one mind on this issue. A few Army officers had supported the re-establishment of the *Masjumi* from the start on the grounds that the New Order could only benefit from an anti-Sukarno organization.

But for a number of other Army officers, who had seen service against the PRRI rebels in Sumatra, a restoration of *Masjumi* was, in any case, unseemly. In this group were also officers of the Christian faith, some with informal ties to the Christian confessional parties. Throughout 1966-7 there was growing alarm in these confessional parties over what seemed to be a new Muslim intransigence in opposing Christian missionary activity. Christianization had quickened in the months after *Gestapu,* in part because of Djakarta's improved diplomatic relations with major Western nations and increased if indirect assistance by foreign missions. According to one authoritative estimate, during the first two years following the 30 September 1965 coup alone the number of Christian converts in Indonesia grew by some 400,000. Allegedly "aggressive" behaviour by Christian missionaries, particularly in strongly Muslim North Sumatra led to several incidents and on 1 October 1967, a score of Christian churches were damaged — some by arsonists — during anti-Christian demonstrations in Macassar.

Fear of the Muslim community was clearly rising in Christian circles, and the establishment of a new Muslim party roused mixed reactions. On the one hand it was thought that yet another Muslim party, one, moreover, with an obvious general commitment to de-Sukarnoization and hence assured of a voice in Suharto's circle, would only strengthen the position of the Islamic community in the *Orba* system generally. This concern was also shared by some leading non-Christian armed forces commanders. For a united Muslim community represented by dominant parties in Parliament, it was believed, might yet again attempt to move toward a new official recognition of Islamic law and indeed, toward a designation of Indonesia as an Islamic state. As we shall see later this concern was not without foundation: Muslim political leaders were still entertaining hopes of getting some new and official recognition of Islamic law in basic State policies. On the other hand, the more modernistic and Reform character of the projected new Muslim party was thought to be a guarantee against the allegedly excessive militancy of Islamic traditionalists. Another Muslim party, politically liberal if not Left of centre in orientation, could well be the small, progressive Christian community's best ally.

Complicating the picture still further were reports of repeated appeals in the course of 1967 made by influential Sumatran and Javanese Muslim leaders to Indonesia's most prominent soldier, MPRS chairman, General A. H. Nasution, to "safeguard" Muslim interests in the country. These appeals reflected various supposed slights suffered by, and frustrations over the *Orba* in, Muslim circles, to be discussed presently. Nasution's reaction is not known. But it did become apparent by the beginning of 1968 that Muslims were increasingly looking toward Nasution as their unofficial champion at the court of the New Order. The ominous implications of a possible new "dualism" in the nation's top executive posts were not lost on some observers.

Amidst all these cross-currents Suharto steered what seemed to many to be an uncertain course, which appeared to please no one and which, in the end, may well have alienated some principal sources of support for his regime. At first, through the closing weeks of 1965 and through much of 1966, Suharto was said to be sympathetic to Prawoto's efforts and to those of the earlier-mentioned Muslim Co-ordinating Body to re-establish the *Masjumi*. But by the end of the year he had made it clear (reportedly primarily because of NU and Army pressures) that he was opposed to a mere restoration of *Masjumi* and he was now reported to be insisting on a "new" party name and organization, one in which former *Masjumi* leaders would remain in the background. Former Vice-President, Mohammad Hatta, who had already been approached earlier, presently also became a front man and organizer of the new Muslim party. But despite his eminence and efforts, opposition continued. Moreover, former *Masjumi* leaders and their younger supporters in other Muslim groups were displeased that they would in effect have to accept a boycott in the new party's upper echelons. Once again Suharto compromised. In April 1967, Suharto agreed to the transformation of the Muslim Co-ordinating Body into a new planning committee of seven prominent Muslim personalities, headed by K. H. Fakih Usman, an older *Masjumi* leader who had, however, not personally participated in the PRRI rebellion. Though Usman was to die shortly, the efforts of the planning committee (which initially included five other former *Masjumi* leaders) seemed to meet with success. All through the second half of 1967 there were frequent reports that the birth of the new *Partai Muslimin Indonesia* (PMI) was imminent.

But unexpectedly Suharto still kept withholding approval, probably not least because the Acting President's relations with Parliament generally were reaching a new level of tension over the elections issue (to be discussed presently). Suharto, in the face of continuing arguments that rehabilitated *Masjumi* leaders ought to have the same political rights as other citizens in "good standing", including the right to be elected to party leadership, nevertheless remained adamant in his opposition to a PMI executive with prominent former *Masjumi* figures. Whether, as was subsequently claimed by the new party's planning committee, Suharto eventually had begun to weaken in this opposition, the fact remains that in the final consultations of the committee with Suharto on 5 February 1968 the latter emphasized again that "for the sake of political stability" no *Masjumi* leaders could be elected to the new party's executive. Controversy was to erupt later in the year over the length of the ban on former *Masjumi* leaders discussed at this 5 February consultation. Some planning committee members claimed that this ban was only to last until the PMI's congress in November 1968. In any case, the PMI planning committee complied with Suharto's demand. Former *Masjumi* leaders who had been intended to serve on the new party's executive board were removed. On 20 February 1968, the PMI was at last formally authorized by presidential decree.

The new party was a federation of sixteen organizations, of which the earlier-named *Muhammadiyah* and the Muslim trade union federation *Gasbiindo* were probably the most important. Both the general chairman and the secretary-general of the PMI were from the *Muhammadiyah* and as indicated no *Masjumi* leaders were appointed to the executive at this time. Already in the "redressing" of the Indonesian Parliament announced by Suharto on 9 February 1968, the PMI had been awarded eighteen (out of a total of 414) seats, though PMI leaders claimed additional support of twelve other deputies representing various "mass organizations". The issue of the former *Masjumi* leadership continued to fester, however, as the new party (now popularly designated *Parmusi* as well as PMI) quickly identified itself with the slightly Left of centre Reform Islamic modernism which had characterized the *Masjumi* before its ban. In November 1968, at the PMI's first congress former Foreign Minister and *Masjumi* leader Mohammad Roem, as well as other old *Masjumi* figures like Hassan Basri and Anwar Harjono, was elected to the party's seven-member central executive. Other *Masjumi* stalwarts were also chosen to a seventeen-man national committee. Already before the congress Suharto had reportedly expressed his disapproval of the election of *Masjumi* leaders as delegates to the PMI congress. After the election of Roem and Suharto's renewed expression of opposition, the PMI released a statement asserting that before the party's congress had been held PMI leaders had been assured by the President's staff that the election of former *Masjumi* leaders to the party's central executive would be all right. Moreover, according to the same statement in their consultation, mentioned earlier, with Suharto on 5 February 1968, the latter had said that while no *Masjumi* leaders could be given prominent positions in the new Muslim party, "on the other hand whoever is chosen at the congress (of the PMI) is your internal problem".

Whatever the accuracy of this version of events, there was no doubt of the depth of indignation, in Parliament and particularly among the more outspoken *Orba*-orientated political leaders and intellectuals, over Suharto's initial failure to recognize the new PMI executive. Former Vice-President Mohammad Hatta flatly declared that Suharto had no right to interfere in such an "undemocratic" manner in party elections. This outcry doubtlessly stayed Suharto's hand and by early 1969 the principals in the dispute seemed to have reached an uneasy truce, with the Government still formally maintaining its opposition to the new PMI leaders who were refusing to step down. A solution was seen to lie — as so often in the case of Indonesian political problems just below the flashpoint — in the face-saving passage of time. There had, moreover, been indications for some time that *Muhammadiyah* and other component groups in the PMI were insisting on a greater autonomy for themselves than the PMI's central executive considered desirable. Throughout the first half of 1969 there was considerable public speculation over the extent of internal fissures in the new party. All the same, even the most enthusiastic civil supporters of *Orba* — elements which the President could ill afford to antagonize if he did not wish to see his regime rely more and more on military power alone — had been shaken by the PMI affair.

Beyond the controversy over the PMI's leadership however, there lay the complex pattern of frustrations and outraged sensibilities in the Indonesian Muslim community as a whole. That community, as has been noted earlier is, neither from the standpoint of its political aspirations, nor of its cultural values, nor even of its religious practices, of one mind. The persistence and — despite considerable opposition — the strength of those favouring the establishment of the PMI clearly alarmed other Indonesian Muslims. Rightly or wrongly the PMI was viewed by more traditional, rural Muslims, from whom (as indicated above) NU draws much of its support, as likely to strengthen the currents of modernism and even of westernization generally. Since the decline of Sukarno and his nativistic guided democracy these currents were believed to be flowing more freely in Indonesia's intellectual and political life. It was well understood that the old *Masjumi* leaders were ideologically close to the intellectuals of the former PSI and of the Independent Group, and that these in turn had powerful friends in the Army. The small but influential Christian intelligentsia, themselves members of, or else with allies in, the *Parkindo* and *Partai Katolik,* as well as enjoying support among the Christian community in the armed forces, also came to be regarded as politically congruent on many issues with the *Masjumi* "modernists", the former PSI and with Independent Group intellectuals and their Army associates. This view persisted even though in fact the Indonesian Christian community was a good deal more ambivalent in its attitude towards the PMI, as we have seen.

Especially in NU and some PSII circles a conviction arose that Suharto, in implementing the New Order, was relying altogether too much on the leaders of the Christian parties for support. Especially the *Partai Katolik's* rising young leader Frans Seda became the Muslim *bête noire.* Other well-known Orba political figures, like Djakarta's Governor Ali Sadikin, had also aroused Muslim ire. Sadikin's legalization of gambling and his deft manipulation of lotteries designed to contribute funds to the capital's improvement, deeply offended Muslim purists worried about public morality. Muslim dissatisfactions culminated in March 1968 in connection with the futile effort to have the so-called Djakarta Charter incorporated in a new basic State policy statement being prepared by an MPRS committee. This Djakarta Charter, originally drafted in June 1945 in the context of the preparations for the independence proclamation of the new revolutionary Indonesian Republic, demands that Muslims adhere to Islamic law. The Charter, rightly or wrongly, has long been interpreted by many non-Muslims and less orthodox Muslims (for example, Sukarno) committed to the principle of a "separation of Church and State" as an attempt to give Islam a pre-eminent position in Indonesia's public legal structure, indeed, as an attempt to transform the Republic eventually into a formally Islamic state (although originally it was seen as something of a victory for secular nationalists anxious to contain Islamic power).

In the late nineteen-fifties discussions in the Indonesian Constituent Assembly over the formal incorporation of the Charter in the proposed new Indonesian Constitution led to a deadlock. This, in turn, resulted in an accentuation of Sukarno's executive powers under the Constitution of 1945, imposed unilaterally by the President in July 1959, and in the proclamation of Sukarno's *Manipol* (Political Manifesto) as the State policy guide-line. In a preamble to his July 1959 decree and in the official version of *Manipol*, Sukarno recognized the Djakarta Charter, without actually providing a formal constitutional place for it, although some Muslims prefer to think of it as having in fact acquired such constitutional legality.

But now, in March 1968, as the MPRS was considering replacing *Manipol* with a new "de-Sukarnoized" statement of basic State policy, the deadlock appeared again in the MPRS committees deliberating on such a new basic policy statement and on a document outlining civil and human rights. The deadlock reportedly resulted from the opposition of Army committee members (in which, it was alleged, Suharto also had a hand), as well as of Christians, and from PSI Independent Group quarters, over the incorporation of the Djakarta Charter in the planned policy statement. In the end the project of drafting such a statement was abandoned for that session of the MPRS and referred to a future one. The bitterness in much of the Muslim community was considerable and had the effect of (1) contributing to some closing of the political ranks between all Muslim political parties, particularly between the new PMI and the NU, and (2) turning even some staunchly *Orba*-orientated Muslims against the Government and its Army and Christian allies. As earlier-mentioned Muslim-Christian tensions remained high, it was the PMI's secretary-general, Lukman Harun, who, in a clear attack on Christian missionary activity, on 10 July 1968, urged in Parliament that all aid to religious establishments in Indonesia coming from "foreign" sources be prohibited. Especially in the *Muhammadiyah*, one of the PMI's principal organizational supports, the anti-Christian, and more mutedly, the anti-Suharto tone became more marked.

In the media of the PMI and of other Muslim parties and their ancillary organizations, it was not so much Suharto himself who by the end of 1968 was increasingly coming under fire but rather those who were said to be in the Suharto "inner ring", Finance Minister and later Communications Minister Frans Seda, the governor of the Central Bank Radius Prawiro, and other members of the Christian-PSI-Independent Group circle. Stories in the Muslim press about alleged evils of Western (read

58

Christian) and secular modernization in Indonesian family life, about supposed slights suffered by Muslim school children at the hands of their teachers in public schools, and about tens of thousands of Muslims being annually converted to Christianity, all tended to add fuel to the flames of controversy. However Suharto refused to be stampeded by these criticisms either into taking action against the Christian missions or — as he was urged to do — into issuing some new kind of acknowledgement of the Djakarta Charter (if only in the comfortably equivocal manner of Sukarno), or in demonstratively diminishing the influence of "modern" expertise in his Cabinet. In consequence, among some Muslim leaders, especially in NU, the PSII and, to a lesser degree, in some of the component organizations of the PMI, an already latent kind of "populist" self-image began to emerge more strongly: Suharto's regime of elitist modernizers was believed to be really out of touch with the rice-roots aspirations of the masses, for Islam (at least as conceived by this segment of the Muslim leadership) was still held to be their spiritual and ideological mainstay.

This Muslim self-conception in turn strengthened the aversion, also in other political circles, to Suharto's allegedly dictatorial tactics generally. There were good reasons for this aversion, despite frequent disclaimers by Suharto that either he or the military was aspiring to dictatorship. For one thing, Suharto clearly had no taste for early parliamentary elections, and alleged Government dawdling in formulating procedures for such elections tended to polarize considerable Muslim sentiment against the New Order. In July 1966, the MPRS, it may be recalled, had decided that the next general elections for Parliament and for the MPRS itself would be held by July 1968. But it soon became obvious that Suharto was reluctant to implement this decision, not least, as his supporters noted, because the constitutional struggle with Old Order forces had not been completed. Criticism of the delay ultimately led the Government to bring a measure governing new elections to Parliament in February 1967. But the proposed bill stipulated one-member electoral districts, making the "regency" (*kabupaten*) the electoral and constituency unit. This proposed law only intensified Muslim protests and that of other main parties as well. For the NU, PSII and PNI have their followings largely in densely populated Java, where those eligible to cast ballots outnumber the combined total of voters on the other Indonesian islands by more than two to one. In the absence of any provision for proportional representation in the Government's proposed electoral measure, a vote in the thinly populated *kabupatens* outside Java would clearly weigh considerably heavier than one in Java. Moreover, since the banning of *Masjumi*, which in the elections of 1955 was shown to have had considerable following outside Java, and since the banning of the PKI which since 1955 probably also had developed significant though undetermined strength in the outlying provinces, no party had arisen with any uniform and distinctively non-Javanese support. Under the circumstances, the vote beyond Java was very much an unknown quantity, arousing further concern among the Java-based parties. Finally, the smaller Christian confessional parties, which have a good deal of their electoral following in specific localities in North Sulawesi, the Southern Moluccas and on the island of Flores, would probably have benefited from the proposed electoral measure.

Shortly the Government's electoral bill became the subject of a months' long confused parliamentary wrangle. By November 1967, at a time when several factions, including government spokesmen, seemed hopelessly deadlocked, a parliamentary committee considering the bill changed it so as to provide for some proportional representation. This aroused the anger of some militant anti-Sukarno elements in and out of the Parliament, and of the Government. After protest demonstrations in front of the Parliament building by KAMI, the Government decided to take the bill back altogether and promised to submit a new measure in the near future. This action in turn caused sharp protests among those supporting a proportional representation provision in the electoral procedure and who argued that the Government had no constitutional right unilaterally to undo the decision of a parliamentary committee. Other critics stressed that the Government's withdrawal action, taken only a little more than half a year before the scheduled elections in July 1968, had the practical effect of making it impossible for the elections to be held on time — something which, it was alleged, the Government had been aiming at all along.

The elections bill issue once again underscored the complexities and frustrations of the Indonesian chief executive's relationship with Parliament all through the country's brief national history, also in the context of the unresolved question of the primacy of the parliamentary or presidential systems, referred to at the beginning of this chapter. Before the 1955 general elections, as well as afterwards during the years of guided democracy, it had become customary for Sukarno to appoint new members of parliament, usually in consultation with party and other political leaders. After the emergence of *Orba*, and as the prospect of early elections began to fade, Suharto followed the Sukarno pattern. What Suharto had to work with at first was the Parliament of 283 deputies appointed by Sukarno in June 1960, from which some thirty Communists and suspected sympathizers were removed in the wake of the anti-PKI pogrom. In January 1967, Suharto, largely because of party pressures, appointed 108 new deputies. There was considerable dissatisfaction over these new appointments. Muslim parties complained that they had not received a fair allocation of the new seats. This was to become an almost continuous NU refrain throughout 1967-8. KAMI and other action front militants, on the other hand, charged that the new appointees were too *Orla* orientated. As the haggling within Parliament and between Parliament and the Government over the elections bill further deepened public dissatisfaction, voices rose that still additional parliamentary changes were necessary, whether elections were held or not.

Sensing the mounting disquiet over the postponement of the elections (in January 1968 there were demonstrations against alleged parliamentary and other governmental ineffectualness), Suharto on 9 February 1968 announced that Parliament had again been "redressed and renewed". Sixty-seven new members were added, raising the total number of deputies from 347 to 414. Political parties had been asked earlier to "review" and replace the personnel of their parliamentary delegations. So-called mass organizations (that is women, youth, labour and professional groups) affiliated to the parties were henceforth to be included as much as possible in party contingents. Unaffiliated mass organizations would continue to be represented separately. The number of deputies from the armed forces was raised from 43 to 75. On 13 February Suharto formally installed 179 new deputies, 67 being new members and the remainder replacements. The relative strength of a few delegations may perhaps be noted. The PNI with 78 seats and NU with 75 had the largest individual party delegations (even so NU and other Muslim leaders complained that Islamic representation had declined relative to that earned in the 1955 elections), followed by the PSII with 20 seats, PMI with 18, *Parkindo* with 17, *Partai Katolik* with 15 and *Perti* with 9. The last-named party, a small independent Muslim group, also with a following beyond Java, was not in fact permitted fully to resume its activities until January 1969, when it was declared to have purged itself from alleged pro-Sukarno and pro-*Gestapu* influence. The Independence Upholders Party (IPKI), strong among West Java's military, and the *Murba* (Proletarian) party, a national Marxist but anti-PKI group, were given 11 and 4 seats respectively. The total party contingent — still the largest single bloc — in Parliament was 247 seats, followed by the armed forces with 75 (the army 29, navy, air

force and police, each 14, veterans 2, and the civil corps 2).
KAMI won 14 seats. Representation of special interest groups
like Balinese Hindus (2 seats) and the inhabitants of the Irian
Barat or West New Guinea region (8 seats) was not overlooked.

Very soon after the new Parliament's first session at the
close of February 1968, much of political opinion in the capital
came into renewed conflict with the Suharto regime, largely it
must be admitted because of the Acting President's own doing.
The appointment of the new Parliament apparently had given
Suharto confidence to consolidate his own position further and
bring the long drawn-out constitutional battle with Sukarno to
a formal but quiet end. Thus in an apparent effort to end the
last vestiges of "dualism" in the nation's leadership, and in order
to give him sufficient time to initiate the rehabilitation of
the country, Suharto, through his parliamentary liaison, was
able to persuade the new Parliament on 28 February 1968
to approve a resolution embodying his chief policy wishes.
According to this parliamentary resolution, which was in fact
really directed at the MPRS, the latter body was to convene as
soon as possible and was to appoint Suharto as regular President
(not just "Acting" President as he had been thus far). The same
resolution also asked for MPRS approval of the Government's new
Five-Year Economic Development Plan and for a postponement
of general elections for a period of up to five years. Only one
of these demands in and by itself could be said to be likely to
arouse considerable public disapproval, namely the one asking for
an election postponement. The rather sudden protests and student
demonstrations (quickly suppressed with some arrests of student
leaders) that followed basically had, therefore, a different cause,
namely a widespread feeling that Suharto and his military "liaison"
staff were treating parliamentarians and MPRS members like
so many puppets, thus justifying the public's gravest fears of an
impending Army dictatorship.

In accordance with Suharto's wishes and Parliament's resolution the MPRS was called into session, however. But its brief
meeting (21-27 March) disclosed, if anything, the political fissures
developing in the New Order. On 27 March the problem of
the nation's "leadership dualism" was at last formally solved
when Suharto, by decision of the MPRS, was granted a five-year
term as "full" President of Indonesia. In substance, the MPRS
also approved the Five-Year Development Plan, putting responsibility for its implementation on the Government, however.
But having made these concessions the MPRS also made sure
that the President was aware of the public disquiet over his
"bulldozer" tactics and over his relations generally with the

legislative arm of Government. Thus the MPRS decreed that elections would be postponed no later than July 1971, a date that would fall well before the expiration of Suharto's presidential term. Moreover, Suharto's emergency powers, dating from Sukarno's 11 March 1966 decree, it will be remembered, and later confirmed by the MPRS, which had given Suharto authority "to take all steps" to ensure domestic tranquillity, were now clipped. The President's special emergency authority, the MPRS decided, was to be used only against the machinations of the *Gestapu*/PKI underground. Clearly the Army's rough handling of recent student and other civilian demonstrators was beginning to arouse some concern.

Yet, even these fairly modest limitations on Suharto's desires seem to have been subjected to occasionally bitter behind-the-scenes clashes between Suharto's liaison staff and MPRS members. Civilian dissatisfaction was particularly deep in Muslim political circles, where, as has been indicated earlier, it was alleged that Army pressure exerted in response to Suharto's wishes, as well as opposition by Christian groups and secular intellectuals, had prevented passage, in the earlier-named MPRS committees on basic State policy and on civil rights, of an acknowledgement of the Djakarta Charter as binding on Muslims. In subsequent conversations with representatives of NU, PMI and PSII, in early April 1968, Suharto was urged to have the Government issue a declaration that the Djakarta Charter was or would be made part of State policy. Suharto declined, however, and after consultations with Christian parties and other groups known to be hostile to the Djakarta Charter portrayed himself in a press conference as "compelled" to "study the matter further". Still, realizing the erosive effects of the unresolved Djakarta Charter issue (now not likely to see another effort at settlement until well after the 1971 elections) Suharto supporters sought to mobilize opinion, also in the parties, for a declaration of adhesion to the results of the March 1968 MPRS session. The then Djakarta military commander, Major-General Amir Mahmud, succeeded on 9 April in obtaining signatures of leaders of all parties, both those who wanted and those who opposed the Djakarta Charter, to a document promising that they would safeguard the decisions of the MPRS. Resentment in Muslim circles continued to simmer, however. As one Muslim students paper pointed out: "Support for what the MPRS has done does not mean approval for what it failed to do."

Clearly, much of the Islamic community remained irreconciled to the *Orba*, deferring open opposition until a tactically more opportune moment in the future. Much the same could be said for other distinctive interest groups in the Indonesian political system. Once again a focal point of controversy became the various draft bills on the future general elections. In October 1968 Suharto, at a public meeting in Pontianak, declared that the Government had begun preparations for the holding of the general elections. But by December parliamentary chairman H. A. Sjaichu said that "unforeseen difficulties" were delaying ratification of the draft legislation on elections. Wrangling over the representation of smaller parties proved especially time consuming. In June 1969, Antara could still report that disagreement among the parties on the composition of new provincial legislative councils as well as on other questions was holding up approval on the three basic election laws already discussed by Parliament for months on end. Three-cornered meetings between the Government, the leadership of Parliament and a special committee on the proposed election legislation were continuing with increasing urgency. Before dealing with some of these and other recent stirrings in parliamentary and partisan political circles, particularly during 1969-70, (see chapter IX), attention needs to be paid first to other developments in Indonesian domestic and foreign policy.

CHAPTER FOUR

The Politics of the New Order: Problems of Constitutionalism and Stabilization

NOT ONLY in its relations with Parliament and the parties, but also in another perennial problem area, that of the relationship between the Central Government and the outlying provinces, has the Suharto regime been having its difficulties. Provincial discontent over alleged neglect by the centre — especially as regards allocations of public expenditures for local development — has plagued Indonesia since the early nineteen-fifties. On several occasions such provincial dissatisfaction spilled over into secessionist or semi-secessionist outbreaks, often led by local military commanders. The latter, virtually having the power of pro-consuls in their respective provincial areas under prevailing emergency regulations (or because of long-established practice), often became rallying points of public discontent and thus reluctant spokesmen in provincial civil relations with Djakarta. This familiar pattern largely continued in *Orba*'s early years as the Suharto regime struggled to rehabilitate the country's badly neglected and mismanaged economy. Within the months from April through June 1968 alone, for example, the Suharto Government was faced with the following developments:

(1) a demand from community leaders, from the Bengkulu district in South Sumatra, urging that Bengkulu immediately be proclaimed a separate province;

(2) a demand, presented by a delegation from the provincial legislature of East Kalimintan (Borneo) visiting Djakarta, and led by an Army Major, that the provinces be given the power to retain all foreign exchange earned on the products and natural resources cultivated or developed by them;

(3) a statement by the South Sumatra military commander, Brigadier-General Ishak Djuarsa, claiming that the United States Government had offered to supply his command directly with

necessary military equipment.   Djuarsa added he would be happy to take the equipment, implying he would, in fact, do so, with or without his superiors' leave;

(4) insistent requests, both from Central Javanese members of the MPRS and the provincial legislature in Central Java, that the Suharto Government introduce into Parliament, as soon as possible, legislation improving the financial relations between the provinces and the centre, and allowing for more provincial autonomy generally;

(5) a decision of the greater-Djakarta local legislative council, and approved by the Djakarta area govenor himself urging wider fiscal and legislative decentralization, and demanding that financial relations between the national and local government authorities be stabilized.

When, however, already early in May 1968, the Government did draft two parliamentary measures providing for greater uniformity and continuity in, as well as for a more clearly defined scope of, regional and local self-government, a bitter partisan political wrangle erupted on the floor of Parliament.   Java-based parties, like NU, seemed especially reluctant to approve increased autonomy for non-Javanese areas.   This bode ill for a speedy solution of the regional autonomy question, and Suharto appeared to have no clear perspective on provincial discontent.

Meanwhile, especially throughout the remainder of 1968, and notably in Sumatra, student groups kept on pressing local governors and military commanders for more provincial self-government as well as for a further purge of Old Order elements in provincial legislatures and in the bureaucracy.   This student agitation, it might be stressed, seemed by this time to be one of the few remaining areas of possibly meaningful action by Indonesia's volatile student movement as a whole.   Because of the importance of student activity in Indonesia's political system a brief digression to account for recent trends may perhaps be permitted.

After the March 1968 MPRS session and the final legitimization of Suharto's *Orba,* the erstwhile *élan* of the student action fronts and their allies among scholars, women and organized labour appeared to diminish dramatically.   The frequent demonstrations over rising prices staged by KAMI and its high school allies in a number of cities in Java and Sumatra, particularly during January 1968, now seemed to be becoming a thing of the past.   Although MPRS chairman Nasution, and leading political intellectuals like Umar Khayam, continued to profess to see new roles for the student organizations, military spokesmen generally were more critical.   Already by the middle of April 1968, such prominent intellectual figures as Mochtar Lubis were saying

66

that student demonstrations were no longer needed. Especially in Djakarta, local military commanders implied that they had had more than their fill of student political activity. In the second half of 1968 some student leaders in the capital themselves began taking a cue from their military critics, and started speaking of the need for a new "moral" or "spiritual" purpose in the Indonesian student movement. Except for the regional and autonomy question in Sumatra perhaps there appeared to be few significant issues around which student agitation could continue to be mobilized. As one KAMI leader in Djakarta put it in an interview with a German journalist in November 1968: "One gets tired of constantly demonstrating about the same old questions like corruption and high prices."

In April 1968, a number of student groups in Djakarta had established a Student Development Task Force to assist in the Government's new Five-Year Development Plan. Elaborate schemes were drawn up for the utilization of student volunteers in the implementation of the Plan, but it was not until the end of March 1969, that the Five-Year Plan itself was actually launched. By this time student ardour had cooled considerably. Increasingly self-criticism within the student movement underscored uneasiness over becoming part of the "establishment": was the value of the movement not being undermined by becoming harnassed to the structure and policies of *Orba*? What was KAMI thinking of (asked student purists), having its own delegation in Parliament, like any other party, in the "corrupt" market-place of politics? Such questions derived added relevancy from each instance of repression of student action by the Suharto Government. In April 1968, elements of the 4,000-member KAPPI (*Kesatuan Aksi Peladjar Pemuda Indonesia* — Action Front of Indonesian High School Youth), one of the principal federations of students of secondary schools and the working youth, demonstrated in Tandjong Priok against the sky-rocketing consumer prices and other alleged Government failures. Local military had not given permission for the demonstration and shortly it came to a pitched battle between students and soldiers which left one student dead and three others wounded. It was by no means the first time that a student demonstration had cost such casualties. But coming at a time when the Government's public relations were particularly poor, as a result of Suharto's attempts, described earlier, to manipulate Parliament and MPRS, the Tandjong Priok incident led to a new upsurge of anti-Government intransigence in student circles. Reading the Indonesian student press in this period, and, indeed, even in following months, gave one the impression that as far as students were concerned Suharto's

Orba had become as bad as Sukarno's guided democracy and that there was nothing for it but to continue an unrelenting student-Government confrontation. Tactless remarks by a few top Army commanders and by the Army paper *Berita Yudha* about "meddlesome children" and about the inherent impropriety of student political participation only exacerbated tensions. Late in January 1969, Suharto stressed to leaders of KAPPI who called on him at Merdeka Palace that further student demonstrations — once effective in bringing down the Old Order — were "unsuitable" in the present atmosphere. Instead, he called on students to "equip" themselves for the demands of national development — in other words, to go back to the classroom.

What probably prevented a really serious explosion between students and the Government was the division within the loosely organized student movement itself. In Djakarta alone there were at the beginning of 1969 at least two dozen major organizations of university and secondary school students, some representing, others cutting across, religious, partisan political and ethnic-racial lines. Many were formal or informal adjuncts or allies of party, trade union and other special interests organizations and constantly subjected to manipulation and schismatic strains by them. Membership might fluctuate severely and activities were often poorly co-ordinated unless major issues arose. Participation in principal federative action front groups like KAPPI was and is nominal in many cases. In 1966-7 when the struggle against Sukarno and the *Orla* was most intense the component parts of the action front complex showed considerable unity, though even then the methods of KAMI and KAPPI had caused disquiet in some of the other fronts. In addition to these two groups KAPPI and KAMI (*Kesatuan Aksi Mahasiswa Indonesia* — Indonesian University Students Action Front), there were KAPBI (*Kesatuan Aksi Perserikatan Buruh Indonesia* — Action Front of Indonesian Workers' Association) with about 5,000 affiliates; KAGI (*Kesatuan Aksi Guru Indonesia* — Indonesian Teachers' Action Front) with a membership of about 3,000; KASI (*Kesatuan Aksi Serdjana Indonesia* — Action Front of Indonesian University Graduates or Scholars) with about 5,000 active members; KAWI (*Kesatuan Aksi Wanita Indonesia* — Indonesian Women's Action Front) with about 6,000 members; and even a KAPNI (*Kesatuan Aksi Perserikatan Nalajan Indonesia* — Action Front of Indonesian Fishermen's Associations) with several hundred affiliates.

Already by the end of 1968 two or three of these action fronts had for practical purposes largely fallen apart, becoming little more than paper organizations. Even within KAPPI and KAMI voices were heard that the two groups should dissolve themselves. Surprisingly, though KAMI like the other fronts was best organized in West Java (where since its founding in October 1965 it had generally enjoyed the encouragement of the Army's crack Siliwangi division), and though it tended to be dominated by its Djakarta branches, it was the pressure from non-Javanese sections of KAMI which contributed greatly to keeping it going. For example, A. N. Adenansi, secretary of the Action Front Co-ordinating Body in South Kalimantan, declared, according to *The Djakarta Times* of 11 February 1969, that outside Djakarta and Bandung, KAMI units were "still performing their original function". He attributed recent demands for KAMI's dissolution to internal jealousies and to an erroneous assumption that New Order conditions in Djakarta and Bandung were developing in the same way in other parts of the country. In January 1969, General Nasution in effect pleaded with KAMI leaders not to dissolve their group and shortly thereafter Foreign Minister Malik asserted that the "polemics" about KAMI's role should cease in the interests of all. In February 1969, KAMI representatives convened in the capital for the purpose of "restructuring and reinvigorating" the student movement. Although it was in principle decided that a national congress of students should be held in the near future, disagreement arose over representation in such a congress. Some KAMI affiliates demanded that only genuine student groups, that is those not part of political or other organizations, be permitted to send delegates. A deadlock ensued and in the end a number of KAMI supporters disaffiliated themselves. In subsequent weeks strenuous efforts were made to heal the rift, but with as yet uncertain success. Whether the expanding pattern of special interest group formation outside Java will be sufficient to keep the action front complex alive remained to be seen. But there is little question that members of organizations like KAGI and KAPBI have increasingly gravitated to other "functional" organizations in a similar line of work. And certainly already by the end of 1967 differences in attitude and tactics toward Suharto's *Orba* had ended any possibility of concerted political action by the action front complex as a whole.

One reason for the growing diversity and ambivalence in public attitudes toward the New Order — apart from such controversial areas as the Suharto Government's relations with the MPRS, Parliament and the parties — was the seemingly unending chain of purges of alleged Old Order officials, and of freshly discovered "plots" and "conspiracies" of underground *Gestapu*/PKI adherents. This aspect of the Suharto regime is more fully dealt with in the next chapter. But it should be noted here that in the ranks of the civil bureaucracy, including affiliated professions like teaching, in the trade unions, and even in the ranks of the armed forces, *Orbasasi* (new orderization) could and often did mean a good deal of job uncertainty and blasted hopes of advancement. Guided democracy favourites, especially if known to have had PKI or PNI connections, were demoted, transferred or disappeared in the ranks of the thousands of political prisoners. And those who had attempted to be the favourites of these favourites were equally in jeopardy, well aware that jealous underlings were closely scrutinizing them. Continuing arrests, even of staff and field-grade officers of the armed forces and the police on grounds of pro-*Gestapu* or pro-PKI sympathy or involvement, contributed much to a climate of public anxiety. It also added to a suspicion that the Suharto Government was keeping the "Communist" bogey alive in order to justify the kind of unseemly political pressuring of which its relations with Parliament and the MPRS were examples. Such suspicion tended to be confirmed further by the manner in which the President, toward the close of March 1969, chose to launch the nation's new Five-Year Plan. For days previously *Orba*'s top leaders, from Suharto to cabinet members and regional Army commanders down, had been issuing statements on supposedly new attempts by the PKI underground to seize power. Then, on 31 March 1969, as he signed the budget for next year and initiated the implementation of the Five-Year Plan, Suharto warned once again of the Communist threat to the nation. Even to *Orba* sympathizers it began to seem as if the Suharto regime was becoming addicted to "Red scare" tactics in order to key up the country.

Is and was Indonesia's New Order as authoritarian and as contemptuous of the rule of law as the Old? With Suharto's ascendancy various previously banned newspapers like *The Djakarta Times* and *Pedoman* have reappeared, and though Communist organs are proscribed Indonesian journalism generally seems much freer than it was. The mindless sloganizing and fatuous ideologizing of the Sukarno era, though by no means wholly gone, have undoubtedly diminished. In schools, in publishing, and in intellectual life generally, there has been a far more critical and self-critical spirit than one was likely to see in the days of "guided democracy". But editors of papers and journals — particularly if known to have connections with the PNI — still run afoul of the military. And *Orba*'s top officials have often been as inclined to arbitrariness in dealing with opponents and critics as were their Sukarnoist predecessors.

An example is the case of Yap Thiam Hien. Yap, a well-known Djakarta lawyer, a member of the Indonesian Institute for the Defence of Basic Human Rights and known in legal circles as something of a champion of the underdog was arrested on 1 January 1968. The reasons for his arrest were never very clear but appeared to involve allegations that Yap had been a member of *Baperki* and hence was somehow pro-*Gestapu*. He was also suspected of involvement in business malversations. *Baperki,* it may be recalled (see chapter I), was the organization of Indonesian residents or citizens of Chinese origin, which had fallen under Communist influence in the early sixties. *Baperki* members and property had been major targets of the post-*Gestapu* pogrom, even though by no means all its members had sympathized with the Communists. One *Baperki* member who had not — indeed, one who had vigorously protested against the PKI's growing influence in the organization — had been Yap. But Yap's membership in the Institute for the Defence of Basic Human Rights, and his general repute as an independent, forthright critic of high-handed government and corrupt officials made him a likely target of official animosities. The Institute for the Defence of Basic Human Rights has long been a thorn in the side of the Government. The institute has consistently and openly criticised the Government's treatment of political prisoners and the judical procedures used in the anti-Communist campaign generally.

As news of Yap's arrest spread, protests from KASI, the press, the legal profession and leading intellectuals began to engulf the police authorities, the prosecutor's office and even the Army's legal department. After about two weeks Yap was finally released, with little or no explanation or excuse. But, in retrospect, what made Yap's case perhaps most important was not the arrest itself, but rather the circumstances surrounding his release. For there is little doubt that the outcry of his professional associates and of the intellectual community in the capital generally was the principal factor in bringing about Yap's eventual discharge from custody. It is here, precisely, that the New Order appears to differ from the Old. For who would, or could publicly protest, say, the confinement of Mochtar Lubis or of the former *Ansor* leader, Imron Rosjadi, in the hey-day of guided democracy? And what paper or journal would have printed such a protest? Nor was Yap's case necessarily an isolated illustration of Government susceptibility to public and press protest in civil rights matters. Toward the close of January 1969, half a dozen Indonesian journalists were arrested in Bandjarmasin, Kalimantan. The journalists were said to have written reports about the recent arrest in the area of various government officials and of some Indonesian Army personnel on grounds of "pro-Communist" and

71

other allegedly subversive activity. When questioned by the Army the journalists refused to disclose their sources and their own arrests followed. A storm of protest by the Indonesian journalists association, in the press, and in intellectual circles shortly led to the release of the arrested and to an embarrassed half-apology by an Army spokesman in Bandjarmasin.

But in the current climate of continuing purges, arrests, and trials of alleged subversives, establishing the rule of law is clearly an uphill fight. Yap and the Bandjarmasin journalists soon found their defenders. But who speaks for the thousands of political prisoners still languishing in jails, some doubtlessly guilty of attempting to revive the PKI and organizing guerilla resistance, and many others guilty — of what? After weeks or even months of detention such a political prisoner may be released without explanation, only to be arrested again later, without a specific charge, when official suspicion of subversive activity in a given area leads to a new pogrom. Except in cases involving prominent *Orla* officials, bringing those charged with subversion or with *Gestapu* sympathy or complicity to trial appears to be a rarity. The treatment of the political prisoners, and the obvious inability of Indonesia's judicial system to cope with them and with the problem of civil and human rights which they pose, had already by the end of 1968 become perhaps the worst unrelieved scandal of the Suharto regime. Despite outraged denials by the Army it had been persistently reported that hundreds, perhaps thousands, of the prisoners had been killed by their custodians in camps and jails in the previous six months. Journalistic insistence on a full official report appeared to have had but little result, and it was mainly because of the courageous protests of political gadflies like Hadji Johannes Princen, and others in the Institute for the Defence of Basic Human Rights, and of a few enterprising reporters, that the issue of the plight of the prisoners and other suspects seemed to remain alive at all.

Meanwhile the Government appeared to be developing an inflexible, back-against-the-wall attitude, inspired by the gravity of the subversive danger that it perceived. Reporting on a visit to one camp of political prisoners near Purwodadi, Central Java, in March 1969, the journalist Frank Palmos quoted a camp intelligence officer as saying:

> "What can we do? We over-arrest because the situation is so dangerous. They're trying to start another Vietnam down here. Tunnels, underground homes, blackmail of former members to return. We can't take the chance. We let most of these people out after their first arrest in 1965 and 1966. After Blitar we had to rearrest them. Biltar township was the centre of a brief PKI (Communist Party) comeback in July and August last year.

72

"I don't take the chance of leaving these men free. They are educated, skilled. Some have given up Communism, but others are still dedicated. They can hang on for years nursing their aspirations."

Reports of a massacre in the Purwodadi area of some 2,000 political prisoners and *Gestapu* suspects, and of extensive torture of victims committed by units of the Army Diponegoro division, led in early March 1969 to the despatch of a special Army investigation team to the area. But given the Army's understandable sensitivity to the question of its members' crimes, few observers counted on a complete disclosure of the nature and extent of the alleged massacre and maltreatment of political prisoners, not just in Purwodadi, but also in other areas. Predictably the Army denied all, and there was little or no satisfaction with the statement coming out of a special cabinet meeting later in March 1969, which labelled the allegations of massacre in the "Purwodadi affair" as a Communist attempt to discredit the Government.

In contrast there has been little Government reluctance in bringing prominent *Orla* personages to trial and in threatening others with court proceedings. Toward the close of May 1968, for example, Achmadi, former Minister of Information, after a long headline-making trial was given a six-year prison sentence. Achmadi had been charged with having "undermined national unity", more specifically with having given public support to the *Barisan Sukarno* and with illegally having made public funds available to the latter organization. The *Barisan Sukarno,* it will be recalled (see chapter II) had been one of the pro-Sukarno mass organizations, inspired by the underground PKI and the PNI Left wing late in 1965, and had been mobilized in support of Sukarno during his political struggle with the New Order forces. At about the same time, Achadi, former Minister of Transmigration and Co-operatives, was meted out a sentence of twelve years, also on grounds of having unlawfully used his office to support the *Barisan Sukarno,* of having permitted Communists to assume a dominant position in his department, and of having thwarted the nation's interests in the co-operative movement and economic development. The charges against both Achmadi and Achadi and the trial procedure they were subjected to probably would not satisfy those accustomed to West European or North American judicial procedures. Indeed, apart from this, some of the charges seem of dubious legal substance even in the context of Indonesia's current highly politicized judicial environment. They inevitably raise the question again, already too apparent in the days of guided democracy, whether merely being of the wrong political persuasion is enough to charge one with a criminal offence.

A high degree of political motivation also seemed to actuate the Suharto Government's threatening attitude toward Sukarno. Toward the close of September 1968, President Suharto confirmed that Sukarno was being interrogated for allegedly maintaining connections with underground *"Gestapu*/PKI" conspirators. On 4 October 1968 Sukarno's second wife, Hartini, was arrested for having acted as a link between the former President and sub-versives in Central and East Java. Though Government sources claimed to have been aware of Sukarno's contacts for some time, it was the testimony of a recently captured, pro-*Gestapu* ex-Army officer, Lieutenant-Colonel Pratomo, which reportedly compelled the Government to take action. Pratomo, reportedly arrested in April 1968, was said to have made an extensive confession on the basis of which the Government intensified its anti-PKI drive (more fully described in chapter V).

It may be recalled that in March 1967 the MPRS had indicated that "further legal procedures" to be taken against Sukarno would be left to the discretion of then Acting President Suharto. Since then rumours that the former President, though reported to be in steadily failing health, would yet shortly stand trial swept the capital with monotonous regularity. But evidently Suharto was not in any hurry. By December 1968, Sukarno had been permanently moved to a house in Djakarta, away from his Bogor residence, where he had been confined, and the Djakarta garrison commander declared that his troops were ready to deal with anyone attempting to restore Sukarno to power. But although the March 1968 MPRS session had reaffirmed that legal action against Sukarno would be taken, and although in more militant *Orba* circles the report of Sukarno's alleged con-tacts with Communists seemed to make such legal action imme-diately imperative, Suharto still seemed reluctant to take further measures against his predecessor. For one thing, a trial of Sukarno might just have provided that spark among the former Presi-dent's cowed and then largely quiescent supporters that might burst into a larger conflagration of public discontent with the Suharto regime. For another, Sukarno's and Hartini's con-tacts reportedly had been relatively harmless, involving some of the hardcore PKI underground to be sure, but more PNI Leftists and purged former *Orla* luminaries. And finally, it seemed prudent to "save" a Sukarno trial for an occasion of more direct tactical benefit to the Government. For Suharto was hardly un-aware of the skepticism, particularly among foreign observers, that met his steady stream of allegations of continuing Communist subversive activity.

That Sukarno could be used to add a new dimension and perhaps lend greater plausibility to some of these allegations became apparent on 31 March 1969. On that day a special government committee, composed of Army officers charged with gathering information on Communist subversion in Indonesia, informed Parliament that the Communists had made the restoration of Sukarno to office a part of their long-term strategy. In this and subsequent revelations the impression was left that Sukarno continued to be the underground PKI's front man, as he had been in pre-*Gestapu* Communist calculations. How effective this Government ploy was cannot be gauged. But it unquestionably outraged some of the former President's then largely mute supporters still further. Already on 17 January 1969 the newspaper *El Bahar*, which is controlled by Commodore Puguh, a nephew of Sukarno, protested that the former President was being shamefully harassed. "The Dutch authorities were clearly more humane than our present authorities," the paper asserted, adding, "how cruel are they toward the pioneers of our freedom". Whether by March or April 1969 a restoration of the ailing Sukarno figured seriously in the tactics of the Communist underground may well be doubted. But the *issue* of the alleged maltreatment of the "freedom pioneer" Sukarno might well have consequences which the Suharto regime would not be able to overlook. Meanwhile, the persistence of certain traditional religio-mystical dimensions of Javanese life were likely to provide Sukarno with the means to keep some of his old charismatic powers. Early in February 1969, for example, a mystic named Embin who had founded a sect in East Bekasi, was arrested for having started an unauthorized religious movement. Among other tenets Embin was reported to have maintained that Sukarno was the offspring of a spirit and therefore could not die but would "live forever".

Even Sukarno's death on 21 June 1970 did not end the question of his lingering political influence. On 8 July 1970, a spokesman for the Command for Restoring Security and Public Order (*Kopkamtib*) in Djakarta declared that interrogation of the former President before his death had revealed that Sukarno had been "involved" in the *Gestapu* affair, but that records would not be made public now that the case had "lapsed" because of Sukarno's death. Was this announcement mainly designed to prevent a future rehabilitation? Government spokesmen warned that no "group" should seek to "exploit" Sukarno's death, and reports that several prominent Army officers, who had been arrested in previous months for allegedly having maintained secret ties with Sukarno, were soon to be released were quickly denied.

Another area of increasing public concern, and one of particular disappointment among the more militant *Orba* supporters, was the Government's handling — or so it was sometimes alleged, its inability to handle — the problems of corruption and general malfeasance of government officials, both civilian and military. In the flush of the anti-Sukarno purges military arrogance and brutality — the summary commandeering of civilian property, the barely concealed blackmail of those suspected of Old Order sympathies, and intimidation and harassment of the public generally — had already reached new lows. With the liberalization of the economy, the influx of foreign capital and the removal of trade restrictions, bureaucratic malversations often carried out in connivance with the military multiplied rapidly. The planned tax-free import of Australian-made Holden motor-cars for the benefit of members of parliament erupted into a black market scandal in November 1967, at the very time when demands for a more intensified tax collection procedure and for a general austerity were being heard in Parliament itself. The "Holden affair" as Indonesians called it, served to underscore the editorial self-accusation of the Djakarta daily *Kompas,* that "most of us have made use of politics and position to enlarge our wealth". The institution of a government "anti-corruption" investigation team (*Team Pemberantasan Korupsi* — TPK) and agitation by student groups against corrupt officials, all have had but minimal effect, however. In April 1968, Attorney-General Soegih Arto asserted that the TPK was unable to do its job effectively because existing laws did not adequately define the exact nature of "corrupt" conduct. TPK sources themselves, at about the same time, complained that the relatively short time (six months) within which alleged "corruptors" had to be charged and brought to trial made the team's work very difficult.

But these explanations did nothing to minimize the odious effects of the persistent, widespread, well-entrenched and well-protected practices of demanding and/or accepting and providing bribes, "percentage inducements" on contracts, "key money", illegal tax levies and "protection payments" and so on, in both the civil and military administrative services, in Java no less than in the outer provinces. Again and again student deputations, in the course of 1968-9, would approach cabinet members, and even President Suharto himself, in order to press for firmer measures against allegedly corrupt practices. Sometimes KAMI and KAPPI leaders themselves would present the Government with their own purported documentary evidence and the results of their own investigations into bureaucratic financial malversations and business frauds. In mid-September 1968, seventeen out of eighteen major importers arrested for swindling, said to involve more than thirty million US dollars in foreign exchange, had to be set free for "lack of evidence". Attorney-General Soegih Arto declared at the same time that a number of government officials suspected of collusion in the swindling also could not be arrested for the same reason. Indonesian as well as foreign observers acidly commented on the ease with which the Government and the Army arrested and held indefinitely those vaguely suspected of political subversion, in contrast to the strict observance of the legal niceties in cases involving corruption.

By the middle of November 1968, the anti-corruption campaign, in Parliament and out, was reaching a new crescendo. The daily *Kompas* published a legal opinion saying that the Government's excuses for not prosecuting cases of corruption were wholly without merit. And a leading Indonesian social scientist, Professor Selo Sumardjan, publicly challenged certain government officials to deny charges of corruption made against them. As evidence mounted of high living by some bureaucrats whose regular salary was clearly but a fraction of their apparent income, and as the cases of fraudulent connivance between government officials and importers seemed to become the staple of the capital rumour circuit and of the press, KAPPI leaders warned the Government that it faced "vigilante action" by the students against "corruptors".

That Suharto was greatly impressed by such threats, given the earlier-mentioned state of disarray in the student movement generally, may be doubted. But it was obviously time to meet the rising public outcry in some way. In subsequent weeks the work of corruption investigation teams intensified, and the number of subsidiary teams in the provinces and in specialized areas of financial activity, such as banking, multiplied. On 18 February 1969, police spokesmen issued a statement in Djakarta saying, "Some 159 officials of Government and private banking enterprises have been found involved in fraudulent practices; 85 cases have been tried, are still being tried or have been submitted to courts of law for trials; the cases involve about 2.5 billion rupiahs." Additionally, some 180 bank depositors had been found to be involved in various unspecified "malpractices". Subsequently similar announcements suggested greatly increased Government activity generally on the anti-corruption front.

But other sources noted that executives of government departments and services were still obstructing the work of the corruption investigation officials. Moreover, it was becoming very clear that few leaders of the political parties or special interest groups, including those in Parliament, really had a clear,

77

consistent interest in keeping up pressure on the Government to clean house. In January 1968, for example, the Indonesian Exporters' Association accused existing political parties with attempting to manipulate and even to destroy the Government's economic stabilization programme for reasons of personal gain. Patronage and political preferments are, as in other countries with party system, inextricably interwoven with the operations of the Indonesian parties. A really intensive and consistent anti-corruption campaign would have incalculable political consequences, as it would have to involve deeply almost all the country's political groupings, and not just the Army, the civil service, or the business community. The question of corruption, moreover, is inseparable from various other economic policy considerations. Trying to rehabilitate the nation's economy by a greater reliance on market forces, and by encouraging indigenous as well as foreign capital, inevitably involves creation of a more permissive business climate, particularly so in an Indonesia trying to manoeuvre itself out of the stagnation of Sukarno's *ekonomi terpimpin* (guided economy) era. Such a permissive business climate is hardly served by endless newspaper headliness featuring the arrest or trials of traders, bankers, entrepreneurs, and bureaucrats on charges of financial malversations which even the State Prosecutor's office admits are from a legal point of view inadequately framed.

Amidst the rising clamour, Suharto in January 1970 appointed a special commission headed by former Premier Wilopo, to inquire into the extent of the corruption problem and make recommendations. By presidential decision of 16 July 1970, the commission was declared dissolved and its members "honourably" discharged while Suharto rejected students' demands that the commission's findings be made public. The relatively short tenure of the Wilopo commission and its allegedly too-cautious method of inquiry had already produced criticism and charges of "whitewashing", and by 24 July 1970, students of the so-called Bandung-on-the-Move organization charged, according to Antara, that "the spread of corruption has reached a critical point of undermining the people's confidence in the Government and impeding development". Certainly readers of the Indonesian press have ample reasons to begin doubting the Suharto Government's ability to root out corruption. During 1969-70 it was particularly such papers as *Indonesia Raya* and *Harian Kami* which kept exposing alleged instances of malversations with government funds, and the questionable business dealings and self-enrichment schemes of prominent political figures. During this period, too, charges of corruption were disseminated in various anonymous pamphlets and handbills in the major cities of Java. Some of these publications were traced to students groups. Whether the accusations contained in these pamphlets are true or not, the climate in which the charges were being made (and believed) can, in a sense, only testify to the declining prestige of the *Orde Baru*. It is especially the alleged involvement of top Army officers in business malversations that continues to arouse public indignation. For example, General Ibnu Sutowo's administration of the Government's Pertamina petroleum corporation, has, according to the Djakarta press, raised serious questions as to his probity, free-wheeling style of living and managerial acumen (one government investigating team reportedly discovered wide discrepancies between actual petroleum exports and export volume recorded in Pertamina's books). But in other government services too there are ample grounds for concern. At the close of April 1970, for example, the Indonesian Attorney-General's office was reported to be investigating some 200 cases of alleged corruption, including several in the Government's telecommunications department, which involved "billions of rupiahs", as well as extensive misuse of funds of the Five-Year Development Plan by some 250 government officials.

A related problem, also fraught with potentially disastrous political consequences, is that of streamlining the swollen government services. The endless duplication of and administrative tangle surrounding offices and poorly paid office holders in the government bureaucracy surely must be considered a major contributing factor to corruption. According to President Suharto's Address of State on the eve of Indonesia's Independence Day on 16 August 1968 to the Parliament, the Central Government (exclusive of the military establishment) employs almost 479,000 civil servants while in the regional civil services there are an additional 647,000 employees. The armed forces number 597,540, and additionally employ 166,000 civilians. There are also some 265,000 casual "workers", including nearly 57,000 in defence and security services, and 336,000 "other" personnel in central and regional government employment. As many as ninety per cent of all government civil employees earn less than thirty US dollars a month.

Since the last years of the colonial era the growth of the Indonesian bureaucracy has proportionally far exceeded population growth in the same period. In 1940, for example, when the estimated total Indonesian population was 68 million, there were 82,000 persons in all types of government employment. By the middle of 1968 when the population was estimated at about 110 million, the total number in government employ was nearly

2.5 million.   Thus in twenty-eight years, while the population did not quite double, the number of government employees increased thirtyfold!   If this comparison is regarded as unfair because of the possible differences in scope and function between colonial and national governments it needs to be noted that between 1958 and 1968 the number of all government employees grew by at least 400,000.   Yet, there are today at least some 3 million unemployed (some estimates go as high as three times that figure) and in 1968 alone about 22,000 students graduated from the country's eighty-eight institutions of higher learning.   It is estimated that ten to fifteen per cent of these graduates will eventually succeed in finding a post in the government service — not a few because of political connections, subtle "inducements" or outright bribery.

Reducing the government bureaucracy and making it more "professional" and efficient has been among the major domestic policy objectives of the *Orba*.   "Overstaffing would only hamper work, cause confusion and greater waste," Suharto said in his earlier-mentioned 16 August 1968 Address of State.   But bureaucratic retrenchment without making significant alternative employment opportunities available would be political and economic folly, and the Suharto Government has been able to make only limited progress (for example in the early pensioning of some civil workers and in providing a measure of civil employment to excess Army personnel).   In February 1969, for example, the Government's National Sea Transport Company (Pelni) which controls most inter-island shipping announced that it had discharged 3,500 of its employees in Djakarta and Surabaya.   This "efficiency measure", a company spokesman stated, would save the Government about Rp.3.5 million per annum.   Although the discharged employees were expected to be absorbed in other Pelni enterprises, including hotels, the wholesale trade and shipyards, in effect such absorption ran into serious obstacles, including the unwillingness of employees to re-train for new jobs.   Trade union pressure on the Government to find "suitable" employment for the retrenched Pelni employees increased, and soon the matter became a political football, raising serious policy questions concerning the whole viability of the Government enterprises.

Clearly, the perimeter of what is politically possible for the Government when confronted with demands to sweep away corruption or modernize the bureaucracy is much more limited than student demonstrators or some academic critics appear to realize. Yet, another illustration of the bind in which the Government finds itself with respect to the problem of corruption in its underpaid bureaucracy has been given by three specialists on the

Indonesian economy, writing in the February 1968 issue of the *Bulletin of Indonesian Economic Studies* of the Australian National University:

> The total number of people in the government's direct employ, as civil servants or military personnel, is about two million. If the *whole* of the government's revenue were divided equally between them each would receive about $320 per year, or $27 per month. If the whole of the *tax* revenue only were divided equally among them each would receive only $217 per year or $18 per month. Only some 36 per cent of all government expenditure (or about 38 per cent of *total* revenues) was used to pay wages and salaries. This means that the average annual income of a government employee was only about $115 per year, or $10 per month.
>
> Indonesia's government servants are the least well-paid in the world. To pay a monthly salary that would permit them to work full time at their designated jobs and/or remove, or at least severely reduce, the temptation to be corrupt would require the government to collect $1.4 billion in taxes for this purpose alone. This is over three times more than the total tax taken in 1967.

Comparatively, it sometimes seems much easier and politically less dangerous to seek modernizing reforms at the top of the public administrative pyramid. To a frustrated public the formation of a new cabinet, or a reshuffling of the personnel of an old one may help create the illusion — if not the substance — of impending new policy departures. Such cabinet alterations have indeed been frequent in Indonesia's brief national history. In accordance with a March 1968 MPRS resolution, President Suharto announced yet another major cabinet change on 6 June 1968 (a minor cabinet structural reorganization and reshuffle had been accomplished in September and October 1967). This new Development Cabinet (*Kabinet Pembangunan*) consisted of five principal "Ministers of State" and an additional eighteen other ministers. In terms of overall membership number there was no change from the preceding Cabinet, but some government departments were reorganized and combined with others. Perhaps more than any other cabinet in Indonesia's history the one appointed on 6 June 1968 begins to approach the idea of a "cabinet of experts". This idea has long had popular currency in academic and intellectual circles. It reflects the dissatisfaction with cabinets constructed mainly on the basis of partisan or special interest group competition and not on the basis of merit and the proven competence of individual ministers. Unfortunately supporters of the "cabinet of experts" notion have often tended to minimize the deep-seated structural problems of the Indonesian economy and society (the persistence of corruption is one) and the limited range of political options of the Government. Select the right men at the top, and the rest of the country will follow — so runs the simple expectation — a hope which despite the *Pembangunan* ministers' considerable achievements was already beginning to be dashed somewhat by the middle of 1969.

Even so there is no denying that the composition of the new Cabinet pleased many. The number of ministers from the armed forces was reduced from nine to six and at least seven cabinet members are or were university professors. Appointment of prominent *Orba* figures like Mashuri, who was given the education and culture portfolio, and of the noted economic expert Sumitro Djojohadikusumo, who became Minister of Trade, generally pleased the restive student community. The appointment of Sumitro and of Ali Wardhana, who became Finance Minister, also met with approval in foreign investment and financial circles. But Sumitro's entry into the Cabinet did cause a muted protest in PNI and other circles which could not forget his leading role in the PRRI rebellion in Sumatra nearly a decade ago. Some, by no means all, Muslim media and groups also continued to complain that the Muslim community was under-represented in the new Government. The retention of the Catholic party's dynamic "modernizer", Frans Seda (who was given the Communications Ministry), particularly aroused Islamic ire, although Seda's tenure of the finance portfolio in the previous Cabinet had also given cause for legitimate criticism.

Perhaps as significant as the appointment of the new Cabinet was Suharto's simultaneous announcement that his personal advisory staff (*Staf Pribadi*) would be dissolved. Composed of about a dozen top-ranking officers the presidential staff had become subject to increasing criticism in Parliament, the press and among the political parties. This criticism stemmed from the allegedly ruthless pressure tactics of staff members, the tendency to encroach on the responsibility of department executives and even of cabinet ministers, and their purported favouritism and "influence peddling" on behalf of certain party leaders. One staff member, Major-General Alamsjah, was also a frequent target of charges of "corruption" levelled by youth groups. The dissolution of the *Staf Pribadi* did not mean the disappearance of some of its leading personnel from the President's inner circle, however. Alamsjah acquired the post of State Secretary while three other former staff members were appointed Presidential Assistants, and yet another became Personal Secretary to Suharto. It is clear that Suharto means to retain his personal liaison network with other power centres in the nation, particularly with the Army.

When in the middle of January 1969, the Interior Minister Lieutenant-General Basuki Rahmat died, he was replaced by Major-General Amir Mahmud, greater-Djakarta area military commander. Mahmud's post, in turn, was filled by the commander of the Sriwidjaja division in Palembang, South Sumatra, Major-General Makmun Murod. These appointments would not merit much attention, were it not for the manner in which the Indonesian news media chose to describe and comment upon them. According to the press Murod's appointment had given Suharto a good deal of concern. For were Murod to become greater-Djakarta area commander this would mean a significant strengthening of the so-called Sriwidjaja group of leading officers in the capital. Among the "Sriwidjajans", for example, are the earlier-mentioned Alamsjah, Major-General Ibnu Sutowo, the director of the Government's Pertamina oil company, Colonel A. Siregar, head of the State news agency Antara, and others. The Murod appointment, the press speculated, thus would be bound to create resentment among top officers from other well-known divisions, like West Java's Siliwangi, Central Java's Diponegoro, and East Java's Brawidjaja. Whether this and similar surmises were more than just journalistic kite-flying or not, there is little doubt that inter-Army and indeed inter-service rivalries are widely accepted facts of Indonesian public life. Since the *Gestapu* affair officers of the AURI (the Indonesian Air Force) have frequently complained that an unwarranted onus of treason has been visited on their entire service. These officers allege that because of the conduct of Dhani, Sujono and a few other AURI personnel, loyal Air Force officers are now being discriminated against in appointments to influential or lucrative public service posts. Sukarnoist sympathies and indeed Communist influence among lower naval personnel and in the ranks of the Marine Corps (KKO) similarly have continued to produce friction. The *Kostrad* (the Strategic Army Reserve), the Siliwangi division of West Java, the RPKAD (the Army's Para-Commandos), as well as small groups of officers closely allied with either Suharto and/or Nasution, have generally been considered to be harbouring the most intensely intransigent and pitiless anti-Sukarno elements in the Army. For this reason *Kostrad* or the RPKAD have aroused a good deal of resentment and enmity among the KKO, the Air Force, or even in the Army's own Diponegoro division.

The most intense factionalism and competition by far, how-ever, is not so much between the major services (including the police), but rather is to be found within the 400,000-man Army. Fissures here probably run less along divisional or regional com-mand lines, as press speculation would sometimes seem to suggest, and more along the lines of service specialization, and of the self-concept and "image" of the Army held by the personnel con-cerned. Almost since the national Indonesian Army's birth in the revolutionary period there has, for example, been a conflict between "political" officers and "technocrats". The former, many of them the products of semi-military "volunteer corps" training in the Japanese Occupation period, often tended to see their responsibilities in ideological as well as purely military terms. In the era of guided democracy this group adopted much of the nationalistic mystiques of Sukarnoism. They also tended to forge close ties with and to look, for protection, to the major political parties. The technocrat group, generally somewhat younger and often trained and retrained abroad in various modern service specialities, conceived of the Army primarily in non-political terms, although these men too occasionally drifted into the orbit of partisan politics. Many in this group long and vainly urged a radical retrenchment of redundant Army personnel, a streamlining of organization, and a general modernization through adoption of new technological and other specialized services. Conflicts between these two groups existed all through the fifties and sixties and tended to intensify during the closing stages of Sukarno's guided democracy when Communist political pressures and infiltration in all branches of the armed forces accelerated. *Gestapu*'s failure inevitably reaccentuated and gave new dimensions to these inner fissures in the Army leadership as *Orba* officers confronted their *Orla* colleagues and as security-giving partisan affiliations fell apart.

More was and is involved in all these conflicts than position within the Army hierarchy alone, however. For personnel of all armed forces branches, but particularly of the Army, have for more than a decade now been increasingly incorporated into all aspects of civil administration and public service, finding posts in every branch of government from the cabinet — indeed from the presidency — down. The range of their responsibilities seems endless. Army officers run or supervise the running of estates, labour unions, or shipping; they can be and are provincial governors and local as well as national legislators; they may control public transport in cities and even the screening of motion pictures and the issuance of market licences, and so on. Directly or indirectly opportunities for graft and fraudulent dealings in many of these posts abound. Not all incumbents have been able to resist the temptation to bolster their meagre and generally totally inadequate salary earnings with a little, and sometimes not-so-little, easy money. In a lecture to the Army's co-operative administration in Bandung, toward the close of June 1970, Transmigration and Co-operatives Minister M. Sarbini candidly noted that the household economy and living conditions of the soldiers were disorganized because the salaries they received were "not enough for daily needs".

The most prominent intellectual critics of Sukarnoism, as they came to the fore in the months after *Gestapu,* were convinced that while the Army was indispensable in bringing the Old Order down with a minimum of domestic turmoil, the Army, no less than the presidency, would eventually have to be "constitutionalized". This meant a reduction in the Army's vast political and civil administrative powers. However, many *Orba* Army, no less than the presidency, would eventually have to be to the Army's non-political function, hesitated. A return to the free-wheeling party politics of parliamentary democracy in the early fifties certainly did not appeal to them. Some were quite convinced that a long Army-dominated "interregnum" led by a figure reflecting sober leadership ("Pak Harto" seemed an ideal choice to them) was necessary before a proper, emergency-free constitutionalism vested in a presidential-parliamentary partnership, could prevail. Party and action front leaders who might concede some truth in this argument nevertheless urged, also in dialogues with their Army allies, that the Army divest itself as much as possible of their special powers lest public fears of *penghidjauan* (literally "greenization", that is domination of public life by green-uniformed military) and even of an impending military dictatorship mount even higher. Such urgings bore but little fruit, however, although Suharto was not unsympathetic.

Already in 1966-7 widespread public criticism had forced local Army commanders to curb and punish summary expropriation of civilian property by a number of Army units, and stricter regulations were issued against intimidation and harassment of citizens. Not until early February 1968, however, did Suharto order district military commanders and governors to stop levying various unofficial "taxes" on goods in transit and to tear down unauthorized "toll barriers" to traffic. In the second half of 1967 Suharto had also progressively ordered the dissolution of various free-wheeling and vaguely constituted regional and provincial military "supervisory" and "administrative" agencies which had been seriously interfering with provincial civil government, including the judiciary. Military attitudes were becoming clearly defensive as a result of such measures. In early January 1968, for example, Colonel Sjahrani, the Governor of East Kalimantan, declared that the recent appointment of members of the armed forces as mayors of cities and heads of "regencies" (districts) in the province was not to be considered as an expression of "militarism" but rather was a "manifestation of the people's trust" in the armed forces.

But attacks on the Army's civil and political function did not abate. In May 1968, *Muhammadiyah* leaders demanded that military personnel holding civil positions withdraw from military service and shortly the KAPPI branch in Djokjakarta urged that military holding cabinet posts sever their service connections. Army "authoritarianism" particularly incensed students who during recent demonstrations had been on the receiving end of the Army's rifle fire and rifle butts. In May 1968, Djakarta garrison troops entered the homes of several students and smashed the transmitters of a student amateur radio station which had been broadcasting jeering criticism of the armed forces and even of Suharto. The incident markedly deepened public concern, and shortly a senior Moluccan police official (the police force is considered part of the national armed forces establishment in Indonesia) castigated the growing authoritarianism of the members of the armed services. Already in January 1968, Suharto, by presidential decree, had prohibited the armed forces from concerning themselves with civil transgressions unless they involved breaches of the criminal code as well. In subsequent months, the demand that the Army "get out of the prosecutor's office altogether", as one student action front paper put it, met with an increasingly larger chorus of public sympathy. Along with this came calls for the end of special emergency and state-of-war conditions throughout the country which, in a general way, had up to now legitimized the powers which members of the armed forces had arrogated to themselves also in their civil positions. At about the same time there were demands to repeal earlier emergency measures which had removed the military from the jurisdiction of civil courts.

The problem is that even in the Sukarno period the involvement of the armed forces in national political life had already been declared an informal constitutional principle. The armed forces' so-called *dwifungsi* (double function) meant not just responsibility for the military security of the State but also participation in the nation's development, in all its phases. The *dwifungsi* concept not only legitimized Army officers holding civil bureaucratic offices and management posts in business, but also the Army's "civic" development, from directing youth groups to constructing roads and schools. *Dwifungsi* also meant guaranteed representation in Parliament and hence continuous interaction with political parties; more, in Suharto's era especially, it has come to mean the role of the armed forces, and in particular of the Army, as a balancer of the parties — that is a function not altogether unlike that once performed by Sukarno. To many, however, Suharto seems unable to stand above the armed forces' *dwifungsi* operations — it was, reportedly, primarily the Army's insistence which led to the regulation, promulgated by the Interior Ministry at the close of 1969, which provided that so-called "functional groups" divest themselves of partisan political affiliations in the various national, provincial and local representative bodies (see chapter IX). The regulation caused a huge outcry of protest among the parties, but the Army was adamant. One of its effects has been clearly to reduce the influence of the parties in the functional groups thus benefiting Army officers, who now, in some instances, have virtually become the principal functional spokesman in local councils.

The obviously mounting public dissatisfaction (some of it even in top leadership circles of the armed forces themselves) over the military's role placed Suharto in a difficult position. A dismantling of' the whole structure of their special powers and the "reconstitutionalization" of the armed forces obviously would be politically suicidal. In the closing weeks of 1968 and throughout the first half of 1969 Suharto launched an accelerating programme of internal Army reforms coupled to a campaign designed to make the Army's "civic image" more attractive. A number of senior officers were either sent abroad on diplomatic missions, or like the Army's intelligence chief, Major-General E. Magenda, were retired. Stricter enforcement of established criteria of efficiency and private morality in determining a senior officer's continuation in the service was also begun. Leading "political" officers and *Orba* activists like the earlier-named Major-General Dharsono who had long been in the public eye were, for good measure, also relieved from their commands though not retired. Early in March 1969, Major-General Dharsono was seconded to the Foreign Ministry in preparation for a foreign service assignment. Lieutenant-General R. Kartakusumah, Chief of Staff of the Army's security department, who earlier had refused Suharto's offer of the ambassadorship to West Germany, was demoted to a lesser post in the defence department in March 1969.

By early April 1969, there were even rumours that Indonesia's best known senior soldier, MPRS chairman General A. H. Nasution, would shortly either be pensioned off or sent to the Army Staff College in Bandung, West Java, for "retraining" (Nasution replied that he was too old to go to school). Clearly the intention of the Army shake-up was not only to weed out marginal senior commanders but also to draw some of the political fangs of a number of high-ranking activist officers and thus give the Army leadership a more professional and disciplined appearance. Concurrently the enforced retirement of a number of older officers undoubtedly opened the frequently badly clogged channels of promotion to restive junior men. Before the reforms the 400,000-man Army had about 8,000 officers of the rank of major and above, including 260 generals. The extent of change in these numbers brought about by the Suharto reforms is not known—one Army source claims that at least twenty officers of the rank of general had already been ordered retired by the end of March 1969. Finally, the sending abroad on various diplomatic missions of politically prominent officers, it need not be stressed, has been many a government's time-honoured device for removing potential threats.

In a vast expansion of its already established "civic mission" programme the Army, under Suharto's prodding, announced in February 1969, that in the near future nearly a third of its soldiers, comprising some 100 battalions, would be sent into the countryside in order to assist the peasantry in the planting and harvesting of rice. To be carried out under cover of a Government call for general, intensified public assistance and participation in helping to make Indonesia's new Five-Year Plan a success, and especially in making the country self-sufficient in food production, the Army's projected involvement in the village economy quite evidently is intended to improve the soldier's standing in the eyes of the public. Though most observers have been justifiably skeptical about the extent and intensity with which this expanded civic mission of the Army will actually be carried out, there is little doubt that this is the sort of tactic which can cut the ground from under Army and Suharto critics. Development of a "people's army"—a force of and from the peasantry and proletariat — was one of the PKI's announced objectives in the years before *Gestapu*.

But apart from the question of whether the Army can strengthen its position and make itself more popular by its going-down-to-the-village tactic, it is already clear that the actual pattern of Army political power has changed but little as a result of these reform measures. Suharto still meets regularly, and either individually or collectively, with several hundred regional top armed forces commanders, most of them in public administrative posts, to discuss and obtain support for Government policies ranging from the implementation of the Five-Year Plan to the staging of the next general elections. Anyone observing the proceedings of these meetings becomes immediately aware where the real political power in Indonesia lies today. There has been no marked diminution of military office holders in the civil or regional bureaucracies and the fabric of emergency regulations remains, to all intents and purposes, as strong as ever. There is also, to be sure, some evidence that President Suharto is not altogether happy with this state of affairs and that he has wished for a more meaningful participation of other power centres, for example the parties, in the process of government. As the President put it in a recent interview with the paper, *Indonesia Raya*: "I believe that the most important problem now is to find out how political parties, as tools of a democratic government, can properly fulfil their functions. . . ." It is no doubt a sincere sentiment. But, it should be asked just the same: how exactly do Suharto and his Army allies view the function of constitutional government? Would the Army, for example, accept a drastic alteration of the present presidential system under which it finds it so much easier to retain its civil administrative powers? And even with the presidential system does the Army believe it should retain special, extra-constitutional authority? Sensitive — more properly one should say "over-sensitive" — as they are to party and special interest group criticism of the Government, neither Suharto nor many Army commanders appear to be sufficiently aware of an adversary element that is both unavoidable and necessary in a proper functioning of constitutional processes generally, and in parliamentary behaviour in particular. That is, such an element is generally essential in states striving to be other than "guided democracies".

CHAPTER FIVE

The Communist Resurgence

"*IL EST des morts qu'il faut qu'on tue*" — "It is the dead who must be killed," wrote the nineteenth-century French publicist, Fernand Desnoyers. To some his observation seems particularly relevant to Indonesia today. Considered superficially, at least, the Indonesian Communist Party (PKI) is "dead". Formally banned since March 1966, its principal erstwhile leaders killed, imprisoned or in exile (only one member of the PKI's nine-man Politburo at the time of *Gestapu*, Jusuf Adjitorop, who now mostly resides in Peking, remains at large), its party and huge front organizational network shattered, its name put at the top of the nation's official demonology, and the propagation of its theories prohibited except for academic study — the party, for the moment, would seem at first blush to constitute little threat to Suharto's *Orba*. Still, the fact is that a strident anti-Communism, a ceaseless probing for and purging of allegedly pro-Communists in all walks of life — but particularly in the government services themselves — and a constant raising of the spectre of supposed Communist subversion, are among the principal dynamics of Indonesian domestic policy at present. There is, for example, considerable evidence that the Suharto Government is increasingly relying on the presumed existence of a Communist threat to mobilize popular support, as in the implementation of the Five-Year Plan. The dangers of a less-than-discriminating anti-Communism of this kind, and the mounting concern in Indonesia about the authoritarian drift of Suharto's regime, have already been indicated in the previous chapter.

But how dead is the PKI really? While there is no question of the alarming ease with which the Suharto Government and its military and bureaucratic allies sometimes invoke the Communist threat, there is also evidence that, though scattered, discredited, and constantly harassed, groups of Indonesian Communists have since *Gestapu* frequently demonstrated remarkable resourcefulness in keeping their underground movement alive. Their influence in sections of the Central and East Javanese rural society, and among militant but now silenced supporters of Sukarnoism and *nasakom,* for example in the Left wing of the PNI and its youth group ancillaries, and even in the armed forces, has lingered on. *Orba's* purges and massacres and the humiliation of Sukarno have left a vast legacy of bitterness which will remain ready for political exploitation by the New Order's enemies for years to come.

Despite the frightful, gradually accelerating anti-Communist pogrom (the wave of killings of Communists and suspects did not really get well underway until late in October and early November 1965, after it had become apparent to youthful Muslim fanatics that the Army's attitude was favourable to a pogrom) small bands of Communists, some of them veterans of the fighting in and around Djokjakarta and Surakarta, had been able to regroup under party cadres and provincial and local party committee members. Already in January 1966, Army sources spokes of underground PKI terrorist groups operating under such names as *Samber Njawa* (literally, "to snuff out life") and *Kutjing Hitam* (Black Cat). At least some of these bands were probably covert second-echelon support and "back up" units originally organized by the PKI for operations during *Gestapu.* Later, as the anti-Communist pogrom spread, they became in a sense "self-defence" organizations. Still later, as the PKI attempted to reorganize itself, they became the vanguard of a new, scattered, underground People's Liberation Army. Already in the early days of October 1965 Muslim youths, students and trade unionists, with some support from Roman Catholic quarters, as well as with the endorsement of local Army commanders, organized themselves for purposes of systematic anti-Communist action in such groups as the KAP-*Gestapu* or Action Front for the Crushing of *Gestapu.* Amid the violent clashes between pro- and anti-PKI and pro- and anti-Sukarno student groups in the post-*Gestapu* constitutional crisis, and during the bloody purges of Communists and suspects, Communist party and front cadres and members also sought protective cover in such political pressure and would-be mass organizations as the *Barisan Sukarno* (Sukarno Front), the *Hidup Nasakom* (Long Live *Nasakom*) and particularly the *Aku Pendukung Sukarno* (I am a Sukarno Supporter).

According to Army spokesmen, provincial and district units of the PKI during most of 1966 attempted to restructure themselves for terrorist action. On 10 May 1966 then Djakarta's commander, Major-General Amir Mahmud, reported that a "Communist plot" to assassinate Suharto had been discovered in the capital. On the following 23 June an Army spokesman announced that yet another plot had been smashed, this one in Surakarta, Central Java, which had been designed to restore a "Leftist regime" to be headed by former Foreign Minister Subandrio (already in detention since March). On 4 June Suharto himself had warned that the banned PKI was reorganizing and remained a continuing threat. He said that the reorganization had already crystallized into a new terrorist network with covert bands operating under such code names as *Gunung Es* (Iceberg) and *PKI Malam* (Night PKI).

Subsequent Army reports, late in 1966, gave a more detailed picture of this alleged underground terrorist network of the Communists. By this time the protection which Communists had earlier sought in relatively "above-ground" organizations like the *Barisan Sukarno* and in Left-wing student and youth groups like the Indonesian Students Movement (*Gerakan Mahasiswa Indonesia—Germindo*) and the National Indonesian Students Movement (*Gerakan Mahasiswa Nasional Indonesia* — GMNI), many of whose members identified themselves with the Ali-Surachman wing of the PNI, had proved rather useless. Under local cadres, die-hard Communists and their allies in the PNI had therefore gone deeper underground, Army information officers asserted. Relying increasingly on the old terrorist structure of the *Gestapu* plot, new action committees and branches with appropriate "project officers" were organized and a measure of functional "specialization" even appeared. In the Rembang area of north Central Java, for example, Black Cat elements, according to the Army, were trained for arson, so-called Creeping Troops were trained for surprise attacks and distribution of poison, and Black Dog Troops were organized for murders, kidnapping and intimidation. To what extent the Rembang underground organization resembled those in óther areas is not clear. But by the end of 1967 captured documents, relating to the planning earlier in the year of a Communist "Indonesian People's Liberation Army" (*Tentara Pembebasan Rakjat Indonesia* — TPRI) in West Java, purported to show a similar division of tactical tasks among different terrorist groups projected to operate in that area.

As early as the beginning of August 1966, Djakarta commander, Mahmud, said that despite the official ban on the PKl the Djakarta branch of the party was still covertly active. Less than half of the party's top leadership had been apprehended, Mahmud added. Mahmud's statement appeared to be the signal for an intensified drive in subsequent weeks against alleged continuing subversion by the PKI underground. Throughout Java, in early September 1966, an Army spokesman announced, some

11,000 "*Gestapu*/PKI" elements had been taken into custody in Central Java, 7,000 alone in the Klaten region between the towns of Djokjakarta and Surakarta, a principal base-area of the Communists during the *Gestapu* coup. A new information campaign was launched by the Central Java provincial governor's office in co-operation with the Army, describing "the political guerilla war conducted by remnants of the PKI" among the village population. This and similar campaigns, wittingly or not, seemed greatly to enlarge the spectre — probably out of all proportion — of the continuing PKI subversive campaign or *gerpol* (from *gerilja politik* or political guerilla war). Such an exaggeration may well have been intended from the start by some Army commanders.

Still, the Communist resurgence seemed real enough. In mid-September 1966, pamphlets inscribed with a hammer-and-sickle emblem and calling for the overthrow of "Fascist dictatorship" were surreptitiously being distributed in Djakarta. Shortly the Army arrested scores of Communist suspects and seized arms caches in various parts of the city. Among those arrested at this time, according to the paper *Ampera,* were leading PNI figures, including two parliamentary deputies, and suspicion arose that the arrests were intended not least as a means of silencing all open or would-be opponents of *Orba*. But Army spokesmen asserted that the arrests had foiled a new, allegedly Communist, plot to kill anti-Communist Army and student leaders on the first anniversary of *Gestapu* a few days hence. Documents purportedly substantiating the existence of this new plot were said to have been obtained during the recent arrest of one of the chief conspirators in the Rawasari district of the capital.

Meanwhile, Major-General A. Mokoginta, then Sumatra's principal territorial commander, declared in Medan that the PKI was also attempting secretly to establish its regional committees on that island. The attempt had been discovered, Mokoginta said, when authorities in Djakarta were trying to stop the reactivation of the PKI's Central Committee in the capital. On 20 September 1966, Army spokesmen in Banjumas in Central Java announced the capture, after an exchange of gun fire, of a purported "Communist stronghold" at Sigelaga which was said to be under local PKI cadre control. On 23 September 1966 the *Armed Forces Daily Mail* announced that according to the Army's regional command of Central Java province, some 70,000 Communists and suspects, among them forty per cent of the PKI's regional committee members and eighty per cent of its committee members of various districts in Central Java, had been captured thus far. Significantly for the type of arrest procedure apparently being followed was the announcement by the same source that of the 70,000 persons apprehended about 18,000 had been subsequently released after it was established "that they have been wrongly seized. Some of them were just innocent followers."

It is difficult to tell whether all these reports of Communists arrested and of plots foiled contributed significantly to the sense of public security or to just the reverse; or, indeed, whether the tensions generated by the reports and the arrests themselves added in fact to the already existing tactical opportunities being presented to the PKI underground. The campaign against Sukarno, meanwhile, and trials of prominent *Orla* figures, like former Central Banking Minister Jusuf Muda Dalam, former Foreign Minister Subandrio and former Air Force chief Marshal Dhani, certainly tended to polarize and harden political sentiments. At the same time reports that the PKI underground was seeking new organizational havens, particularly in the PNI and its affiliates, appeared to contribute further to an already alarming conspiratorial dimension in domestic Indonesian politics, one that apparently justified the endless search for new alleged subversives. In the middle of November 1966 there were new press stories, obviously being circulated with military approval, of yet another just-discovered plot, this one purportedly designed to kill principal religious leaders, overthrow Suharto, and kidnap leading generals in order to prevent the execution of Subandrio, who had been condemned to death three weeks previously. The plot was said to have been hatched by PNI leaders, in collusion with the PKI underground, at a meeting in Rogodjampi, East Java, and reportedly included also a number of high-ranking Army officers who were subsequently arrested for having fallen under "Communist influence". The officers allegedly had been assigned the task of infiltrating anti-Sukarno student groups, inciting them to violence and thus providing an official excuse for severely repressive measures against them. The cloudy reports of this alleged conspiracy became still further confused when Army spokesmen subsequently denied that any Army personnel had been involved in the Rogodjampi conspiracy. Through the closing days of November 1966, the Army continued to conduct house-to-house searches in Djakarta, and indeed, on 25 November, as tanks rumbled into position around a supposed Communist "stronghold" in the city, the Chief of Staff of the Djakarta military command announced yet additional "security operations" against "*Gestapu*/PKI remnants" as well as against ordinary criminals, and appealed for public calm.

The close of 1966 also saw anti-PKI operations continuing beyond Java. On Bali where the PKI had had a significant and growing following just before the *Gestapu* incident, and where the anti-Communist purge had initially been particularly bloody, Communists and their sympathizers had begun to strike back. In early August 1966, a Communist "counter-terror" campaign had been launched in Bali; grenades were hurled, and shops and public buildings were burned down. By the beginning of December 1966, additional troops had to be flown into Bali from West Java to cope with the unrest. Shortly, too, a Communist guerilla insurgency was to flare up in West Kalimantan, along the Sarawak border (to be discussed presently). But the heart of PKI activities continued to be in Central and, subsequently, East Java. On 4 December 1966 the *bupati* (head of a so-called regency administrative district) in Bojolali, Central Java, reported that "two companies" of "*Gestapu/PKI*" forces were still operating in his area, which is situated at the foot of Mounts Merapi and Merbabu, referred to earlier as a major base of PKI operations before and after the *Gestapu* affair. In Semarang, meanwhile, the Public Prosecutor's office disclosed that a new, allegedly Communist, organization had been uncovered with "numerous branches throughout the city" and that Communist propaganda materials from abroad were being disseminated.

In the middle of January 1967, Djakarta military commander Mahmud gave a report on PKI underground operations during the previous year. According to his statement the PKI had been able to re-establish a central committee headed by Sudisman, a prominent party Politburo member before the *Gestapu* affair. Sudisman had been particularly active in Djakarta and he was arrested there early in December 1966, subsequently tried, and executed on 29 October 1968, along with another captured Politburo member, Njono. Even before Sudisman's arrest, however, there had been other efforts at a central reorganization of the party. Perhaps the most important of these was the one which got underway in the second half of 1966 and which was led by Rewang, alias Karto, occasional contributor to the Prague-based, Soviet-orientated *World Marxist Review* and the PKI's Central Java province chairman, and by Ruslan Widjajasastra, the party's chairman for East Java. A rudimentary "agitprop" department led by Robby Sumolong, a former party youth leader, had also been part of the Rewang-Widjajasastra operation and had had some success in spreading its propaganda sheets called *Mimbar Rakjat* (People's Forum).

In this period of PKI underground resistance (1966-7) apparently considerable effort was made by surviving cadres and supporters to retain the party's erstwhile influence in some segments of the armed forces. In preparation for the *Gestapu* affair PKI leaders had established a *biro chusus* (special bureau) in order to establish closer liaison with Army sympathizers, although the relative effectiveness of this agency in winning support among the military remains unclear. According to some reports the Rewang-Widjajasastra operation, independently or jointly with the Sudisman group in Djakarta, sought to reconstitute the *biro chusus* channel; certainly the PKI's lingering influence among East Java military and particularly in the Marine Corps (KKO) suggests a close and continuous contact. Other sources, however, claim that until their arrests the *biro chusus* remained under the leadership of three shadowy party "specialists" in armed forces infiltration, namely, Sjam, alias Kamaruzaman, who as indicated in chapter I was one of the chief *Gestapu* plotters (and who went on trial in February 1968); Muljono, alias Walujo (tried in October 1968); and Pono (whose capture was announced in March 1969).

Although the Rewang-Widjajasastra group was continuously decimated by arrests (Rewang himself was erroneously reported killed by the middle of 1967), it and the remnants of Sudisman's underground apparatus in and around Djakarta were able to consolidate their organization during 1967, incorporating much of the earlier-named Indonesian People's Liberation Army (TPRI) in West Java as well as elements of such relatively scattered terrorist groups as the Surabaya People's Guerilla Movement (*Persatuan Gerilja Rakjat Surabaja*) and the *Kutjing Hitam* (Black Cat. There was no dearth of leadership. Well-known, pre-coup second-echelon PKI leaders — among them Oloan Hutapea, former editor of the PKI's chief theoretical organ *Bintang Merah* (Red Star); Mohammad Munir, secretary-general of the PKI's principal labour front SOBSI; Sukatno, alias Teguh, one-time leader of the party's principal youth front; and eventually also the earlier-named Sjam — most of them separated and in hiding in the second half of 1967, gravitated towards the Rewang-TPRI-terrorist organization complex. Their participation was to provide still further structure and direction to Communist operations which were to become dramatically apparent in the first few months of 1968. Hutapea shortly appeared to have become the principal leader of this new party organizational complex, eventually heading his own reported Central Committee in the south Blitar region of East Java.

In selected places in Central and East Java a network of covert encampments, meeting places, shelters and even bunkers connected by underground tunnels in the Viet Cong manner were constructed. In 1964 the PKI reportedly had sent a team of fourteen cadres to North Vietnam to master Viet Cong guerilla tactics. Most returned before the *Gestapu* affair, and though the team leader, one Satir, had been killed before the PKI's underground reorganization under Hutapea and Rewang significantly got underway, the expertise of the remaining North Vietnam returnees became clearly apparent in subsequent Indonesian Communist tactics. Some of this expertise was also imparted at an underground People's Liberation Army School (*Sekolah Tentara Pembebasan Rakjat*—STPR) in the Klaten area, with "branches" around Blitar. Tactics involved division of operational zones marked "red" (safe or Communist controlled), "pink" (successfully infiltrated), "white" (neutral, but open to infiltration) and "green" ("enemy" controlled, that is particularly suggesting a strong anti-Communist Islamic community or organization), and concentrated especially on so-called "persuasive" front techniques in making white zones pink, and on creating disturbances and disruption in the green sectors. A hierarchical structure of *kompro* or project committees supervised these operations, and by the beginning of 1968 an enlarged provincial committee for East Java (including the eastern portions of Central Java), which eventually was to call itself the party's new Central Committee headed by Hutapea and located south of Blitar, was providing a measure of tactical guidance. The location of caches of arms and other supplies uncovered later often showed considerable planning. There is also no question of the co-ordinated nature of the PKI's counter-terror campaign unleashed with particular ferocity early in 1968 in some of the so-designated green zones, in the Central Java border region, including killing and kidnapping of village offcials, *kiajihs* (Muslim religious leaders), prominent members of NU and of the largely Islamic Indonesian University Students Association (*Himpunan Mahasiswa Indonesia*—HMI).

The same relative co-ordination — including ambushes of Army convoys and other hit-and-run clashes — later was apparent in the Communist guerilla resistance in the Blitar region and elsewhere in East Java, in the middle of 1968. Some Indonesian sources claimed to the author to see in this co-ordination the hand of the former Brigadier-General Suharjo, erstwhile military commander of East Kalimantan, a political radical and Sukarno sympathizer who was studying at a Soviet military staff college at the time of *Gestapu* and who reportedly subsequently made his way back to Indonesia in secret via Hanoi. Suharjo reportedly also lent his talents to the Communist guerilla insurgents operating along the Sarawak-Indonesian border. Other reports, however,

97

note that military training in Blitar was chiefly directed by Lieutenant-Colonel Pratomo, the former military commander of Pandeglang district in West Java. Pratomo, who appears to have been involved in the *Gestapu* conspiracy in a manner not yet fully disclosed, was captured in April 1968. His confessions were to have widespread repercussions in the West Java Siliwangi division of the Army, to be discussed presently. In this connection the influence of the party's earlier-mentioned *biro chusus,* which after the capture of Sjam (Kamaruzaman) came largely to be directed by Pono, also should not be overlooked. In February 1968, for example, some 330 Army, Navy, Air Force and police personnel in East Java province, most of them from the Malang region, deserted to the Communist underground, taking their weapons with them. In making white zones pink the new PKI offensive appears particularly to have relied on sympathizers in the Left wing of the PNI and its organizational fronts (the fugitive Surachman, principal leader of the PNI Left, was caught and shot on 20 July 1968, during the Army's operations against the Communists in the south Blitar region) and on an underground press campaign, which saw extensive dissemination, particularly in East Java, not only of the earlier-named *Mimbar Rakjat* but also of such new action publications as *Front Anti-Fasis, Suara Demokrasi* (Voice of Democracy) and others.

Already during July and August 1967, there were dozens of arrests of Army officers, including top-ranking ones like Brigadier Sukendro, a leader of the IPKI party which, though small, has been quite influential among the military, especially in West Java. Sukendro was accused of having allowed *Orla* elements, including pro-PKI Sukarno sympathizers, to find a haven in IPKI. His arrest and that of other officers were coupled with seemingly ceaseless official warnings, including some by Generals Nasution and Suharto, that the Old Order elements, in league with *Gestapu*/ PKI/*gerpol* activists, were still burrowing on and undermining the State. These arrests and warnings served to heighten public concern at the very time that the Hutapea-Rewang reorganization of the PKI was beginning to gain momentum. In November 1967 the Army announced increased activity by the TPRI in West Java, as nearly simultaneously the arrest was announce of the members of a "West Java PKI Emergency Committee". At the close of 1967 increasing attention was also focused on alleged Communist activity beyond Java, including the Minehassa area of North Sulawesi, and especially North Sumatra, where in and around Medan more than 200 were arrested in October and November for unspecified attempts to revive the PKI. As the Maoist sympathies of Chinese insurgents along the Indonesian-

Sarawak border also seemed to be becoming increasingly prominent in this period, anti-Chinese sentiment, seemingly endemic in Indonesia, flared into the open again, and in a number of locations Indonesian officials stressed the connection between the Communist upsurge in the country and the subversive activity of Chinese in Indonesia and abroad. Thus in November 1967 there were press reports of Chinese Communist infiltration through the islands of Bangka and Belitung, while at about the same time in Semarang, Central Java, local Chinese support for the resurgent PKI there was alleged. Then, in January 1968, the arrest was announced of nine leaders of the "Semarang PKI underground organization" and the following month five allegedly leading Communists were apprehended in Djakarta.

But, as the months went by with their seemingly regular quota of press reports of ever more arrests of PKI suspects and alleged *Gestapu* sympathizers, an unwary reader could easily get the impression that the Communist underground seemed but to thrive on all these apparent obstacles to its organizational expansion. The daily *Kompas* on 26 March 1968, for example, carried yet another report on new arrests, this time in connection with the Army's *Operasi Kalong* (Operation Bat) against the Djakarta Communist underground since the beginning of the year. More than 300 supposedly PKI members (more than two-thirds of them in the military) were reported to have been apprehended in this new drive in Djakarta, along with a number of prominent leaders of the party's former SOBSI labour front and *Pemuda Rakjat* youth front, as well as former party Central Committee members. The same report alleged that five Djakarta district committees of the party had been established recently, along with branches of new covert terrorist organizations, including yet another Indonesian People's Liberation Army (*Lasjkar Pembebasan Rakjat Indonesia* — LPRI). The point is that already in December 1966, at the time of Sudisman's arrest, announcements by military spokesmen in Djakarta led one to believe that the attempt to revive an underground PKI organizational structure in the capital had been definitely, if not definitively, crushed. To some observers it seemed that the Communists were indestructible or the Army had a stake in keeping the issue of PKI subversion alive, or that perhaps even both were the case.

About four weeks before the March 1968 mass arrests in Djakarta the city's military command asserted that no less than twenty-seven "meeting places" used by the Communists had been discovered in the city as well as a party training centre for a projected "people's army" just outside the capital; and near the conclusion of the trial of Sjam, in early March 1968, an Army spokesman declared that the trial proceedings had "proved" that twenty Communist "cells" were operating in the capital. Presumably appropriate action was taken in the wake of these discoveries. But a year later, in March and April 1969, Army spokesmen in Djakarta were still urging public "vigilance" and were quoted as saying that a "shadow *Gestapu*/PKI organization" was still very much alive in the city. Meanwhile, during March 1968, disquieting reports of stepped-up PKI terrorism in the heart of East Java province — that is around Kediri, Malang and Blitar — were also beginning to appear in the press. The chairman of NU's youth affiliate organization, *Ansor,* whose members it will be recalled had played a major role in the mass killings of Communists and suspects after the *Gestapu* affair, claimed that Communist terrorism was becoming ever more frequent in East Java and another NU spokesman said that some forty members of his party in East Java had recently been murdered by Communist terrorists.

Perhaps most noteworthy in the published accounts of all this alleged Communist activity during this period was the appearance of PKI tactical innovations or new organizational departures, suggesting that the effects of the Hutapea-Rewang restructuring process were becoming increasingly apparent. Already in a so-called "self-criticism" reputedly published by a "PKI Politburo" in September 1966, and subsequently reprinted in the January 1967 issue of the Albania-produced periodical *Indonesian Tribune,* Indonesian "Marxist-Leninists" were urged to hold aloft "three banners" namely, building a party free from revisionism, opportunism and subjectivism; waging the "people's armed struggle" which was said to be essentially the anti-feudal agrarian struggle of the peasantry under the leadership of the working class; and forging the "revolutionary united front", based on the worker-peasant alliance, and also under working-class direction. To what extent the Indonesian, Mao-orientated, Communist refugee element around *Indonesian Tribune* influenced or maintained liaison with the Hutapea-Rewang movement in Java, or with the PGRS in West Kalimantan, cannot now be specified, although some such liaison undoubtedly existed. The underground publications and captured tactical directives of the Hutapea-Rewang group have with few exceptions a strong Maoist flavour and also, beyond Java, Army commanders in the early months of 1968 revealed a number of seized PKI underground directives cast in distinctively Chinese Communist style. The East Kalimantan district military commander, for example, declared in March 1968 that in his area the PKI underground had raised its own three banners, that is adopted its own threefold programme, consisting of organizing for armed revolt by the peasants; forming cells among the masses, and mobilizing a "national front" against the authorities.

However one chooses to interpret the actual implementation of these respective banner directives or programmes by underground party units, it readily appeared that the resurgent PKI seemed to be inexhaustible in forming new "revolutionary united front" groups and also was steadily becoming more aggressive in its conception of people's armed struggle. In April 1968, Djakarta military authorities declared that a new secret PKI front, the *Kala Tjakra* movement, with its own fighting group or *barisan* designed for street brawls and demonstrations, had been uncovered. *Kala Tjakra* reportedly had sought to bring Sukarno back to power in co-operation with the PNI Left wing and was said to have attempted to infiltrate both the armed forces and anti-Sukarno action fronts. In Central and East Java the situation was becoming more and more disquieting by April 1968, leading to new and more frequent consultations between President Suharto and local security officials. During April a band of allegedly TPRI members attacked a civil defence guard (*Pertahanan Sipil* or *Hansip*), near Tulungagung, East Java, while in Surabaya two dozen reputedly "strategic cadres" of the PKI underground attacked an Air Force armoury. Fifteen Air Force personnel were subsequently arrested for having aided the latter venture. In early May more Air Force personnel, this time at the Panasan air base near Surakarta, Central Java, were arrested along with a score of civilian PKI sympathizers for complicity in a plot to capture the base. Near Kediri, Madiun and Malang, all in East Java, there were regular attacks on villages, guard houses and rural police posts by self-styled TPRI guerillas from May onward.

By this time there were also increasing reports of a functioning Communist shadow "government", formally headed by Hutapea as "President" of an "Indonesian People's Republic" with headquarters near Blitar. The paper *Harian Kami* claimed, on 6 June 1968, that in Surakarta local armed forces had been effectively penetrated by the PKI and Communist sympathizers. The Communist plan, as Central Java military spokesmen put it at this time, was to "disengage" (that is win over to the Communist cause) elements of local Army and police units, then with their help set up control over relatively isolated but contiguous rural areas and villages, and from these bases, in Maoist fashion, eventually proceed with plans to attack small and larger towns. Constant militancy, according to captured PKI documents, was the best way to defend the embryo People's Republic. Other seized documents urged, in this connection also, an intensified consolidation of scattered guerilla and terrorist groups, such as the earlier-named Black Cat, and LPRI organizations into the TPRI, as the "Republic's" official fighting arm. During May, June and July 1968, as the Indonesian Army's operations against the insurgents in East Java province were greatly stepped up, and as reports on Hutapea's People's Republic began to circulate more widely, it was also quite evident that the stepped-up PKI activity was not confined to Central and East Java. During April and May 1968, for example, several scores of military belonging to the Army's South Sumatra Sriwidjaja division were rounded up on charges of having attempted to establish a PKI organization, and in West Java, particularly in Djakarta, arrests continued of TPRI suspects, some of whom, according to the capital city's military command, had recently infiltrated both Army and student action front units. Army personnel in West Java said to have been involved in the *Gestapu* coup (as opposed to more recently "disengaged" military) and whose hiding places were only recently reported to have been revealed, similarly were rounded up in successive arrest campaigns. Toward the close of May 1968, Major-General Pranoto Reksosamudra, whom Sukarno at the height of the *Gestapu* coup on 1 October 1965 had originally appointed as Army chief in place of the slain General Yani, was also ordered confined to quarters, preparatory to trial on charges of having been a key figure in the *Gestapu* conspiracy. In South and East Kalimantan in June several scores of military and civil government personnel were discharged because of alleged Communist sympathies. Numbers here were small compared to East Java province where no less than 8,725 civil servants, both at the provincial and local government levels were discharged between March and the beginning of June 1968 for alleged *Gestapu* complicity.

The on-going Communist plot, one might well be led to believe from these developments, seemed to have spread its tentacles everywhere in the country, among the high- and low-placed, and in the civil as well as the military services. Who, one could ask, was to be trusted? Had any of the security measures taken in the past two years really been adequate? Pessimistic answers to such questions came from a special investigating delegation of the provincial legislature of West Java, which after an on-the-spot study of developments in East Java, published its findings in early August 1968. Quoting East Java's police commander, the West Java legislators declared that "in East Java we have been negligent of the danger" from the Communists, who, it was alleged, with financial aid from Chinese in Surabaya and other cities had been able to establish a covert network of guerilla organizations in the Viet Cong manner. There had been no difficulty in getting a popular following, the same report claimed: no less than ninety per cent of the inhabitants in the south Blitar area, where Hutapea had had his headquarters, were reported to have assisted the PKI underground. Communist influence had also been considerable in the Army in East Java, it was noted, and while most "disengaged" military had subsequently been arrested, most of the weapons they had taken with them had not been recaptured. Clearly the West Java report suggested that the PKI had been able to reconstitute itself under the very noses of the authorities, and from the number of suspects, or of those purged because of purported disloyalty, one could say with little exaggeration that the Communists had been well on their way to establishing a "counter government" in sections of East Java.

By the time that the West Java legislative investigators had issued their findings, however, the Army was already and once again claiming success in its *Sambar Raga* and *Trisula* operations during the previous three months against the Communists. Hutapea was reportedly captured and stoned to death (others say he was shot by a local village "defence force") in south Blitar at the beginning of July, while in the next few days, Rewang, Sukarno, Munir and a small number of lesser East Java party leaders (two of them former Army men) were also apprehended. Also, as indicated earlier, on 20 July — two days after Rewang's capture — the PNI Left's principal figure, Surachman, was shot by the Army. With these developments came additional Army information on the PKI underground's evident tactical penchant for developing a network of strongholds on the slopes of mountains. The complex of Mounts Merapi and Merbabu in Central Java had already served such a Communist purpose on several occassions in the past. Prior to his arrest, Sukarno, it was now disclosed, had responsibility for developing a similar Communist redoubt along the slopes of Mount Semeru, East Java (the so-called Gunung Banjak complex), while at Mount Lawu, on the border between Central and East Java provinces, Mohammad Munir had served as "project officer" with a similar assignment. The three complexes, along with one south of Blitar, had been developed not just because of the local population's tacit or open support, but also, as East Java's military commander Major-General Jasin charged on 13 July 1965, because of the connivance and cover provided by local officials and even by members of the East Java provincial legislature.

In his disclosures of and comments on the recent arrests of leaders of the Hutapea-Rewang PKI organization, Jasin at this time also, whether by accident or design, revealed what he and other Army commanders evidently considered to be the great advantage of the continuing waves of arrests and inter- rogations in the country: sooner or later one might come across a seemingly innocuous statement or confession, a conspiratorial "loose end", so to speak, which when properly pulled would unravel a whole new and unsuspected network of subversion. The "loose end" in this case was reportedly former Army Lieutenant-Colonel Pratomo, one-time military commander of Pandeglang in West Java and implicated in the *Gestapu* affair. Pratomo's capture — according to most reports near Blitar in April 1968 — and subsequent confession revealed not only key details of the network of Hutapea (including its links with Sukarno and his wife Hartini), but also provided additional information highly damaging to top-ranking officers in the Army's Siliwangi division in West Java. Whether or not it was inspired by Jasin's views on the relative advantages of mass arrests, the Army certainly did not restrain itself in making arrests in its *Trisula* campaign: by 9 August Jasin claimed that more than 800 Communists had been arrested in the south Blitar region alone and that some 500 "underground" meeting places, dwellings and various "project command headquarters" of the PKI had been destroyed. At least fifty PKI members had been killed also, some of them said to be prominent party district and front officials. Arrests else- where in East Java by this time stood at least at 2,500. Captured Communist cadres were quoted in Army press releases to have said the party had failed to build a mass following — a statement contradicted by some of Jasin's own earlier comments.

But this was by no means the only instance of inconsistency in official comments. As early as 16 August, for example, Jasin was quoted as saying that the Army's campaign against the Com- munists was being stepped up. But four days later, according to *The Djakarta Times,* Information Minister Budiardjo averred that conditions in south Blitar had returned to normal. In sub- sequent weeks, moreover, especially in the middle of October 1968, new security operations were launched in the Banjuwangi region of East Java, where remnants of the Hutapea-Rewang organization were said to be making yet another "last stand".

Then, too, the repercussions of the anti-Communist drive in East Java continued to be felt in other areas of the island. As a result of Pratomo's confessions, a purge began in early August 1968 in the Army's Siliwangi division in West Java and by the end of the month more than fifty officers, of whom a dozen were of field grade, plus several scores of non-commissioned and other personnel, had been arrested for current or past com- plicity in Communist (and/or *Gestapu*) activities. On 10 August the military mayor of Bandung, Colonel Didi Djukardi, was apprehended, and the Army subsequently put it about that according to a former West Java PKI leader Djukardi had been a member of the Communist party since 1953. Twelve days later the list of prominent recently arrested officers in West Java was published; among the names were those of Djukardi, Major-General U. Rukman, formerly East Indonesia commander and now in semi-retirement at central Army headquarters, Colonel Abdul Sukur of the Army Staff College, and Major Achmad Santoso, Chief of Staff of the Bandung West Java military district. Additionally, thirteen officers of the Pinad (an Army industrial plant) in Bandung were arrested in mid-September. By this time there had also been for several weeks stepped-up arrest drives aimed at the alleged PKI underground in Bandung, Bogor and other West Java towns. But the results of these campaigns in terms of numbers apprehended were, at least according to published reports, quite meagre, and in any case the Siliwangi arrests and official comment upon them drew virtually all of the headlines. Whether the relatively few arrests of alleged PKI civilians were due to a shift of the party's theatre of operations to East and Central Java, or due to the circumstance that such West Java PKI activity as presumably existed had not as yet been brought to light, is difficult to say. It is noteworthy that in the relatively mountainous and inaccessible southern sections of Bantam and other West Java areas no Communist complex similar to those of Mounts Lawu and Semeru has thus far been discovered, though the West Java terrain is in some respects even better suited to such a purpose.

In Central Java, on the other hand, Communist underground activity, formally supervised, according to captured documents, to some degree by Hutapea's south Blitar headquarters, equalled that of East Java; and so did the scope of the Army's *Kikis I* and *Kikis II* operations against the insurgents. The PKI's new tactics based on the earlier-noted zonal grid (red, pink, white, and green), the STPR (People's Liberation Army School) with its dispersed network of underground "extension" and "accelerated" courses in "people's war" and of village guerilla schools run by small special cells or *kompro* (project committees), and even the organizational structure of roaming bands of TPRI (the previously mentioned Liberation Army) and terrorist groups, like the Black Cat, had all to a considerable extent been developed first in Central Java. Though by the end of July 1968, some 1,500 alleged PKI members had also been arrested in Central Java and claims were made by Army spokesmen that "sixty per cent" of party members in this town or "seventy-five per cent" of party members in that rural area were now in custody, there seemed to be no end to the Communists' hidden resources. Hardly would a network of tunnels and hiding places be uncovered in one area — as, for example, near Klaten, in August 1968 — and arrests of suspects duly made, than another similar network would be found — as, for example, in Purwodadi, in November. Army and police personnel, village officials and members of district councils, prominent local PNI leaders (some of whom already had made their homes into PKI sanctuaries) were among the arrested, and evidently resurgent Communism in Central as in East Java had been able to extend its tentacles most everywhere.

One gets the same impression from arrests in other parts of the country during the remainder of 1968. For example, more than 1,000 employees of Garuda, Indonesia's national airline, were dismissed early in September 1968. Most of them had belonged to the Communist-dominated SOBSI labour federation. Nearly simultaneously about 1,100 postal workers were discharged for alleged complicity in "*Gestapu*/PKI activities" and an additional 2,500 were reported to be "under close scrutiny". As Army arrests continued all the while — a number of officers were apprehended in August and September 1968, for allegedly having attempted to establish a PKI base in the Riau islands, located off Sumatra's east coast — the Navy too announced several scores of personnel dismissals and detentions for subversive complicity, and a new purge in the KKO (Marine Corps) lasted until well into November. Even the Justice Department itself reportedly proved not to have been immune to PKI encroachments. The Attorney-General's office, where a bitter factional struggle between Attorney-General Soegih Arto and senior subordinates had erupted, announced late in September 1968 that Major Subowo, subsequently identified as a Communist party member and Soegih Arto's private secretary, had been put behind bars. He was accused of leading a PKI group right into the Attorney-General's office itself.

Among the welter of dark accusations and warnings by local military commanders throughout Indonesia at this time (many of them stressing that their respective area was about to be used as the base area for a new Communist come-back attempt, or else announcing that PKI "guerilla training centres" had been discovered), one deserves more attention, perhaps than the others, This one came from South Sumatra, where the territorial commander Brigadier-General Ishak Djuarsa, as well as local commanders of the Army's Sriwidjaja division, repeatedly called attention to a disquieting pattern of rapidly developing PKI activity in the Lampung district of South Sumatra. The Lampungs have long been a major resettlement area of migrants from overcrowded Central and East Java (the heartland of PNI and PKI strength before the *Gestapu* affair) and the migrants' political and cultural ties with Java have remained strong. Already in 1955, when Indonesia's first general parliamentary election was held, the Communists proved to have considerable following in the Lampung migrant sections. The plight of migrant communities since then certainly has done little to mitigate radical tendencies among them.

It now appears virtually certain that already during the Rewang-Widjajasastra reconstruction of the Communist party in Central and East Java in 1966-7, which it will be recalled preceded and became the basis for the Hutapea movement in Blitar and elsewhere a year later, PKI cadres had been sent to the Lampung district to reorganize the party there. Among the more than 400 alleged party members arrested by the military in the Lampung area in June and July 1968, at least nine were subsequently identified as cadres having recently come from Semarang, Bojolali, and other Central Javanese towns. There is but little exaggeration in Djuarsa's claim in August 1968 that the PKI had selected the Lampung region as its most important theatre of operations, next to East Java. During December security operations continued, and on 11 January 1969, Antara reported that in the previous year more than 4,000 "Communist suspects" in the Lampungs had been apprehended, while Army spokesmen were quoted by the same news agency as saying that the PKI had attempted but failed to launch a "people's revolution" in the area during the previous November. From the little that can be gauged authoritatively from this PKI activity in the Lampung region, it would seem that essentially the same tactics had been used there as in Central and East Java. Nuclei of cadres or *kompro* had penetrated receptive Javanese immigrant settlements; accelerated people's war courses of instruction had been covertly instituted; and from secure red areas, party activities and sympathizers had swarmed out to white neighbourhoods to win followers, or else engaged in a few hit-and-run terror attacks upon green or enemy villages. Earlier arrests of a few top party project officers had apparently not stalled the movement; only fairly indiscriminate mass detentions of suspects in November and December 1968 seemed, for the moment, to have accomplished that.

Perhaps the emphasis in the preceding sentence should be put on the words "for the moment". Because well before the complete break-up of Hutapea's short-lived counter government in Blitar, and of the party's underground network in Klaten, top Indonesian officials had already underscored again the persistence of the Communist threat. Speaking to Riau's regional legislature at the end of August 1968, for example, President Suharto had not only noted alleged PKI plans to make Riau into a new staging area for its future operations, but he had also said that in the country as a whole about 220,000 members of the Communist party were still at liberty — presumably ready to do new mischief. Almost simultaneously Major-General Amir Mahmud, then Djakarta's military commander, declared that recent Communist operations in East Java and elsewhere had been a kind of preliminary exercise for an expected major party drive at the close of 1968, which in turn would be a rehearsal for an even more elaborate attempt to seize power in 1970. The cadres prepared by Sudisman and Hutapea, respectively, Mahmud declared, were the first of two waves of new party leaders, and a third wave was now being trained. Mahmud also cautioned that some fresh party activity might flare up during 1969 in connection with the forthcoming act of free choice of the Papuan population in West Irian (see chapter VI).

The truth of all these and similar allegations is, as yet, difficult to verify. There was, for example, no significant increase in PKI activity during the critical months preceding the West Irian referendum process in the first half of 1969. On the other hand, the physical evidence of Communist activity during 1968 — from tunnels and emplacements to terrorist attacks and printed propaganda — is too substantial not to warrant belief in the existence of a sizeable, frequently well-co-ordinated and quite extensive subversive operational network which might be damaged but which would not be easily destroyed. At the same time the most zealous *Orba* spokesmen in the Army and in other departments of government cannot but have entertained suspicions from time to time that there was an element of "propaganda overkill" in the anti-PKI campaign. During the first week of July 1968, South Sulawesi's military commander, Brigadier-General Solichin Purwanagara, ordered the destruction of an allegedly dangerous group of insurgents in his area calling themselves the Volunteer Army of the Unitary Republic of Sulawesi. Solichin termed the group as Communist directed and declared that some Chinese in Tawau, Sabah, who he said maintained affiliations with Peking, were helping the rebels. Within a few days, however, Solichin was quoted as saying that (1) the rebels numbering about seventy did not constitute a serious security threat after all, and (2) that far from being Communist, the Volunteer Army in fact was a remnant of the well-known anti-Communist *Darul Islam* insurgent movement in the South Sulawesi area! In mid-September, 1968, a South Sulawesi military spokesman disclosed that an Indonesian Army officer in the area, charged with screening allegedly Communist detainees in the town of Kendiri, was himself discovered to be "a Communist". Who in fact was, was not or had not been "a Communist" in this unhappy affair, seemed in the subsequent controversy to become a problem less and less amenable to satisfactory solution. About the middle of September, 1968, also, the military commander of Sumatra, Major-General Kusno Utomo, disclosed that a recent "trade fraud", which had reportedly cost the Government more than thirty-five million US dollars in lost foreign exchange earnings, was discovered to have been linked to "China's subversive network to undermine the Indonesian economy". During the following weeks it was found, however, that these alleged links with Chinese subversives were in fact so tenuous as to be non-existent and that the trade fraud in question also involved high-ranking military.

In August 1968, Indonesia's Army Commander in Chief, General Maraden Panggabean charged that it had become part of underground Communist strategy to "weaken rival political parties through subversion" and to "exploit group conflicts" in the country. But while such strategy historically can indeed be attributed to Communist operations, Panggabean offered no specific evidence to skeptical observers. Subsequent allegations, that it was the PKI which was fanning such "group conflicts" as those existing between Christians and Muslims in Indonesia, were similarly made without any corroborating details.

A related question had arisen with respect to the conduct of former President Sukarno, already discussed in the previous chapter. There was some evidence that since his confinement in 1967 Sukarno maintained covert contact, through one of his wives (Hartini) as well as through friends in the PNI, with various, including anti-Suharto, political elements, among them the PKI underground. In so doing Sukarno clearly broke an MPRS regulation barring him from political activity. But the charge made in March 1969 by a special Army committee looking into PKI activities to the effect that the Communists were trying to bring Sukarno back to power, and were arming the peasantry in Java to that end, and subsequent overheated press speculations that Sukarno had in fact established an informal political alliance with the Communists, were again of a nature calculated to raise the eyebrows of less partisan observers and to cause even some of the Suharto Government's more ardent supporters to refer in conversation with the author, to *Orba*'s "anti-Communist credibility gap."

Deserving of a separate, if necessarily brief, treatment is the problem of the Communist guerilla insurgency along the border of the Malaysian state of Sarawak and the Indonesian province of West Kalimantan. During Indonesia's confrontation campaign against Malaysia this border area had witnessed periodic crossings by several hundreds of young dissident Sarawak Chinese, informally affiliated with what Sarawak authorities have called the CCO (Clandestine Communist Organization) or SCO (Sarawak Communist Organization). In Indonesia during 1963-5 these young Chinese were trained in special camps by Indonesian military and also, established contact with local Kalimantan PKI branches and front groups. For several months after the *Gestapu* affair Indonesia's confrontation campaign against Malaysia formally continued, if at reduced levels of intensity. Not until May 1966 did Suharto and his associates undertake steps to bring anti-Malaysia hostilities to an end. As late as March 1966, however, a Sarawak government official could claim that Sarawak Chinese youths were still slipping across the Indonesian frontier for training in sabotage and guerilla warfare. There is little doubt that as the anti-PKI pogrom gained momentum in Java in late October 1965 and during the following months, the Sarawak-Indonesian border area became a haven for fleeing Communist cadres. Pro-Sukarno Army officers and KKO units in West Kalimantan, unenthusiastic about the deceleration of the anti-Malaysian confrontation and about *Orba*'s changes in domestic and foreign policy generally, provided a sympathetic environment for the PKI refugees, for the Sarawak Chinese, as well as for the scattered elements of such groups as the National Army of North Kalimantan (*Tentara Nasional Kalimantan Utara* — TNKU) which had first emerged in the anti-Malaysia uprising in Brunei, in early December, 1962. On 4 October 1966, then Malaysian Premier Tunku Abdul Rahman declared that units of Indonesian regular military, acting on their own authority, had joined TNKU elements in "incursion" operations in Sarawak and were threatening Malaysia's security.

The fluid complex of underground PKI cadres and/or dissident Maoist Chinese on both sides of the border, undisciplined Indonesian military, and TNKU and other anti-Malaysia elements, formed the original base of what came to be known loosely as the Sarawak People's Guerilla Movement (*Pasokan Gerilja Rakjat Sarawak* — PGRS) which, though formed earlier, first came into prominence early in 1967. Later the PGRS took on an increasingly Chinese character, although the PKI underground has continued to maintain affiliation with it. On 16 July 1967, a PGRS force of about 100 launched a surprise attack on an

110

airstrip and munitions depot at Singkawang, in Indonesian West Kalimantan, killing four Indonesian soldiers and capturing quantities of weapons. It was the beginning of a chain of guerilla ambushes and other clashes with Indonesian Army units in West Kalimantan, including attacks at Sanggauledo (where in earlier days some of the young Sarawak Chinese "border crossers" had had their training by Indonesian military) and at Tanggal Laboh. On 20 October 1967, the PGRS ambushed and virtually annihilated a platoon of regular Indonesian Army near Mount Merabuk in the Bengkajang area; and on 28 November 1967 outnumbered regular Indonesian forces, battling against, reportedly, some 500 PGRS guerillas in the same area, were compelled to call for air support and other reinforcements from the nearby Siliwangi division of the Army, because the heavy mortar and and automatic-rifle fire of the insurgents was decimating the regulars' ranks.

Only a few weeks before, demands had already been voiced in the Indonesian Parliament that the PGRS should be prevented "from becoming a Viet Cong-type terrorist band". In October 1967, Antara reported that Army units had recently discovered in the forests near Sajung Kampong, Sebaloh, and Punti, various guerila arms caches which also contained "insignias with quotations of Mao Tse-tung's teachings inscribed on them". By the following December Peking media were hailing the PGRS as "people's forces" which were engaged in "an important breakthrough in lighting the torch of armed struggle" in the Indonesian countryside. A pattern of Maoist-inspired PKI-CCO insurgency steadily appeared to be developing and *The Straits Times* editorially observed on 25 September 1967, that "armed bands" from various parts of Indonesia were landing in remote areas along the Kalimantan coast and attempting to join the guerilla insurgency. The stringent control measures implemented by the Indonesian Army in the course of 1967 over Chinese residents in West Kalimantan — including a ban on border crossings, enforced resettlement and relocation of groups of border Chinese — had the effect of winning sympathy for the PGRS, just as earlier similar measures in Sarawak had further inflamed young Chinese radicals there.

Then, in mid-October 1967, a PGRS attack on the village of Uduk in West Kalimantan unleashed a bloody and indiscriminate anti-Chinese pogrom throughout much of the province by the indigenous Dayaks of the area. By the end of the year several hundred Chinese, including many with no proven PGRS connections, had been slaughtered, while thousands of others had become refugees, and had been crowded, with gravely insufficient food and medical attention, in a few district towns. Though the Indonesian Government had made some effort to abate the Dayak fury and protect the Chinese, the rapid deterioration of diplomatic relations between Indonesia and People's China in this period, and the constant allegations by Indonesian military spokesmen that PGRS guerillas were devotees of Maoism and, indeed, might be getting arms from Peking, rendered every Chinese in West Kalimantan an object of official suspicion as well as a legitimate target of the endemic, popular anti-Chinese sentiment.

As early as September 1966, Malaysia and Indonesia had begun implementing a joint border security programme. But the persistent pattern of grievances of minority Cninese in Sarawak, and their echo across the border among the Chinese of West Kalimantan, as well as the proven viability of the PKI under-ground and rebel pro-Sukarno Army elements in the area, con-tinued to provide a favourable atmosphere for a Maoist-orientated guerila operation. In early September 1968, West Kalimantan regional commander, Brigadier-General A. J. Witono, said that over 1,000 "Communists and supporters" involved in the border insurgency had been killed, captured or had surrendered by the previous July, and that more than 220 weapons, including some of Russian and American manufacture, had been seized. The following October, Antara claimed that Indonesian troops had killed "421 guerillas in a year of operations against Chinese-led Communist rebels in West Borneo province", and through the following months there were Antara reports of additional small groups of rebels — including "Chinese girl-guerillas" — being killed.

Then on 21 January 1969, Witono announced that the PGRS in West Kalimantan "had now been entirely crushed". Those who might be led to conclude from this statement that the pro-vince's insurgency problem was now over soon discovered that they were mistaken. For immediately Witono declared that a new campaign had begun, this time against the guerillas of the North Kalimantan People's Army (*Pasokan Ra'ayat Kalimantan Utara — Paraku*). Almost simultaneously Witono also announced that 140 *Paraku* elements had already been "eliminated" leaving some 200 "still lurking along the border". The distinction be-tween the PGRS and *Paraku* Witono did not explain, although on 24 January 1969, *The Sarawak Tribune* asserted that *Paraku* was "regarded as less militant and less under Communist influence" than the supposedly crushed PGRS. But not only did subsequent operations disclose that former PGRS leaders were now directing *Paraku* bands; on 5 May 1969, *The Djakarta Times* also quoted Witono as saying that the PGRS which had been declared des-troyed five months earlier still had some sixty members in the

112

jungle. At the same time other reports suggested that whatever their differences in name or in the degree of their "militancy" the *Paraku* and PGRS bands appeared operationally interchangeable and shortly before Witono's replacement in May 1969, Indonesian regulars were described as being compelled to step up their drive against the insurgents. In August 1969 some two dozen *Paraku* rebels were reported shot. Nor was there any abatement in the Chinese Communist influence in the insurgent movement, judging from continuing disclosures by Indonesian military of the capture of Maoist literature, badges and ' other propaganda items in rebel jungle caches. On 2 August 1969 Antara reported that yet additional Indonesian forces had been deployed along the Sarawak border in order "to give Chinese Communist terrorists in the area a final blow". The deployment of these new troops seemed to contrast with the assertion in Kuching at about the same time of the new West Kalimantan military commander, Brigadier-General Jumadi, that the border insurgents were now "a spent force".

Suspicion has remained that the rebels have friends among the Indonesian regulars supposedly operating against them. Already in January 1969, Witono announced the arrest of thirteen officers in the West Kalimantan military command "believed to be former Communist cadres", and later investigation revealed that the rebels had been obtaining regular Army weapons from a second-lieutenant in the command. These arrests preceded several waves of arrests in South Kalimantan, which included nearly three scores of Army personnel as well as civilians. The South and West Kalimantan arrests were at first thought to be unconnected with the PGRS-*Paraku* problem — a captured PKI cadre, one Ahmad Ismail, had earlier told Bandung authorities of alleged PKI connections of the arrested — but later West Kalimantan military spokesmen intimated that a "network" of subversion embracing the border insurgents had been established in West and South Kalimantan Army units with the connivance of local civilians.

Whatever the truth of such allegations it is quite evident that the problem of the PGRS-*Paraku* in West Kalimantan, like the PKI problem of Central and East Java, is deeply rooted in the particular, unresolved socio-economic imbalances and popular frustrations of these areas. From the endless, frequently one-dimensional reports issued by the military, by other government agencies or by the Antara news agency, of ever more new arrests of "Communists" or *"Gestapu*/PKI plotters" in the past few years, one easily gets a misleading picture of mere conspiracy, of the existence of scattered aggregates of devious and unrelenting plotters working throughout the country to subvert the State. Personal motives or environmental matrices of those arrested rarely come to light in these reports, and considering the heavy curtain of security that shrouds all accounts of the arrests and which impedes any attempt at more than a superficial analysis, it is hardly likely that greater clarity is to be had in the near future. Even so, it is as impossible to separate continuing PKI activity in Central and East Java from the pattern of Muslim landlordism, rural un- and under-employment, and the extensive evils of tenant farming prevailing in those regions, as it is to consider the insurgency in the Sarawak-Indonesian border area apart from the difficulties of the local Chinese, especially the youth.

One has the impression that the Indonesian authorities are insufficiently alert to such inter-relationships, and, in consequence, that their methods of dealing with political prisoners merely add to already severe existing problems in domestic stability. By the end of 1969 there were still perhaps some 110,000 political prisoners in Indonesia, and in the vast majority of cases the Government, as correspondent Neill Jillett has put it, "lacks the evidence to win convincing verdicts of guilty of treason. Nor, as it seeks to maintain political stability, does it want to stir up popular emotions with mass trials." Hundreds of prisoners, in Java as well as in Kalimantan, Sumatra and other islands, have, according to statements by local military commanders and by Army and civilian prosecutors, been released without trial, only to be apprehended again in a new wave of arrests. "Over-arresting" for reasons of security has been common, and informers, particularly if they themselves are known to have or have confessed to Communist antecedents, too often tend to be given unqualified credence.

The cost of maintaining the large political prisoner population (food costs per year alone amount to nearly two million US dollars) led to a consideration of various control schemes, ranging from a suggestion as early as 1967 to ship several thousands of prisoners to a remote "Devil's Island" in Indonesia, to employment of other, less dangerous prisoners in new reclamation and rural development schemes in Kalimantan, to a new "extra-mural parole" system in which prisoners return to their homes to live and work but regularly report to local authorities. Such schemes may well in many cases aggravate the bitterness, already so severe because of the earlier, bloody, indiscriminate anti-Communist pogrom, and they do not touch on the real reasons why the Communist underground in Indonesia today continues to be able to find new recruits, despite the waves of arrests. By early 1969 the Government had launched an intensive programme of assistance and development of the rural "infrastructure" in Central Java and in Bali. By early August 1969 more than 1,000 villages in Central Java were reported to have received 100,000 rupiahs each in cash for construction of schools, road improvement, housing, and so on. A similar sum had been made available to each of some 500 villages in Bali. However it remains to be seen whether such money grants are the answer to the problem of Communist influence. Meanwhile, by November 1969, the first 2,500 political prisoners in the "B" category (relatively hardcore PKI or front activists, many also suspected of some complicity in *Gestapu*) arrived on Buru island, in the Moluccas. Annual contingents of 2,500 or more are to follow, until, presumably, the total "B" group (about 13,000) has been relocated. Some 5,000 "A" group prisoners (known party and coup leaders) are presumably to be tried in the future, while the less culpable "C" and "D" groups of detainees are to be eventually released. Amnesty International, among other organizations, has for several years protested against these political imprisonments and the conditions in the prison camps.

An unknown quantity in this Communist underground, and in the PKI's resurgence generally, is the concern shown by both the USSR and People's China in the Indonesian party's continuing operations. There are today two groups of PKI *émigrés*, ideologically orientated respectively toward Moscow and Peking. Each has published its account and explanation of the debacle of 30 September 1965, and each is busily engaged in belabouring the other for tactical and doctrinal errors. The Moscow group's evaluation, published either late in 1966 or early 1967 by a self-styled "Marxist-Leninist Group of the PKI", some of whose leaders reportedly have found a haven in India and Ceylon, criticized the increasing influence of "petty bourgeois" and "adventurist" influences in the pre-*Gestapu* PKI, accompanied, on the one hand by an over-indulgence in "Leftist phraseology", such as, "Let us turn Indonesia into the revolutionary beacon for Asia, Africa and Latin America", while on the other hand true mass revolutionary work was neglected and there was a growing and dangerous "class collaboration" with the bourgeoisie. With respect to its "international line", the PKI, according to this Moscow-orientated self-evaluation, developed "an antipathy toward the struggle for peace and peaceful co-existence". The party presumably forgot that the struggle for peace does not necessarily mean that "the revolution should choose any one definite way" but rather that tactical alternatives should always be kept open. Without mentioning the Sino-Soviet rift as such, the critique of the Marxist-Leninist Group notes that the disappearance of friendship between "the two major parties", had an adverse effect on the PKI and forced Indonesian Communists henceforth "to subscribe to a lopsided point of view".

In the Prague-published *World Marxist Review* (also published under the title *Peace, Freedom and Socialism*) which, as is known, is a principal international mouthpiece of Soviet-orientated Communist parties in the world, there have been published, since 1965, a number of short pieces, most of them presumably written from Djakarta, or by Moscow-orientated Indonesian Communist *émigrés*. Emphasis has tended to fall in these articles on the anti-Communist pogrom and the repressive measures of the *Orba* era, particularly on the harsh fate of political prisoners. Yet these accounts and those by Soviet writers on conditions in Indonesia, appearing particularly in such Russian organs as *Narody Azii i Afriki* and *Literaturnaya Gazeta*, as well as in *Pravda* and *Izvestiya*, are worded relatively mildly, compared to those flowing from the pens of the Pekingites. The alleged dominance of Indonesian politics by "the extreme Right" (by which is meant especially the action fronts), and the influx of private Western capital for development of the economy, are singled out for particular condemnation. But one does not find in these accounts the open praise for "people's revolutionary" movements and other avowed anti-Government action in Indonesia which are the stock in trade of 'the publications of the Peking-orientated group of PKI *émigrés*, or of Chinese Communist authors.

In September 1966, a group of PKI *émigrés* and Indonesian student supporters in Peking, led by Jusuf Adjitorop (a leading PKI Politburo member and the party's former expert on relations with intellectuals, who was in Peking at the time of the *Gestapu* affair) formally adopted an *otokritik* or "self-criticism", entitled "Build the PKI along the Marxist-Leninist line to lead the People's Democratic Revolution in Indonesia". The previous month had already seen the issuance of a "statement" by a purported new Politburo of the PKI. Both documents were subsequently published in the *Indonesian Tribune*, the principal organ of Maoist Indonesian Communists, and the publication address of which is Tirana in Albania (although much of the editorial work seems to be done in Peking).

Taken together these two documents amount to another indictment of earlier PKI policies. It is alleged, for example, that since the Indonesian Communist Party was inadequately grounded in theoretical training and lacked understanding of "concrete conditions of Indonesian society" it "did not develop guerilla warfare that was integrated with the democratic movement of the peasants", this presumably being the only certain way to defeat imperialism. Stress is also placed on the party's improper policy toward the national bourgeoisie. Minimizing the inherent contradiction that remains even between the progressive or "national" bourgeoisie, on the one hand, and the proletariat, on the other, for the sake of establishing a "pro-people" front, led the PKI allegedly to abandon "its position as a proletarian party that had to take an independent attitude towards a bourgeois government". The PKI's incorrect united front tactic thus brought it to a dangerous and uncritical collaboration with the party's "class enemies", a development which in turn could not but lead to wrong tactics and "revisionism", and which "reached their climax on the eve of the September 30th events".

Particularly noteworthy in the September 1966 *otokritik* is the reference to "revisionist" influences in the PKI. These influences are said to have led to a mistaken preferenec for the "peaceful road" to socialism, and hence to an improper and ineffective party effort on behalf of those restive peasants who, in the course of 1964-5, were rising against landlords. The PKI, it is charged, failed to "develop" these peasant actions into a "higher form" of revolutionary struggle. The lesson to be learned from such past party errors, according to the September 1966 self-criticism is plain: the peasants' struggle must be transformed into an anti-feudal and anti-imperialistic "agrarian revolution", under "the leadership of the proletariat". Hence, as both the September 1966 *otokritik* and Jusuf Adjitorop's speech to the Fifth Congress of the Albanian Workers' Party in November 1966 emphasize, the new PKI must raise "three banners" (already noted earlier in this chapter), namely, build a genuine Marxist-Leninist party uncontaminated by "revisionism" and other evils; wage an agrarian-based "people's armed struggle"; and develop a proletarian-led united front opposed to the Suharto Government.

On 23 May 1968, a so-called "delegation" of the Central Committee of the PKI based in Peking issued a statement, mainly through Chinese Communist media, commemorating the forty-eighth anniversary of the Indonesian Communist Party. Party and people, the statement asserted, were commemorating the PKI's birthday "by waging heroic struggles against the Suharto-Nasution Fascist military regime, by taking up arms in the countryside and in the mountains and jungles, by persevering in the struggle in the prisons and concentration camps", all with an unshakable spirit. "Mao Tse-tung's thought", according to this statement, was now recognized "as the sole guiding ideology of the PKI in building itself anew into a Marxist-Leninist party capable of leading the

Indonesian revolution". In a "message of greetings" to Mao and the Communist Party of China, on the occasion of the latter's ninth congress in April 1969, Jusuf Adjitorop, now designated as "Head of the Central Committee Delegation" of the PKI, noted that the Chinese people and proletariat "armed with the invincible thought" of Mao "staunchly stand by the side of the Indonesian people and consistently support the Indonesian revolution".

The conviction that Communist China is indeed "staunchly" standing by the side of the PKI, and is in fact aiding the latter's "heroic struggle" in "the mountains" and in "the countryside" in Indonesia, has, by now, rightly or wrongly, become a matter of policy for the Indonesian Government. Already in August, 1966, the paper *Ampera* accused Peking of training Indonesians living in People's China to be cadres for a fresh Communist drive in Indonesia and by November of the same year Antara news agency reported that an estimated "700 *Gestapu*/PKI fugitives from Indonesia" were in Peking training for or otherwise assisting and directing subversion in Indonesia. In the group were said to be Indonesians who had left the country before *Gestapu*, PKI *émigrés* fleeing the anti-Communist pogrom since *Gestapu*, and several scores of Indonesian students. In the last category were some who had been studying in the USSR and in Soviet satellite countries, and who had had their visas cancelled after the coup, but who had made their way to Peking via Albania. On 24 November 1967, Army authorities in Djakarta charged that a major of the Army of People's China was leading Communist insurgents in Central Java. At about the same time Army newspapers in Djakarta asserted that a Peking-directed plot of nationals from People's China, who had recently surreptitiously landed at Tandjong Priok in order to assist the PGRS in West Kalimantan, had been discovered and smashed.

For Indonesian military and other government spokesmen there is no doubt that People's China has been exporting both the tactical revolutionary ideas and some of the weapons of the insurgents operating in Java and Kalimantan. On 1 August 1968, for example, the then Djakarta military commander, Major-General Amir Mahmud, categorically asserted that the underground PKI was now adopting "Maoist tactics", that is attempting to encircle towns from rural bases, and, shortly, the Djakarta command announced that even a local Muslim Institute of Enlightenment had to be closed by the authorities because it was "Communist controlled", and in its courses of instruction it had allegedly been praising Mao Tse-tung. Elsewhere, several local military commanders charged that Chinese in their vicinity were in effect agents of Peking and had been caught supplying the

PKI underground. Such an accusation was made, for example, on 30 July 1968, by Colonel Eri Supardjan, Army commander in Central Java. Again in February 1969, military spokesmen in the Riau islands area accused unnamed Chinese Communist agents "coming from the mainland" of seeking to establish channels of supply for insurgents in West Kalimantan, South Sumatra and Central Java.

How difficult it is to assess the relative degree of propaganda overkill in these and similar accusations has already been noted. But what lends such charges further credibility, however, is the fact that compared to the Moscow-orientated PKI *émigré* group, the Peking faction is much more articulate and gives the impression of much more extensive co-ordination and leadership. For one thing, the Adjitorop group's principal organ, the earlier-mentioned *Indonesian Tribune*, makes a consistent effort to provide a revolutionary ideological rationale — drawn from the Chinese Communist experience to be sure — for a particularly Indonesian resistance movement. For another, there is no question that this ideology is now permeating the chief underground PKI publications in Indonesia itself (for example *Suara Demokrasi* and *Mimbar Rakjat*), giving the underground as a whole a distinctly Maoist character. In organization, the Peking faction, unlike the Moscow-orientated *émigré* group, now does seem to possess a clear and identifiable leadership (the self-styled "delegation" of the PKI's Central Committee) and a single acknowledged spokesman (Jusuf Adjitorop), and there have been some indications that their influence is felt in the resistance in Central and East Java. Finally, because of Peking's demonstrable material and directional assistance to Communist insurgencies in other areas of Southeast Asia, it would be difficult to believe that such assistance was wholly bypassing Indonesia, although without doubt Indonesian military spokesmen have a stake in magnifying such Chinese Communist help.

The USSR, too, continues to be suspected of aiding subversion. Early in December 1968, for example, the paper *Nusantara* reported that the fugitive Brigadier-General Suharjo had recently been discussing the "revival" of the PKI with a Soviet diplomat in Surabaya, and that a number of Indonesian employees of the Soviet consulate in that East Java city had been arrested. Suharjo was said to have been repeatedly seen entering the Russian consulate, where a number of former PKI members were also reported to have found employment. On 11 October 1968 the Soviet Union warned Indonesia of "baleful consequences" if it carried out the death sentences imposed on some twenty persons convicted of participation in the *Gestapu* affair. Later that month an Indonesian military spokesman announced the execution of former Politburo members Sudisman and Njono, and of the PKI Djokjakarta leader Wirjomartono. While the Soviet press denounced the executions there were no discernible Soviet diplomatic or other reprisals. But Soviet criticism did serve to underscore publicly expressed opinion in Indonesia that the USSR remained interested in protecting and assisting subversives and, hence, that Soviet-Indonesian diplomatic relations, like Sino-Indonesian relations, should be suspended.

Throughout 1969 the familiar pattern of arrests of suspected "Communist elements" in widely scattered areas of Indonesia continued. In January and February there were scores of arrests in the Pattimura military command in the Moluccas where the PKI underground was alleged to have formed a number of cells. The chief editor of the Moluccan edition of the daily *Pelopor Baru* was also arrested for supposed participation in the "Communist movement in the area" and for having encouraged publication of exaggerated accounts of religious conflicts on the island of Amboyna. At about the same time arrests were also made in Garut, West Java, where Communists were reported to have infiltrated legitimate organizations like the *Angkatan '45* ('45 Generation — a revolutionary veterans' group). On 1 February 1969 the arrest was announced by military authorities in the Riau islands of 119 alleged Communist "activists", who according to regional military commander Brigadier-General Widodo had been attempting to develop a local subversive "people's army" and had established a covert training centre for that purpose. Major-General Sabirin Mochtar, commander in South Kalimantan, at about the same time announced arrest of some forty new suspects, both military and civilians, and in Central Java the Army continued to clash with roving bands of suspected guerilla terrorists, particularly in the Klaten district.

On 9 February 1969, police in Bandung announced the apprehension of more than a score of Chinese on grounds of illegal entry and suspicion of Communist activity. A police spokesman asserted that the arrested Chinese had gone to People's China in 1959, later had gone to Macao and Hong Kong, and with false passports had then attempted to re-enter Indonesia. It was intimated that there were "hundreds of similar cases" of Chinese returnees in West Java. Public suspicion in Indonesia about the political bona fides of local Chinese, already high, rose still more after this incident — and rose yet further when the Attorney-General's office shortly afterwards accused the embassies of a number of Communist states in Indonesia of helping to spread Communist literature in Indonesia. The embassies themselves were not named, but the distributed Communist materials were said to originate in the People's Republic of China, Albania, the USSR, as well as to be coming from the Peking-orientated Malayan Communist Party. To some Indonesians it seemed that Communist and Communist-sympathizing "foreigners", including and in particular local Chinese, were flooding the country with subversive propaganda. On 17 July 1969, North Sumatra military commander Leo Lopulisa, in a meeting with Islamic youth leaders, urged that a close watch be kept on resident nationals of People's China in the area. He declared that Chinese Communists had masterminded recent disturbances in Malaysia and Singapore, and added that North Sumatra was one of the regions of Indonesia nearest to places "where Chinese Communist elements have established their bases".

Reports of a new Communist plot to assassinate President Suharto during a forthcoming visit to Masohi, in Central Moluccas, of the seizure of a PKI arms cache in Krawang, near Djakarta, and the arrest of some 100 suspects of yet another foiled attempt to reorganize the PKI in Central Sulawesi — all seemed to provide justification for repeated warnings by President Suharto, during March 1969, that Communists were attempting to stage a come-back. The most notable of these repeated warnings came on 31 March 1969, the day when Suharto formally launched Indonesia's new Five-Year Plan. Foreign observers were virtually unanimous in describing Suharto's stress on the continuing Communist threat to his country as exaggerated, and as motivated primarily by a desire to mobilize Indonesians on behalf of a determined effort at national reconstruction and development. Suharto's warnings coincided also with the news of the arrest of the earlier-named Pono, believed to be a top underground Communist liaison cadre with the armed forces and to have collaborated, it is presumed, with *Gestapu* leader Sjam (Kamaruzaman), and with revelations of continuing PKI burrowing in the Navy and the police force. To some skeptics the official report that Pono was also said to have been captured during security operations in Purwodadi, Central Java — an area also much in the news during March 1969, it will be recalled, because of the alleged maltreatment and even of the massacre of hundreds of political prisoners — seemed hardly accidental.

In April 1969, there were new waves of arrests of "Communist suspects" in Southeast Sulawesi, whose identity, military spokesmen said, had only recently come to light during anti-subversive operations by the Army in East Java. In the Lampung region of South Sumatra the round-up of suspects also continued in subsequent weeks, and throughout 1969 there were intermittent clashes in "the southern hills region of Central and East Java" as military communiques put it. President Richard Nixon's visit to Indonesia, late in July 1969, was the occasion for new official warnings of Communist activity (subversives were reported to have planned to disrupt Nixon's official reception). Djakarta authorities also arrested numerous beggars and tramps in the capital, ostensibly because the PKI underground was using them as a cover, but probably also to improve the city's appearance during the American chief executive's brief stay.

Up to the end of 1969, however, no new pattern of PKI complexes similar to those developed by Hutapea's movement in Blitar had made its appearance, and the Communist underground in Central and East Java seemed for the moment to have fallen back largely on sporadic terrorist activity by scattered units of the self-styled TPRI, Black Cat, and similar groups. The rupture of party activities in the Lampung area had, for the moment, also weakened the Communists' principal new hold on Sumatra, although in and around Medan, in the north of the island, the PKI underground continued to remain active, aided reportedly from across the Straits of Malacca by cadres of the underground Malayan Communist Party. In West Kalimantan, fast-moving bands of the PGRS-*Paraku*-SCO organizational complex also persisted in operating back and forth across the Sarawak-Indonesian frontier, and periodic Indonesian Army announcements that the bands were now *in extremis* were becoming increasingly more difficult to believe, not least because Sino-Dayak tensions and the frustrations of younger Chinese obviously continued high.

In view of the scattered and furtive nature of the PKI underground at present, little is known for certain about its organizational structure. By August 1969, captured PKI documents suggested that yet another new Politburo had come into being but its membership is still unknown. In Central Java the Communist TPRI guerillas appear to have decided on a degree of operational division of labour — definite "rayons" or zones of activity appear to have been assigned to certain units. Propaganda activity is at a standstill, however, although there is some evidence that the "people's army's training courses" continue to be given in the Klaten area. Early in July 1969 an Army spokesman in Semarang charged that in the rural areas around Rembang underground Communist "tax collectors" had made their appearance, but that village defence guards had driven them off. Whether the PKI was embarked on a new tactic of extortion and intimidation remained to be seen.

Arrests and headline-making trials of alleged PKI and *Gestapu* participants are likely to remain a distinctive feature of the Suharto regime for many months to come. Within a period of five weeks, for example, from the middle of June to the end of July 1970, Antara announced:

(1) the arrests of twenty-six underground Communists", among them a "retired Army lieutenant", in the Wantji sub-district of South Sulawesi, who were charged with attempting "to reactivate the PKI";

(2) the arrest of Siswojo (lias Sardjono), former director of the *Universitas Rakjat* (People's University) and Central Committee member, who was caught while attempting to distribute Communist propaganda in Djakarta;

(3) the impending trial of a number of Navy personnel, "including senior officers", some of whom. had held "important positions" in the PKI, and who had been involved in *Gestapu;* and

(4) the forthcoming trial of Adi Sumarto former secretary of the *Partindo* (a Left-wing and subsequently PKI-infiltrated offshoot of the PNI), accused of having taken part in the *Gestapu* coup.

Meanwhile, the daily Kompas, on 16 June 1970, reported that the Sriwidjaja military commander had warned that the Night PKI in the Lampung area had been forming so-called "Red Ray troops", an underground terrorist organization composed of former "C" category political prisoners who had recently been released. The "Red Rays" were also employing ordinary criminals to add to the confusion they were creating. In Kalimantan, meanwhile, joint Indonesian-Malaysian security operations (called Operation Highway) netted several hundred "Communist guerillas", killed and captured, mostly Chinese from Sarawak. There is little indication that the limited but persistent PKI underground activity, whether in Java or beyond it, is abating.

Perhaps mindful of this, and in a clear effort to improve the bad impression which its policies toward political prisoners have been creating abroad, the Suharto Government has sought to bring some order and consistency in detention procedures. During the early months of 1970, the Attorney-General's office, in conjunction with local prosecutors, police and, indirectly, also with military security personnel, began developing new ground rules for those under detention. All arrests would have to be reported to the local prosecutor's office within eight days "in order to guarantee individual freedom and legal responsibility", a new regulation asserted. Temporary release of those whose cases have not been submitted to the courts should be permitted, and clear lines of responsibility should be set for the physical well-being of all prisoners. Satisfaction over the promulgation of these directives in organizations like Peradin, the Indonesia trial attorneys' association (which at its August 1969 congress adopted a resolution asserting that the rule of law still did not prevail in the country, and urging the Government to release all those prisoners detained without lawful cause), is tempered by dismay that, with thousands of prisoners on its hands, the Government has waited so long to announce such directives.

Strange as it may sound, the level of Communist activity appears at present to be more of a relative asset than a liability to the Suharto Government. For that activity is sufficiently intense (or is made to appear so) so as to serve as a pretext for the retention not just of formal and more or less constitutional internal security powers by the executive, but, more important, also of the hardened network of informal and extra-constitutional social and political controls exercised for years now by the armed forces throughout the country. Yet underground PKI operations are not so extensive at the moment as to constitute a real threat to the Government, whether in the capital or the outlying provinces. It should give some pause to the PKI *émigré* groups, orientated toward and dependent on Moscow or Peking, as well as to the Communist insurgents and their sympathizers operating within Indonesia itself, that what they have been doing thus far has, in fact, mainly strengthened the position of their opponents.

On the other hand, the persistent presence of Communist subversion may yet provoke the Government to the kind of over-reaction of which the Purwodadi affair was an example, and thus augment the disquiet already existing in many circles over the Government's security powers. To provoke such an over-reaction and reap the possible political benefits accuing from it — either in terms of an eventual weakening or even a replacement of the Suharto regime, or in terms of a broad liberalization of all partisan activity — may well be, therefore, an immediate tactical objective of PKI activity. For the long haul, however, the Communist underground must depend on the inability of the Suharto Government or its successors to accelerate the nation's economic rehabilitation and modernization, and on the endemic and seemingly deepening problems of land tenure relationships, rural and urban unemployment, and minority-group frustrations, that have provided much of the seed-bed of PKI activity in recent years.

CHAPTER SIX

Irian Again — and Again

INDONESIA has its share of naggingly persistent and seemingly insoluble problems: its rapid population growth and demographic imbalance, for example, or the disharmony between the centre and the outlying regions. Among such problems must surely also be reckoned the continuing controversy over the status of and the persistent unrest in West New Guinea or West Irian, or Irian Barat as Indonesians call it. Early in August 1969, the Suharto Government professed to believe that the Papuan inhabitants of West New Guinea, through a recent United Nations-supervised "act of free choice", had now fully accepted permanent Indonesian control over their land. But continuing Papuan unrest since then, and the sympathy for rebellious West Irianese among Papuans in the eastern, Australian-administered half of New Guinea island, the Territory of Papua-New Guinea, suggest that the world may not yet have heard the last of the Irian Barat question.

To understand the situation in West New Guinea it is necessary first to go back a few years. West New Guinea, it may be remembered, was the one part of their erstwhile East Indies possessions which the Dutch retained when they transferred formally their sovereignty over these possessions to the fledgling Indonesian Republic at the close of December 1949. There is no doubt that Dutch retention of the territory was a concession to conservatives; even so the sovereignty transfer barely squeaked through the Dutch Parliament. At first moderately and by diplomatic means, including repeated but futile efforts to get the United Nations to support its claim, Indonesia sought recovery of the territory. By 1960, as attitudes had hardened on both sides, an Indonesian confrontation campaign got underway, complete with paratroop landings, commando infiltrations by sea, and an international press and propaganda drive, all designed to create a "war scare". This campaign particularly had its effects on the Kennedy administration in Washington, then becoming increasingly embroiled in Vietnam, and strong American pressure came to be exerted on the Dutch to abandon the disputed territory. The US let it be known that neither Australia, which had by and large supported the Dutch, nor Holland itself could count on American military help if hostilities over West New Guinea were to increase significantly in the future.

On 15 August 1962 Dutch and Indonesian representatives in New York reached agreement on the transfer of West New Guinea to Indonesian control by 1 May 1963, after a brief United Nations interim administration. The agreement provided among other clauses that Indonesia would "guarantee fully the rights, including the rights of free speech, freedom of movement and of assembly of the inhabitants of the area", and that "an act of self-determination" (that is some sort of plebescite) would be held before the end of 1969 among the Papuans of West New Guinea in order to determine whether they wished to remain under Djakarta's control or whether they desired "to sever their ties with Indonesia". It cannot be said that the agreement was very popular among many, or, perhaps, even among most emancipated Papuans, and particularly in Hollandia (soon to be called Sukarnopura, and since March 1969, Djajapura), the territory's capital. There were several reasons for this.

For one thing, in the last decade or so of Dutch control over West New Guinea, a Papuan political awakening had gradually begun as the Dutch expanded their educational and economic development efforts in the territory. Elected local councils and ultimately establishment of a semi-legislative body for the entire territory (the *Nieuw Guinea Raad* or New Guinea Council) stimulated the emergence of about half a dozen small indigenous political parties and other interest groups, some of them in different ways expressions of a belated but unmistakable Papuan nationalism. To be sure, in the western coastal area, particularly in and around Sorong, there remained a signficant pro-Indonesian political undercurrent, dating from the period of the Indonesian Revolution against the Dutch (1945-9). Still, by the time of the August 1962 Dutch-Indonesian transfer of sovereignty agreement, a growing, modern-educated Papuan lower-middle and middle class had begun to come into existence, among many of whose members long-standing ethnic animosities toward Indonesia provided added impetus to aspirations for an independent state of *Papua Barat* or West Papua.

These Papuan animosities should not be underestimated. For many Indonesians, even after Djakarta acquired control over the territory, the Papuan was and had been, for a long time, little more than a benighted savage, and the popular Indonesian image of the *Papua bodoh*, that is the "dumb Papuan", inevitably triggered off frustration and resentment. In a pamphlet written by West Irianese Papuan nationalists entitled *Voice of the Negroids in the Pacific to the Negroids throughout the World*, and published in the middle of 1962, one reads for example:

> The Nationalist Papuan Movement was started in 1907. The missionaries of the Netherlands Reformed Church soon found that the Papuan students (Johan Ariks and others) at the Seminary of the Protestant Mission at Depok near Djakarta were not liked by the Indonesian students. So the Papuan students were soon transferred to the Seminary at Tobelo on the island of Halmaheira. There too they were ragged and derided by the Indonesian students, so that finally the Rev. van Hasselt was compelled to start a Seminary for Papuans, which was opened in 1923 on the island of Mansinam. In 1925 the Seminary was transferred to Miei near Manokwari. Henceforth the Papuans received their training there. Consequently, West Papua is now electing as its leaders Papuans who studied at that Seminary.

One knowledgeable Australian observer, Mr Peter Hastings, writing in the Australian news weekly *The Bulletin* of 2 March 1963, and describing a recent visit to West Guinea, noted how the incoming Indonesian officials detested their new post: "Homesick for the beauties of the main island and the attraction of their big cities", Hastings wrote, "Indonesians regard West Irian and its people as just about rock bottom, which is not surprising although it is signficant that so many were taken in by their own propaganda."

In New Guinea the foreigner's sense of having reached "rock bottom" is, indeed, not surprising. The territory is among the world's least developed and internally most isolated regions, a land where the writ of government issued in the coastal centres penetrates only with difficulty up-river or into the mangrove swamp, or into the equally forbidding forested and mountainous interior. As virtually every emancipated Papuan in West New Guinea realized only too well at the time his land was transferred to Indonesian control, the sustained economic development programme and the artificially high wage level maintained by the Dutch would soon be things of the past. Indonesia's stagnating economy and fiscal mismanagement under Sukarno's adventurist guided democracy held little promise. West New Guinea's budget expenditures under the Dutch had grown from about 36 million florins (about US$11 million) in 1952 to more than 120 million florins (about US$37 million) in 1961, with a corresponding increase in the Dutch Government's budget subsidy (from US$4.5 million to US$18 million). Despite Sukarno's promise that he would make "Irian Barat into the pearl in the emerald necklace of the Indonesian islands", there were few knowledgeable Papuans who believed that Djakarta would be able to match the Dutch development effort in the territory.

In the following years of Indonesian control these Papuan apprehensions proved more than justified. Shortly after the formal Indonesian take-over in May 1963, West Irian came under a political quarantine which not only prevented the free exercise of political rights of its Papuan inhabitants as stipulated by the original August 1962 Dutch-Indonesian sovereignty transfer agreement, but which also made travel to, in or away from the territory difficult and often impossible, particularly for foreign observers. News of conditions there now became hard to come by. Yet a few foreign journalists did manage to visit the area from time to time. Around the middle of 1968, for example, the Australian journalist Peter Hastings visited West Guinea again after an absence of five years. In the September-October 1968 issue of the Australian periodical *New Guinea*, of which he is editor, Hastings gave his impressions:

> Indonesia's administration of West New Guinea in the last five years has been nothing short of calamitous. While many members of the West Irianese elite were prepared to try and work with the Indonesian Administration nothing prepared them for what was to follow. Indonesia quickly abandoned all pretence of maintaining either a proper Administration or the economic development projects started by the Dutch. Indifference in Djakarta, the compulsions of Confrontation and sheer logistical incapacity led to rapid administrative breakdown in an area more than ordinarily dependent upon high-grade administrative skills and effort and upon good communications.
>
> President Sukarno rapidly lost personal interest in the area and with Djakarta's declining concern the Administration, backed by the Army, was left to its own heavy-handed devices. Shops were looted, consumer goods disappeared and development projects either languished or in many instances were totally abandoned. Imported foods disappeared and urban Papuans used to artificially high wages and full employment under the Dutch were forced to return to subsistence gardening in order to get enough food to eat.

In the same article, he also noted the "sporadic brutality" of the Army which carried out "numerous beatings, shootings and goalings" of Papuans "in order to ensure a passive population".

There is little to be put on the other side of the ledger. Indonesian officials have claimed a marked expansion of the territory's educational system since 1963, including the establishment of the Tjenderawasih University at Sukarnopura. At the time the Dutch abandoned the territory, however, there were already some 1,300 schools (from village schools to college preparatory, vocational and technical secondary schools) and the number of Papuan students had risen from 26,400 in 1952 to 40,600 in 1961. But by early 1967 the total number of students was reported by Indonesian education officials to be only 42,400. Moreover, questions might well be raised regarding the quality, the technical facilities and the purpose of the educational plant, given the general economic stagnation of the territory.

Perhaps even more alarming were the indications that Djakarta, now having acquired West New Guinea, had little intention of living up to the plebescitary and other provisions of its August 1962 agreement with the Dutch. Already in November 1962, some Indonesian spokesmen indicated that the formal Indonesian take-over from the United Nations interim administration over the territory should take place before the agreed date of 1 May 1963, and that there was really no need for a Papuan plebescite. Shortly too, Sukarno said that West New Guinea would have "internal" but not "external" self-determination (that is, would not be allowed to vote itself free from the Indonesian flag). And as early as January 1963, Max Maramis, the chief Indonesian civil representative in West New Guinea, when questioned about the Papuan act of free choice asserted, on the one hand, that "it will be carried out, according to law", but, on the other hand, that "when the people decide much earlier that it is no longer necessary to have the aforementioned plebescite isn't that also the people's voice?" Foreign observers have commented on how Indonesian officials in West Irian, even during the last weeks of the United Nations interim administration, attempted to intimidate and threaten Papuans into abandoning the provision for self-determination in the 1962 agreement.

Then, when Indonesia formally announced its withdrawal from the United Nations on 2 January 1965, the Djakarta English-language daily, *Indonesian Herald*, which at the time closely reflected the views of the Foreign Affairs Ministry, promptly commented that among the "great number of advantages" derived from this move was the fact that Indonesia was now "freed from all commitments made under the auspices of the United Nations. Holding of a plebescite in West Irian in 1969 is one of them." On 24 May 1965, President Sukarno, in a broadcast interview with a Dutch correspondent, declared that an act of self-determination in West New Guinea was no longer necessary, since all Papuans there now favoured the Indonesian Republic. To the correspondent's question of how he, Sukarno, intended to prove that the Papuans wanted to remain part of Indonesia, Sukarno replied: "Have you seen any reports to the contrary?"

Sukarno's answer was disingenuous, to say the least, because by May 1965, even the Indonesian press itself was carrying heavily censored "reports to the contrary", while at about the same time visiting foreign correspondents in West Irian also filed

129

reports of Papuan discontent. Already in the course of 1964 there were minor skirmishes and anti-Indonesian demonstrations in several places around the Geelvink Bay area, including the island of Biak, and in such towns as Manokwari, Warèn and Ransiki. Also in some sections of the Bird's Head peninsula, for example, in and about the town of Ajamaru and along the Arfak Range, anti-Indonesian sentiments ran strong (elsewhere in the Bird's Head, for example the town of Sorong, and around the McCluer Gulf, pro-Indonesian feelings seemed more common). Some, though by no means all, of the leaders of the developing Papuan resistance movement were Papuans with civil or military experience during the Dutch period. As early as January 1965 one such Papuan leader, Nicolaas Jouwe, who had been a vice-chairman of the earlier-mentioned *Nieuw Guinea Raad* before the transfer of the territory to Indonesia, directed a plea to then British Prime Minister Harold Wilson asking for aid in stopping Indonesia's alleged campaign of repression and intimidation in West New Guinea. According to Jouwe, the chief spokesman of the Holland-based Freedom Committee West Papua/West New Guinea (a group of some four dozen or so anti-Indonesian Papuan exiles and sympathizers), the Indonesians (1) had been forcibly conscripting about 20,000 Papuans to fight against British and Malaysian forces in Borneo, in the context of Indonesia's then prevailing anti-Malaysian confrontation campaign, (2) were resorting to "Gestapo style midnight arrests, beatings and shootings of Papuan nationalists", and (3) had been suppressing all freedom of Papuan political expression except that of which Djakarta officially approved. In May 1965, the Indonesian press reported that several scores of Papuans connected with the *Organisasi Papua Merdeka* (Free Papua Organization) or OPM, said to have recently emerged in the Ajamaru region, had been arrested.

Foreign press accounts, at the same time, suggested growing tensions. In *The Straits Times* on 17 May 1965, Creighton Burns reported from Sukarnopura that Indonesian rule over West New Guinea "perhaps subsconsciously" had drifted "into something very like nineteenth-century colonialism"; that the local population "is shrinking protectively from contact with their new Indonesian administrators"; that once-cultivated fields around the main towns "have now gone back to *kunai* grass and weeds" as Papuans "continue to retreat to their jungle villages"; that there were rumours "of growing West Irian resentment and sterner reprisals"; and that Papuan "Students have been forbidden to discuss even among themselves, Indonesia's decision to abandon its agreement to allow the West Irian people 'an act of self-determination' before the end of 1969"

By June 1965, the "political quarantine" in West New Guinea was reportedly being eased somewhat, at least to the extent that some political organizations and parties, officially approved in the rest of Indonesia's guided democracy system at the time, would henceforth be permitted to open branches in the territory. This planned lifting of the ban on political activity was said to have been particularly due to pressure from — and was expected especially to bring benefits to — the PKI, by that time Indonesia's largest and most powerful political party. Papuan dissatisfaction was moderated as little by such political palliatives as by Djakarta's periodic announcements that new plans were being made for the development of West Irian's cattle industry, vocational schooling or health services. Indonesia's continuing chaotic financial condition had long since rendered all such announcements of a piece with the rest of Sukarno's bombast and sloganizing.

Shortly the extent of Papuan dissatisfaction became too deep to be ignored even by the censor-ridden Djakarta press. On 24 August 1965 carefully worded reports appeared in Djakarta newspapers about new "unrest" in Manokwari and on Biak island, where OPM raiders were said to have attempted to blow up a number of oil dumps and other military installations. Brigadier-General Sutjipto, the Indonesian "Co-ordinator" for West Irian, spoke of *nekolim* (a Sukarno acronym, standing for neo-colonialism, colonialism, and imperialism) plotters, the Antara news agency, at this point strongly PKI influenced, referred to subversive American missionaries, but still other Indonesian press circles roundly mentioned the "unsympathetic" behaviour of Indonesian officials in West Guinea as the principal cause of recent explosions of Papuan discontent. Though Indonesian para-commandos had little difficulty in initially clearing Manokwari of Papuan rebels, the OPM obviously not only remained active in the area but also was finding followers in and around Fakfak. The *South Pacific Post*, published in Port Moresby, in Australian-administered eastern New Guinea, reported on 7 March 1966 the remarks of an Indonesian security official which were to the effect that West New Guinea Papuans were continuing to flee to and seek political asylum in Australian New Guinea, and that the dream of a Papua state and the notion that the Papuans are citizens of such a state and not of Indonesia were still clearly being nourished in Irian Barat.

By this time, it might be emphasized, the anti-Sukarno and anti-*Orla* reaction following the abortive coup of 30 September 1965, was well underway in Indonesia. The birth of the post-*Gestapu* era, however, seemed to have but little influence on Papuan discontent with the possible exception perhaps of giving it more widespread prominence, since press and political restrictions in Indonesia generally were somewhat relaxed. In the middle of November 1966, for example, the Roman Catholic daily *Kompas* in Djakarta carried a series of articles by a special reporter sent to West Irian. These articles gave the impression that, politically and economically, conditions were becoming critical in the territory. "Fights often break out between the local people and government officials and it is not surprising that anti-Indonesian feelings are raging among the natives," *Kompas* declared. From Australian New Guinea, reports continued of West Irianese refugees crossing the border, some of whom claimed that there had been extensive arrests in Sukarnopura. Some of the refugees also claimed that, along the poorly marked border and just inside Australian-held territory, informal refugee "transit" camps had been constructed by Papuans escaping from Indonesian rule and that in some of the camps OPM activists were busy recruiting.

Perhaps most significantly, there now also began to flow a steady stream of complaints from West Irianese Papuans with some official standing in the Indonesian Government. On 24 November 1966, a West Irianese delegation led by N. L. Suwage told Foreign Minister Malik that the territory's economy was stagnating and that Papuans were complaining about chronic shortages of basic consumer necessities. A month later, yet another delegation, led by N. Ohey, met with General Suharto and urged greater autonomy for West New Guinea. Suharto reportedly replied that present difficulties in West New Guinea were due to the neglect of the previous administration and asked for Papuan help in overcoming them. But this appeal had little effect and Papuan political leaders continued to warn Djakarta that it was losing whatever Papuan following it once might have had. F. Karubuy, an MPRS member from West Irian, not only demanded, on 10 March 1967, that rocket and other military installations be removed from the territory, but also added that Papuans were increasingly taking up arms against the Government because of shortages of food and clothing. Karubuy sharply criticized allegedly rapacious Indonesian officials who were going to West Irian "for business and not to build up the territory". Two days later another MPRS member from West Irian, Silas Papare, appealed to the Government to end Indonesian strafing and rocket attacks on Papuan villages, claiming that as many as 1,000 Papuans had already been killed in such actions.

Papare's appeal was in a way the first official report of new fighting in the territory, and on 16 March 1967, Foreign Minister Malik admitted that Indonesian troops had recently opened fire on rebellious Papuan tribesmen in the northern Bird's Head area.

He denied, however, that 1,000 Papuans had been killed, saying "it is not as many as that" and adding that "when our troops were attacked they had to open fire". A month later, when confronted again with reports that Indonesian troops had met with persistent Papuan resistance and allegedly had claimed some 2,000 lives, Malik said, "I think the number was exaggerated, the troops might have killed 200." On 27 April 1967, West Irian military commander, Brigadier-General Bintoro, admitted that the Indonesian Air Force had recently been compelled to strafe the town of Manokwari and that forty persons had been killed. The difficulties in Manokwari, said Bintoro, had begun the preceding 3 January when "Awom, a dissident Papuan leader", had proclaimed himself a leader of a "Free Papua". For two days, beginning on 18 January, the town had to be strafed because the rebels refused to end their resistance, Bintoro said.

These developments attracted a measure of international attention. In Australia-administered eastern New Guinea, the increasing influx of West New Guinea refugees presented the Government there with a difficult problem. For humanitarian reasons the Papuan border crossers could obviously not be forced back, at least not at once. On the other hand Canberra was most anxious to stay on the right side of a Djakarta which now had abandoned its anti-Malaysia confrontation policy. Because of Australian defence support for Malaysia, and the presence of Australian troops on Malaysian soil, the confrontation seemed at one time likely to bring Australia into open military conflict with Indonesia. But now, relations between the two countries were gradually improving again and, for example, work had begun to delineate the border in New Guinea between the two countries more clearly. Perhaps most disquieting to Australian officials was the gradually growing sympathy for the West New Guinea rebels among elements of the eastern New Guinea Papuan political elite, including leaders of the House of Assembly. Meanwhile, in Britain, on 5 April 1967, Lord Ogmore of the Liberal Party demanded in the House of Lords that the English Government take steps to initiate a United Nations investigation into the reported killing by Indonesian military of several hundreds of rebellious Papuan tribesmen.

In the Netherlands, conservative Protestant political circles, and also a number of anti-Suharto Left-wing radicals, expressed sympathy for the West New Guinea "freedom struggle", and there is much truth in subsequent accusations by Indonesian officials that Papuan exile leaders Nicolaas Jouwe and his rival Marcus Kasiepo (the latter heading the *Front Nasional Papua* in the Netherlands and in New Guinea) were fomenting "resistance and subversion" in West New Guinea from abroad. In Holland the *Stichting Door de Eeuwen Trouw* (The Foundation "Faithful Through the Centuries"), an organization of political conservatives, many of them orientated toward the principal Protestant confessional parties, and heretofore mainly concerned with the interests of the exiled Ambonese minority from Indonesia in the Netherlands, became a principal supporter of Papuan national aspirations, seeking to stir Dutch and, in effect, world interest on behalf of an independent West New Guinea. Late in September 1967, members of Jouwe's West Papua Freedom Committee, travelling with Dutch travel documents, approached United Nations' officials in New York, requesting investigation of alleged massacres by Indonesian military of Papuans in West New Guinea. The Freedom Committee spokesmen also demanded an inquiry into the alleged torture and imprisonment of prominent Papuans, among them the former Governor of West New Guinea, Eliezer Bonay, first appointed and then removed by the Indonesians after he resisted Djakarta's "Indonesianization" policies in the territory. Queried about all these allegations, Indonesian Foreign Minister Malik denied that there had been a massacre, but admitted to "isolated incidents" and to the arrest of Bonay on charges of "corruption". The West Papua Freedom Committee's public appeal was considerably bolstered, however, by reports at this time of continuing anti-Indonesian resistance by some 2,000 Arfak tribesmen led by Lodewijk Mandatjan, a veteran of both the Dutch colonial and later Indonesian military services.

Whether or not all this, for Indonesia, unwelcome international attention to West Irian played a decisive role in the diplomacy surrounding the territory's future is hard to say. However, by this time Djakarta had already indicated that it intended to abide by the provision in the 1962 agreement with the Dutch giving West New Guinea Papuans the opportunity for an act of self-determination by the end of 1969. Already on 30 September 1966, when Malik came to United Nations headquarters in New York to facilitate Indonesia's return to the world organization, he declared that, although during a recent visit to West Irian he had been handed a petition saying that all Papuans desired to remain with Indonesia, there nevertheless would be a plebescite. Yet, on 7 December 1966, the then Indonesian Home Affairs Minister, Lieutenant-General Basuki Rahmat, was quoted as saying that a plebescite would not be held in West New Guinea and that this was in accord with the wishes of the Papuan population. Rahmat's remark led to a demand by the Dutch Government for an "immediate explanation" (the Dutch, notably, had kept silent, when, a year and a half earlier, Sukarno had said that a plebescite in West New Guinea was no longer necessary). On 12 December 1966 Malik again affirmed that a plebescite would be held in 1969: "This is not just a local agreement", the Indonesian Foreign Minister explained, "with which we can do as we wish. We shall carry out the wish of the West Irian people, and if they want a plebescite we shall hold a plebescite."

Yet within a few days the Provincial Council of West Irian — the reconstituted successor to the *Nieuw Guinea Raad* — adopted a resolution rejecting a plebescite, and on 23 August 1967 several hundreds of students demonstrated in Djakarta demanding that no consultations be held with the Papuan population about West New Guinea's future because the "West Irianese people want to stay in the Indonesian Republic", as a student spokesman was quoted as saying. This demonstration came in the wake of several expressions of loyalty to Indonesia, and/or demands that no plebescite be held, by a West Irianese youth group and by the territory's branches of Indonesian mass and patriotic organizations.

Effective Indonesian control over and manipulation of public life and approved organizations and institutions in West New Guinea seemed to become more evident toward the close of 1967, causing many observers to question whether there would be an untrammelled expression of Papuan opinion even if Djakarta now seemed ready once again to abide by its earlier agreement to allow a Papuan act of self-determination. For under Suharto Djakarta's policy clearly seemed to be one of allowing the Papuan act of free choice, while at the same time making it plain that any idea of secession of West Irian from the Indonesian Republic would simply not be countenanced.

Already in his 16 August 1967 general policy message to the Indonesian Parliament, on the eve of the country's independence anniversary, Suharto spoke of Indonesia's "obligation" to provide a "free choice" in West New Guinea by the end of 1969, but he also asserted that the Papuans ought to be helped (presumably by Indonesia) "to realize their resolve, affirmed many times in their statements, to remain part of the Indonesian nation and territory" and remain "inseparable from the territory of the unitary Republic of Indonesia". A year later, in his 16 August 1968 message to Parliament, Suharto again declared that although the act of free choice would be held, "This does not mean that we are going to abandon the principle of the unitary state of the Indonesian Republic with a territory extending from Sabang to Merauke". The natural culmination of this policy position came on 3 February 1969, only a few months before the act of free choice would finally get underway, when Suharto said that he would regard any decision by the people of West Irian to leave the Republic of Indonesia as "treason". Suharto added that it had "always" been the aim of the Indonesian independence struggle "to have and to create a unitary state" from Sabang (on the western tip of Sumatra) to Merauke (on the eastern border of West New Guinea).

There is some reason to believe that behind this policy, behind the confident predictions of various Indonesian officials that West Irianese would vote to remain in the Republic, and behind the categorical assertions by public organizations in the territory that no plebescite was needed, there was a good deal of uncertainty in the Government. There was considerable, if muted, soul-searching in intellectual circles in Djakarta on the wisdom and morality of Indonesian policy in the territory. In the press, too, doubts were openly expressed. On 22 September 1967, for example, *The Djakarta Times* carried this editorial:

> Observers returning from West Irian some time ago frankly said that the situation in that territory is quite different from official reports received here. The behavior of the Government officials 'imported' from other parts of Indonesia was reportedly more repugnant than that of the colonial rulers. Many people having returned from that territory are pessimistic that, should fair chances be given under the present conditions, the local people would choose to remain in the Republic.

Similar press reflections persisted in the following months. As late as 9 May 1969, for example, shortly after the anti-Indonesian Papuan uprising in the Enarotali area, the paper *Warta Harian* recommended that the *Pepera* (the Indonesian acronym for the West New Guinea act of self-determination) be cancelled altogether, on the grounds that Indonesian intentions were hypocritical and false: "We pretend to be 'democratic'. We pretend to be faithful to 'international commitments'. If we are 100 per cent honest in wanting to implement the Act of Free Choice, that is all right. But, often, there, is a difference between wishes and deeds. The result is that we are suspended in mid-air, a nation without integrity and determination."

This was not the first time, it might be added, that a suspension of the Papuan act of self-determination had been mooted in the Indonesian press. Also, around the middle of 1968 there had been reports in Dutch newspapers — reports denied by Djakarta — that the Suharto Government had vainly approached UN Secretary-General U Thant in order to win approval for a postponement.

In considering Suharto's policy on the Irian question it is well to stress the narrow range of his options. All during the complicated constitutional struggle with Sukarno after the *Gestapu* affair, Suharto and his backers could never permit their Left flank to be turned on them. Coping with the residual influence of the PKI and the PNI meant first of all that on such volatile issues as West Irian there could be no room for flexibility or compromise. Indeed, for the Suharto Government to agree to the Papuan act of free choice at all — even if only as a formality — was to provide political opponents with ammunition at a time, as would have been apparent from previous chapters, when Suharto's relations with other power interests in *Orba*, or with other parties and the outlying regions, had for various reasons already become strained. On 23 May 1968 the executive board of *Nahdatul Ulama* (NU), perhaps the most influential Islamic party at the time, declared that the holding of the act of free choice in West New Guinea "would be an act of treason to the proclamation of Indonesia's independence". NU maintained that under international law a nation already exercising *de facto* and *de jure* control over a certain region could not be subjected to "foreign intervention".

The effect of NU's move, clearly designed to embarrass the Government, was to a considerable extent undercut during July 1968 and the following months by a spate of Djakarta-induced proclamations by the various Government-appointed regional and local legislative councils in West New Guinea and by groups of tribal chiefs, all of whom either expressed continuing alliance to the Indonesian Government or else declared the act of free choice to be unnecessary, and by similar statements by such groups as the Movement to Maintain the August 17 Proclamation of National Independence, the Red and White Movement, and the '45 Generation organization. These various avowals of Papuan loyalty, carefully contrived as some of them seemed, in effect placed the Suharto Government in the relatively comfortable position of being able to affirm, for formality's sake, its obligation to hold a Papuan plebescite while at the same time enabling it to answer its critics to the effect that there could and would be no "treason" to Indonesia's independence since the West Irianese were, presumably, overwhelmingly in favour of remaining within the Indonesian fold.

Privately, however, the Suharto Government continued to be worried about the state of Papuan opinion. The much-publicized expressions of loyalty by various official West New Guinea councils and organizations seemed to contrast with official Indonesian acknowledgements that the territory's development had stagnated and, indeed, had led to Papuan resistance. On 22 March 1968, Suharto said, for example, that the Government was "paying the closest attention" to improving the public

137

administration and welfare in West New Guinea. By May of that same year Foreign Minister Malik admitted that "technical difficulties" had delayed allocations of Papuan development funds and added that recent Papuan uprisings were in protest against the scarcity of daily necessities. Early in May Economics Minister Sultan Hamengku Buwono, after a visit to West Irian, said that the economic situation in the region was "very bad" and noted that groups of dissatisfied Papuans had fled into the jungles and were creating "disturbances". Directly following the Sultan's return from West New Guinea, President Suharto, according to an Antara despatch from Djakarta on 8 May 1968, sent a message to Papuan leaders declaring that the Government was "making serious efforts to improve present conditions" in the territory.

It was not until February 1969, however, that Djakarta announced the beginning of the implementation of a US$230 million long-term development plan for West New Guinea. The plan would presumably operate in conjunction with the US$30 million development programme (the funds of which were originally provided by Holland) already framed late in 1967 by the Fund of the United Nations for the Development of West Irian (FUNDWI). The combined allocations would, at least on paper, make available a greater per capita expenditure on welfare and development than anywhere else in Indonesia. But execution of the development programme obviously would require time and, toward the close of March 1969, one West New Guinea youth leader, Bakri Abdulgani Tianlean, Secretary of the United West Irian Students and Youth Organization, in a Djakarta press conference, declared that the situation in West New Guinea was "becoming worse". He added that there was no freedom in the territory and that one would be courting arrest as an agent of the anti-Indonesian Free Papua Organization (OPM) "if he talks about economic improvement".

By this time a new area of contention was beginning to develop over the manner in which Indonesia planned to carry out the West Guinea act of free choice. The August 1962 Dutch-Indonesian agreement says little about the plebescitary procedure beyond specifying "the eligibility of all adults, male and female, not foreign nationals, to participate in the act of self-determination. . . ." By the middle of 1968 this "eligibility" was being defined publicly by Indonesian spokesmen in terms of a method other than a one-man-one-vote system. The latter was not considered practical in view of West New Guinea's undeveloped state (for example, the enormous communications difficulties, and the illiteracy and isolation of much of the territory's population). The lack of a specific voting procedure in the 1962 agreement was, in any case, well appreciated by the Indonesians. According to an Antara despatch from Djakarta, on 3 June 1968, Foreign Minister Malik in a press interview frankly admitted that "one advantage for Indonesia" in the West New Guinea question was that the New York agreement made "no mention" of a one-man-one-vote system. Later that same month Dutch Foreign Minister Joseph Luns, similarly commenting on the plebescitary provisions, declared that the self-determination procedure of the 1962 agreement was "somewhat vague", but recalled that the Indonesian delegation at the New York talks which produced the 1962 agreement "would not accept any other wording".

On 15 February 1969, the Indonesian Government officially detailed what the forthcoming Papuan act of free choice would involve (a general intimation of the procedure to be followed had already been given some two weeks previously by the Information Ministry). In the first step of the official plebescitary procedure a special consultative assembly would be formed in each of the eight *kabupaten* (regencies) in West Irian. The number of representatives in each assembly would depend on the regency's total population (which ranges from about 35,000 to about 165,000), but would not be less than 75 nor more than 150. The representatives would not be popularly elected in a general election. Rather, in each regency, the regency representative council — a semi-legislative body appointed by the Indonesian Government — formed a committee to organize popular meetings (where feasible or considered desirable) and at such meetings representatives for the special consultative assembly in each regency would be chosen. However members of the regency representative councils automatically became members also of the special consultative assembly in their regency; members of the West Irian Provincial Representative Council — the territory's semi-legislative body — also automatically became members of the special consultative assembly of the regency from which they originated. This meant that, right from the start, the special consultative assemblies harboured staunch pro-Indonesian leadership contingents. Additionally, acknowledged tribal chiefs more or less automatically became members (if they were acceptable to Indonesian officials) of the special consultative assembly in their respective regencies. Approved political mass organizations, like the earlier-named Red and White Organization or the '45 Generation, also sent representatives from among their midst. UN officials were present at only a fraction of these formative procedures for the special assemblies.

In the second step the eight special assemblies would meet separately and individually, in order to decide the question formulated in the 1962 agreement: whether to stay or sever all ties with Indonesia (the agreement text provides for no other choice). In effect then, a little over 1,000 delegates (Antara reported on 31 July 1969 that the exact final number was 1,025), distributed over eight special assemblies, would determine the political future of West New Guinea's total population of about 800,000. In the deliberations in the eight special consultative assemblies it was announced, moreover, on 15 February 1969, the Indonesian principles of *musjawarah* (mutual discussion) and *mufakat* (concensus) would prevail. This meant that there would be no formal voting but contending views would be aired and discussed until general agreement was reached. (In the event, the voting on the plebescitary question in the special assemblies in each of the *kabupaten* — Merauke, Djajawidjaja, Paniai, Fakfak, Sorong, Teluk Tjenderawasih, Manokwari and Djajapura — held between 14 July and 4 August 1969 resulted, according to the Indonesian Government, in a "unanimous decision" in every case to stay with Indonesia.) As if anticipating demurrers, Indonesia's Deputy Foreign Minister for West Irian Affairs, Sudjarwo Tjondronegoro, declared in Djakarta on 25 February 1969, that the Indonesian concept of *musjawarah* was also known to the people of West New Guinea.

Pari passu, one may perhaps note the irony of the anti-Sukarno Government of President Suharto applying the principle of *musjawarah* to the West New Guinea question. For whatever its roots in rapidly eroding indigenous Indonesian traditions, *musjawarah* had been one of the deposed Sukarno's favourite guided democracy tactics, used essentially as an authoritarian device to enforce political and ideological unanimity. *Musjawarah*, rather than voting by "ayes" and "nays", thus even came to be imposed on the proceedings in the Indonesian Parliament in guided democracy's hey-day. But after Sukarno's fall it was precisely the abandonment of *musjawarah* that was urged in many paliamentary and political circles. In the middle of July 1970 leaders of the PSII party urged parliamentary leaders to "restore" the principle of making decisions "by majority vote", arguing that the *musjawarah* and *mufakat* procedure in Parliament was only producing "endless debate" and deadlock. Earlier that same month former Vice-President Mohammad Hatta had denounced the unanimity concept prevailing in Indonesian representative bodies as "nonsense and most reactionary". It should perhaps also be stressed that while the 1962 Dutch-Indonesian agreement mentions the word *musjawarah* the latter refers to Indonesian

Government consultations with local representative councils in West New Guinea *about* the Papuan act of free choice, and does not refer to the *method* by which the act of free choice itself is to be carried out.

There can be little doubt that Indonesian officials, including the military, from the start, sought to make sure of the outcome of the act of free choice. Brian May, the correspondent of Agence France Presse, reported from Djajapura in *The Australian* on 4 June 1969 that "West Irianese complain that they are forced to stick up paper Indonesian flags that decorate many houses. Some say they have been ordered to sign declarations of allegiance to Indonesia. Pupils have been warned that if they oppose Indonesia they will get no education. After the 11 May (anti-Indonesian) demonstration, army officers went to schools and the university and ordered students to take part in a counter-demonstration." By the beginning of April 1969 several hundreds of Indonesians described as "teachers of history" and "politics" by Djakarta were being sent into West Irian in order, as Indonesian spokesmen candidly admitted, to "help make a success" of the act of free choice.

Still it cannot be said that the Indonesian plebescitary procedure did not run into opposition. Particularly some of the Australian, West German and Dutch press were critical. But officially neither The Hague nor Canberra, nor for that matter Washington, nor any other capital, expressed public dismay. Typical, perhaps, of the reaction of the powers once chiefly concerned with the Irian problem was the statement of Australia's then External Affairs Minister Gordon Freeth, on 18 February 1969. Freeth emphasized the difficulties of a one-man-one-vote procedure in West New Guinea and the need for maintaining harmonious relations with Indonesia. In a letter to the principal daily in Australian-administered eastern New Guinea, signed by exiled members of the anti-Indonesian *Front Pembebasan Papua Barat* (West Papua Liberation Front) sharp issue was taken with Freeth's statement and with the Indonesian plebescitary method which was characterized as "unjust and unacceptable" and "dictatorial". The *Front Pembebasan* letter, while in the main favouring a one-man-one-vote type of act of free choice, did recognize significant existing differences in political sophistication among West New Guinea's Papuan population. Hence, the letter proposed that illiterate inhabitants of the territory's hinterland might elect representatives to voice their wishes, but that coastal dwellers and urban residents be given the right to a direct and secret ballot.

This proposal was of more than usual interest because it paralleled one made by none other than the United Nations' supervising representative for the West New Guinea act of free choice, the Bolivian diplomat, Dr F. Ortiz Sanz. In accordance with Articles 16-12 of the 1962 Dutch-Indonesian agreement of West New Guinea, Sanz had been appointed by United Nations' Secretary-General U Thant, in early April 1968, for the purpose of assisting and advising in the preparations of the act of free choice as well as to report on the results. Sanz soon proved to be no mere rubber stamp. He criticized Djakarta on 18 September 1968 for its failure to publicize sufficiently the machinery of the forthcoming plebescitary procedure among the Papuan population of West Irian. Then, early in 1969, Sanz suggested to the Suharto Government that a one-man-one-vote method be used in the more developed coastal regions of the territory, although he admitted that such a system would be impractical in the interior. But Indonesia rejected this suggestion. *Inter alia* it might be noted that in West Irian itself, as well as in Djakarta, there were protests against the Indonesian act of free choice procedure. Some 200 Papuan demonstrators, with placards reading, "One man one vote", marched on Sanz's residence in Djajapura on 11 April 1969. Indonesian troops had to fire warning shots to disperse the protesters. Perhaps it was suggestive of the state of "free speech" and of the right of "assembly" in West New Guinea that after this demonstration a spokesman for Sanz declared that the latter had been assured by Indonesian authorities that no reprisals would be taken against the demonstrators. Meanwhile, in Djakarta, some West Irianese students, who had been distributing leaflets in the capital protesting the act of free choice procedure, were arrested, reportedly at gun point.

But though it had long since become quite clear that Indonesia meant to have its own way in the act of free choice, Sanz continued to be a thorn in the Suharto Government's side. In May 1969, for example, when the act was only a few weeks away, the Bolivian requested that the Indonesian Government provide certain fundamental safeguards for Papuan freedom of political expression and for an impartial judiciary. The request was denied on the grounds that the safeguards requested did not prevail elsewhere in Indonesian territory, and hence a special act of the Indonesian Parliament would have to be required in order to grant them to the West Irianese. It was again at Sanz's insistence that late in June 1969, in four *kabupaten* in West Irian — Sorong, Fakfak, Teluk Tjenderawasih and Merauke, the selection of members for the special consultative assemblies was held once again, because the previous selection had occurred without supervision of observers from Sanz's staff.

Sanz was also instrumental in persuading Djakarta to grant amnesties to several scores of West Irianese political prisoners, most of whom had originally been apprehended for participating in anti-Indonesian demonstrations. But additional scores of Papuan detainees have remained behind bars, however (Papuan informants estimate there may be as many as 1,200 in various prisons and camps in Java). And whatever concessions Djakarta may have felt it could or had to make to the United Nations' observation and supervisory team were at no time likely to alter the carefully orchestrated score of events. As *The New York Times* reporter in Indonesia evaluated the act of free choice on 7 July 1969, "Jakarta's diplomatic community insists and members of the Indonesian government frankly admit in private that the entire process is a meaningless formality."

To the end, however, Sanz was not to be denied: his final report to U Thant, after the completion of the act of free choice, raised serious questions. For one thing, according to Sanz, "United Nations observers" were only able to attend the election of twenty per cent of the total membership of the eight special consultative assemblies. And though Sanz noted that Indonesia had agreed that the assemblies should have as large and as varied a membership as possible, the Bolivian declared, "I regret to have to express my reservation" regarding the implementation of Article 22 of the 1962 Dutch-Indonesian agreement "relating to the 'rights including the rights of free speech, freedom of movement and of assembly, of the inhabitants of the area'. In spite of my constant efforts, this important provision was not fully implemented and the (Indonesian) Administration exercised at all times a tight political control over the population." Sanz also took note of West Irianese petitions protesting further Indonesian control.

It was partly because of Sanz's report that, during the deliberations in the United Nations General Assembly on the outcome of the act of free choice in November 1969, Ghana called for yet another act of free choice in West Irian by the end of 1975. Ghana's proposal was rejected, however, and instead the General Assembly on 19 November 1969, by a vote of eighty-four for, none against, but with no less than thirty abstentions (most of them African states), approved a Dutch-Indonesian resolution which noted (and in effect endorsed) the results of the act of free choice. The large number of abstentions in the Assembly reflected the quandary many nations felt themselves in with respect to the West Irian situation. Clearly, on the one hand there was (and is) little or no desire to postpone still further a solution to a long-term, troublesome, international problem. On the other hand it can hardly be denied that anti-Indonesian and Papuan nationalist sentiment, no less than the *musjawarah* procedure used in West Irian, demanded forthright comment at the bar of international opinion.

There have been other, unmistakable signs of Papuan discontent with Indonesian rule, for example, border crossings from West Irian to Australian-held eastern New Guinea. Between 1963, the year of the formal Indonesian take-over of West Irian, and the end of 1966, when the anti-Indonesian Papuan resistance began to take significant flight, 573 West Irianese Papuans had crossed into the eastern half of the island. In 1967 alone, however, there were 866, in 1968, 801, and by November 1969, some 850. *The Sydney Morning Herald*, on 11 September 1969, reported that nearly 500 West Irianese Papuans had crossed into eastern New Guinea the previous month alone, and that a number of these were dissatisfied with the outcome of the act of free choice, as an Australian administrative officer put it, while others were said to have crossed over because of "economic motives".

Australian officials in past years have tended to stress the accidental nature of these border crossings, ascribing them to the ignorance of a primitive people of the importance of national boundaries. But as early as 1966 Australia was also granting "permissive residence", that is political asylum, to some West Irianese refugees, and, despite announcements that groups of the border crossers had subsequently returned to West New Guinea, the group of "permissive residents" and asylum seekers by the end of 1969 had grown to at least 280. In April and May 1969 Indonesian patrols, in pursuit of West Irianese refugees, crossed into Australian territory, firing at Australian officials and killing two of the fleeing Papuans. The incidents significantly contributed to a new rise in popular sympathy among eastern New Guinea Papuans — including some members of the House of Assembly at Port Moresby — for the West Irianese and their anti-Indonesian independence aspirations.

Meanwhile, by the end of 1968, there was developing a network of jungle camps, on both sides of the border separating the two halves of the island, used by refugee "squatters" as well as increasingly by the underground West Irianese Papuan resistance movement. Most of the camps were temporary and some were broken up by patrols. But it appeared that the anti-Indonesian underground in West New Guinea slowly but unmistakably might be moving toward mobile, jungle guerilla warfare tactics and that the pattern of border camps might well begin to play a prominent role in these tactics.

Certainly there was no dearth of evidence that, despite reverses, the West Irianese resistance was continuing. In June 1968, under the doughty paratroop commander Brigadier-General Sarwo Edhie Wibowo, a new "pacification" campaign was launched, directed primarily, though not exclusively, against the Arfak rebel movement, led by the brothers Lodewijk and Barend Mandatjan, active in the Bird's Head region of West Irian. By September Indonesian spokesmen claimed that "thousands" of Papuan insurgents were giving up their fight and that Lodewijk Mandatjan himself was asking for the terms of surrender. Djakarta gave the impression that Papuan resistance was virtually over. But two months later the rebellion was still continuing, and Edhie, on 9 December 1968, after a visit to Port Moresby, announced a new drive against the dissidents, a drive, he said, which would involve some 6,000 men. Meanwhile Edhie deprecated the fighting capabilities of his Papuan enemies, describing them as being in possession only of some antiquated fire-arms which "cannot fire farther than thirty feet".

On 1 January 1969, the two Mandatjans surrendered and during their subsequent visit to Djakarta President Suharto said that the Indonesian Government had never regarded the Mandatjans' past conduct as "treachery" but rather as a result of "misunderstanding". But expectations that Papuan resistance had now ended were once more dashed with fresh reports that groups of Arfak rebels, this time led by Frits Awom, a former sergeant in the Dutch-trained former Papuan Volunteer Corps, were keeping up the resistance. In the middle of January 1969, two additional Indonesian infantry battalions were sent from Makasar, South Sulawesi, to West New Guinea in order to help "restore peace and order". The South Sulawesi military commander, Brigadier-General Sadjiman, commenting on the sending of these new forces, said that with the Mandatjans' surrender the task of the Indonesian Army was not yet over. "Our job now is to win the forthcoming act of self-determination in West Irian," he added — a candid statement, perhaps, but one which, in the context of the despatch of fresh troops, hardly seemed calculated to remove the serious doubt in the minds of some observers as to Indonesia's intention and methods in the act of free choice.

A special Indonesian mission, meanwhile, sent to talk with Papuan *émigré* leaders in the Netherlands, returned without success: the resistance would go on, and by the end of April 1969 Awom's rebel band of some 300 was tying down five to six times as many Indonesian troops. In April 1969, also, some

30,000 Kapakau tribesmen, in and around the town of Enarotali, in the western central highlands of West Irian, rose in revolt against Indonesian officials, driving them from their posts, raising the West Papua flag over their encampments, occupying airstrips, and making preparations for a new guerilla campaign. Djakarta claimed that the personal *pique* of a district chief who refused to be transferred to a new post, as well as the low salaries of local Papuan policemen, were chief causes of the Enarotali rebellion. Yet Djakarta also asserted that fighting persisted and that Awom was, in fact, co-ordinating the Papuan resistance. Observers of the Enarotali rebellion particularly noted a new degree of tactical co-operation among the rebels. As Brian May, a reporter for Agence France Presse in West Irian, put it in early May 1969: "Primitive tribesmen, supposedly ignorant bow-and-arrow natives, not supposed to know the difference between their country and any other, have shown a marked degree of sophistication."

In July 1969, another revolt broke out at Moanamani, near Enarotali. Armed only with bows and arrows, but assisted by dissident members of the local Papuan police force, the highlanders at Moanamani reportedly killed some twenty Indonesian military, as meanwhile a new spirit of resistance was spreading to neighbouring Papuan communities.

To be sure, Papuan refugees in eastern New Guinea, as well as Papuan independence leaders in the Netherlands and at the United Nations, have often tended to exaggerate these rebellious outbursts. Particularly difficult to verify is the claim of some of these dissidents that by the middle of 1969 several Papuan resistance groups had come into being. According to these claims the previously mentioned OPM (*Organisasi Papua Merdeka*) is now little more than the generic term for the whole Papuan resistance movement. The real fighting is said to be carried on by smaller, mobile groups like the *Gerakan Papua Merdeka* (GPM) or Free Papua Movement, and the *Gerakan Nasional Papua* (GNP) or National Papua Movement. Both these groups are reported to be operating mainly around the Geelvink Bay area, including on Biak island. Other resistance groups, for example the one led by Awom in the Bird's Head, and those operating from the jungle camps at the eastern New Guinea border supervised by a shadowy West Papua Liberation Command (*Kesatuan Kemerdekaan Papua Barat* — KKPB), appear to have little or no contact with the GNP and GPM. Periodically West Irianese refugees in eastern New Guinea, in touch with dissidents along the border, have issued covert manifestoes or made public statements over the names of other supposedly established resistance groups, like the Freedom Front of West Papua (*Front Pembebasan Papua Barat* — FPPB), but these seem no more than paper organizations.

Much the same can be said of the groups of Papuan exiles in the Netherlands. Some forty of these exiles established, in Holland, in early April 1963, the earlier-named *Front Nasional Papua* (FNP). Most of the group had been in the Dutch civil service in West Irian, having served in local councils or in the all-territorial *Nieuw Guinea Raad*. Marcus W. Kasiepo, the oldest of this group of exiles and the *Nieuw Guinea Raad*'s first vice-chairman, became the FNP leader (Marcus's brother Frans is now the Indonesian-appointed Governor of West Irian province). In August 1964, a schism arose, however, and Nicolaas Jouwe, the former *Nieuw Guinea Raad*'s second vice-chairman, and half a dozen followers left the FNP in order to form their own West Papua Freedom Committee (*Komité Kemerdekaan Papua Barat* — KKPB), which since then has claimed contact with the West Papua Liberation Command (KKPB) operating along the West Irian-eastern New Guinea border. Jouwe's group in particular has enjoyed the support of certain Dutch conservatives, concentrated in segments of the principal Protestant confessional political parties. These earlier had taken up the cause of another group of Indonesian exiles in the Netherlands, namely the inhabitants of the South Moluccas, in east Indonesia, who fled to Holland during 1950-1.

Jouwe's group has been particularly active in appealing to African states, to the Organization of African Unity and to the OCAM (*l'Organization Commune Africain et Malgache*). But as shown by the November 1969 vote on the Dutch-Indonesian resolution in the United Nations General Assembly, which endorsed the outcome of the act of free choice in West Irian, such African sympathy for Jouwe's cause as exists was not enough to produce a repudiation of Indonesian rule in the the territory.

Immediately after the completion of the act of free choice in West Irian in early August 1969, Indonesian Foreign Minister Adam Malik visited a number of African countries, including Niger, Dahomey, Ivory Coast and Liberia, where Jouwe had been able to elicit a measure of support. The purpose of his visit, Malik said, was to explain why the Indonesian Government had to refuse a one-man-one-vote procedure in the West Irianese act of free choice. During his journey, Malik also stressed his Government's unqualified support for the Government of Nigeria, in her struggle with rebellious Biafra. Evidently Malik was able, through this visit, to neutralize much African opposition to Djakarta's policies and to prepare the way for a United Nations' endorsement. Elsewhere, too, Indonesian spokesmen stressed the lack of real support for the OPM among the Papuans of West Irian and noted that under Indonesian administration "the Papuans" of the interior areas, who formerly lived in isolation and lacked outside economic contact, are now absorbed in the country's economic system which "the Government is trying hard to put on a sound basis so that the community can be enabled to increase its standard of living". As for the exercise of political freedom in West Irian, the Indonesian Embassy in London, for example, in a statement published in the May-June 1969 issue of *Eastern World*, put it this way:

> It would be unfair to accuse the Indonesian Government of manipulating freedom of expression in Irian when it is forced to suppress ... violence and terrorism so as to protect law and order. Indonesia as a state upholding the rule of law, cannot possibly tolerate practices of intimidation and armed disturbance on the part of an irresponsible group at the expense of the common people, especially when this group is clearly encouraged and supported from outside (all the leaders of the OPM are Dutch citizens).

One is tempted to raise several questions about this and similar apologias issued by the Indonesian Government, particularly as regards the question of who exactly in West Irian has been engaging in "practices of intimidation" of the "common people", or whether indeed "all leaders of the OPM" are in fact Dutch citizens (some whom the author has met definitely are not). But there is no denying that now, and particularly after the concurrence of the United Nations in the result of the act of free choice, a number of significant factors clearly operate in favour of Indonesia's retention of her West Irian *irredenta*. These may now be considered briefly.

The Papuan resistance, like West Irianese tribal society itself, remains badly dispersed and, despite evidence of some co-ordination, continues in a relatively haphazard way. Though many claim to speak for the OPM, its formal organization is hard to find, and major refugee leaders, like Jouwe and Kasiepo, are deeply divided. Moreover, the insurgents, at least at this juncture, do not have significant material support from abroad. The vocal sympathy of Dutch conservatives for the Papua Barat cause does not offset the steady determination of the Dutch Government not to risk its new and advantageous diplomatic and investment relations with Indonesia through yet another West Irian imbroglio. The weekly of the Peking-orientated wing of the Australian Communist Party passed on a report, in June 1969, which implied that West Irianese might be receiving Chinese

Communist aid. Hong Kong informants have told the author that two Papuan representatives from West Irian had conversations with Peking's emissaries in the colony the following month. While some Communist Chinese support for an insurgency in West Irian would, in principle, be in harmony with similar Chinese tactics elsewhere in Southeast Asia, it is too early to tell whether such support will in fact materialize in this case and, if it does, whether it will be sufficiently significant to prevent the eventual withering of the Papuan resistance now expected by many observers. Some African sympathy for the Papua Barat cause lingers, but is unlikely to translate itself into new diplomatic pressures unless the insurgency in West New Guinea takes a new and dramatic turn.

Then, too, it is recognized even among the OPM's strongest sympathizers abroad that an independent West Irian would not be economically viable for a long time to come. The world already has too many, recently "decolonized", pauper states, heavily dependent on foreign largess. Considering the not insignificant advances which Indonesia has been making in her economic rehabilitation since the fall of Sukarno (see chapter VII), West Irian's future development — it can be reasonably argued — could well be structured much better in an Indonesian context than if the territory were independent. The new foreign interest in Indonesian petroleum resources includes also potential reserves in West Irian, and Japanese lumber concerns meanwhile remain interested in the territory's forest assets. Such interests must, however, take account of the prevailing political climate: an independent West Irian which would — as seems likely — be a continuing target of an aggrieved and frustrated Indonesian nationalism in its immediate neighbourhood would hardly provide an attractive investment setting.

Furthermore, to many foreign observers of the West Irian problem, the force of this Indonesian nationalism must realistically be accounted to be of more importance in the international arena, considering Indonesia's size and strategic location, than that of the Papuan variety. After all, acquisition of West New Guinea has been an important dynamic in post-revolutionary Indonesian politics. Although, as indicated earlier, in the period 1967-9 the Indonesian press often expressed skepticism about the Suharto Government's policy in West Irian, the question may well be raised whether the Suharto regime, considering its political problems and liabilities (see chapters III and IV), could have survived the emergence of an independent *Papua Barat* in 1969, or would survive it at any time in the near future. Certainly for the USA, Australia and the Netherlands, to name but three nations closely concerned with the Irian question in the past, a marked aggravation of political instability in Indonesia would seem to be too high a price to pay for the appearance of a weak and politically unpredictable new state of West Irian.

Indonesia, finally, has survived more serious provincial insurrections than the one now going on in West Irian: there was the rebellion of the South Moluccas, for example, in 1950-1, and the counter-government of the "Revolutionary Indonesian Republic" in parts of Sumatra and Sulawesi during 1956-9. In these areas secessionist sentiments which once seemed as deep-seated and as morally persuasive as those evident in West Irian today slowly diminished as a result of Djakarta's judicious mixture of repressive force and policy reforms. Does it not seem likely, Djakarta's supporters ask, that the younger Papuan generation will also be absorbed in a broader Indonesian nationalism as education and economic integration proceed?

All these factors and considerations may well prove to be decisive in the perpetuation of Indonesian rule over West Irian. But some formidable obstacles remain. There is first of all the fact that for many politically conscious West Irianese the Indonesian *musjawarah* procedure in the act of free choice was little better than a fraud, a carefully contrived imposition of the will of the foreign occupying power—not an honest attempt at self-determination. The experience of Geoffrey Hutton (writing in the 26 July 1969 issue of *The Sydney Morning Herald*) is representative of the impressions of other reporters who were in West Irian during the act of free choice:

> Several correspondents have been handed letters, slipped to them by someone who beckons at a window. The one I received was addressed to the foreign correspondents, and handed over with three others addressed to the United Nations representative, Dr. Ortiz Sanz, the foreign ambassadors, and the "Free Papuans" living abroad (in Holland). It contained detailed accusations of bribery of delegates, arrest of three local council members and four public servants, and wholesale murder of villages in the interior. Although marked very secret it was signed with five names, giving each man's occupation.

Indonesia's complex method in the forming of the special consultative assemblies which were to carry out the act of free choice also appears to have left something to be desired. On 4 July 1969, for example, in Bosnik, on the island of Biak, four Papuans who demanded a new election and a one-man-one-vote procedure during a public meeting gathered to elect representatives for the local special consultative assembly, were arrested by Indonesian military. Immediately after the meeting there were seven more arrests in Bosnik in order, as an Indonesian spokesman explained, to prevent "internal fighting while feelings were running high"

An AAP-Reuter's correspondent, Hugh Lunn, who attended the act of free choice process in West Irian, has described not only how in Manokwari he was given a letter containing some 5,000 names of Papuans in the area who were allegedly opposed to further Indonesian rule, but also how he personally witnessed "desperate fights" in the city on the day that the act of free choice was held there. "Young Papuan men, shouting 'alone, alone' (that is separation) in Indonesian, fought with baton-wielding Indonesian and Papuan police," Lunn recounts, "some tried to tear down a red and white Indonesian flag." Yet despite such incidents the seventy-four members of the Manokwari assembly reportedly voted "unanimously" for the continuation of Indonesian rule — as Indonesian security forces meanwhile kept a watchful eye outside the assembly's meeting place! It is incidents such as these which not only cast doubt on the veracity of the outcome of the act of free choice, but which underscore once again that Papuan nationalism in West Irian is much more extensive than some observers appear to believe.

On 1 May 1969, during demonstrations and covert meetings in and near Djajapura, Papuan dissidents reportedly proclaimed a "National Republic of West Papua", and on 10 May 1969, an Indonesian Army spokesman disclosed that recently captured documents revealed that exiled FNP leader Marcus Kasiepo had been named "President" of the new "Republic". The substance of such reports is as difficult to verify as the trickle — since 1963 — of stories of Indonesian maltreatment of and brutality toward the Papuans (for example, according to one reporter, Michael Donald, in London's *The Observer* of 1 June 1969, Indonesian military in West Irian had killed "thousands of primitive tribesmen", an accusation also frequently made by Papuan refugee leaders).

Whether or not a West Papuan "Republic" exists, and whether or not large numbers of West Irianese have been killed, such reports continue to have influence in Australian-administered eastern New Guinea. It is particularly the interaction of repressed nationalism and resistance in West Irian with the nascent nationalism of the eastern half of the island that is likely to become an important new dynamic of the whole Irian question in the future. It is quite clear that the flow of West Irianese refugees to the east, referred to earlier, and the inadequacies of the Indonesian *musjawarah* procedure in the act of free choice, have evoked considerable sympathy for the anti-Indonesian Papuan resistance movement in the Territory of Papua-New

Guinea, that is eastern New Guinea. (To be sure the influx of West Irianese squatting on lands not their own in eastern New Guinea has also produced some resentment.) On 27 June 1969 the House of Assembly of the Territory of Papua-New Guinea in Port Moresby passed a resolution expressing "deep concern" over Indonesian policy in West Irian as well as "deep dismay" over the alleged failure of the United Nations to insist on a better way of determining West Irian's political wishes. The resolution caused considerable embarrassment to Australian authorities, in view of Canberra's general policy of acquiescence to Indonesian policy in West Irian. But anti-Indonesian protests were also voiced by students and clerical leaders in Port Moresby. And well before the act of free choice one commentator in Port Moresby's *South Pacific Post* (24 March 1969) observed: "What possible assurance is there that after Suharto and his regime have rehabilitated the potage left by Sukarno and Subandrio they won't once again move against North Borneo and Sarawak and East Irian?" Pan-Papuanism, that is advocacy of a possible political unity of both eastern and West New Guinea in a single state, is diffused and by no means general. But it does figure prominently in the thinking of some eastern New Guinea political leaders with whom this writer talked in the middle of 1969.

It may well be that all this eastern New Guinea interest in and sympathy for his West Irianese neighbour will gradually be attenuated or vanish as the development of West Irian itself steadily advances and relations between Australia and Indonesia remain good. On the other hand, the long-term problem posed by the different political perspectives of the two halves of the island is not always fully understood abroad. For eastern New Guinea has been promised more and more autonomy by Australia; indeed, if its Papuan inhabitants desire it, independence will eventually be granted and the United Nations Trusteeship Committee — a thorn in the flesh of some of the more seasoned Australian administrators in the Territory — will always be there to keep prodding such a development. But, while in the eastern part of the island increasing recognition is and will be given to the maturing nationalism and political consciousness of the Papuan inhabitants, at the same time in the western part of the island such Papuan nationalism is and will likely continue to be repressed and diluted. West Irian is now an "undisputed" part of Indonesia, as Suharto has insisted. Whether these contradictory developments within the same island-area, and in the context of the anti-Indonesian and Pan-Papuan sentiments just described, can long continue without conflict may well be doubted. This is all the more so, because there is little indication that Indonesia understands the significance of Papuan nationalism. The enactment by the Indonesian Government, shortly after the act of free choice, of a vaguely worded measure, providing for provincial "autonomy" for West Irian, has done little to allay skepticism toward Indonesian policy intentions, not least because the measure leaves unaltered the powers of local military commanders in the territory operating under prevailing emergency regulations.

Indonesian officials formally regard the OPM as a terrorist organization, charging it with attempted murder and kidnapping, as well as with sedition. Other Indonesian spokesmen have at various times stressed that it is difficult to apply "democratic principles" of government in West Irian and indeed have cautioned that even the introduction of a modern "democratic education" would be a violation of Papuan traditions (see, for example, the remarks of Sudjarwo Tjondronegoro, the Indonesian Deputy Foreign Minister for West Irian Affairs, in *The Djakarta Times*, 23 June 1969). Moreover, the "backwardness" of West Irian is a popularly accepted fact in Indonesia, which cannot but colour relations with the Papuan community. One reporter, Bob Hawkins, writing in the 14 August 1969 issue of the *Far Eastern Economic Review* has noted typical Indonesian reactions: "Most Indonesians know where West Irian is. Few seem to want to go there. Almost everyone I spoke to in Djakarta had little good to say about the place ('Very primitive you know'; 'It doesn't make anything for us'; 'It's going to cost us a lot of money'; 'The people don't have much sense')." Still, Hawkins notes, Indonesians regard West Irian as properly part of their territory. Revealing also perhaps was the announcement by Indonesian Information Minister Budiardjo at the close of July 1969 that Indonesian civil servants from other regions of Indonesia who were stationed in West Irian would be relieved at the end of their "six-year term of hardship assignment". Budiardjo said that the reason for this policy was that living conditions in West New Guinea "are really tough for civil servants". One wonders if conditions in West New Guinea are more difficult for Indonesian officials than, say, a posting in the interior of the Borneo provinces, or on Sumbawa or Flores in the Lesser Sunda Islands.

Meanwhile, despite official Indonesian assurances, Papuan resistance against Djakarta's rule goes on. On 8 April 1970 Antara reported from Djakarta that the newly appointed territorial military commander for the Moluccan-West Irian region, Rear-Admiral Subijakto, in a press interview in Biak had said that there were still bands of rebels in the Biak and Manokwari areas, led by Awom. At the end of May 1970 a new combat task force was airlifted from a Bandung airport, destined for the Baliem

Valley, ostensibly for "rehabilitation" of the Almena airport there, but actually to launch a new drive against local insurgents in the area. By early June military spokesmen claimed that a number of prominent OPM leaders, among them Lodewijk Sariba, had recently been killed during the Indonesian Army's *Pamungkas* operation against Papuan rebels. Later that same month the arrest was announced of five Indonesian Chinese in Biak who reportedly had been supplying the OPM with rice, clothing and money. OPM insurgents had planned to sabotage water and electricity facilities in Biak, according to the Army. In November 1970, Awom and 154 of his followers surrendered to the Indonesian authorities, followed, early in January 1971, by two other Papuan resistance leaders, Louis Bony and Joseph Wanmau. Despite such defections, however, intermittent Papuan guerilla resistance is continuing.

The plan proposed by President Suharto at the close of October 1969 under which 200,000 West Irianese children would be taken from the island and housed with Indonesian families in other parts of Indonesia aroused such a storm of protest — not least because of its implication that the West Irian environment was somehow inadequate for a proper education — that on 24 November 1969 Antara reported that Suharto's plan had been misunderstood. Suharto "only wanted to collect money to finance the education of West Irian children, whereas the children themselves remain in their province", an Antara release put it. This episode has done as little to improve West Irianese-Indonesian relations as the repeated instances of corruption among Indonesian officials in the territory. Cases of fraudulent diversion of goods (destined for West Irian from Hong Kong and Singapore) into private channels — sometimes with the connivance of local military — do not fade from Papuan memories because official corruption elsewhere in Indonesia also continues to flourish. West Irian's military commander, Brigadier-General Sarwo Edhie, conceded in mid-September 1969 that some of his forces "have been involved in malpractices", though he denied charges by a West Irianese member of parliament, Lucas Rumkorem, of more extensive malversations. Clearly Djakarta is far from having won the confidence and support of its easternmost province's inhabitants.

Still, it must be conceded that the Suharto Government is anxious to promote West Irian's development. The Fund of the United Nations for the Development of West Irian (FUNDWI) in its 1968 report pointed out that Dutch economic policies and subsidies created an unrealistically high wage level for the urban Papuan out of all proportion to the territory's development plateau and resources. The twenty-two initial large-scale projects to be undertaken under Djakarta's and FUNDWI's supervision in the territory in the next few years at a cost of US$100 million, and as part of the earlier-named. longer-term US$230 million development plan, will significantly widen vocational training, commercial fishing and agricultural development. But meanwhile communications remain poor, and, in June 1970, former Vice-President Hatta, after a tour of the territory, stressed that goods often piled up in places like Merauke while in many other areas ships would not appear for months on end. Already in January 1970, Major-General Harun Sohar, assistant to the Minister of Internal Affairs in charge of West Irian projects, declared that in so far as West Irian was concerned implementation of the national Five-Year Development Plan would be some nine months late, mainly due to transportation bottlenecks and bureaucratic delays. On 16 February 1971 the Indonesian Government's director-general of sea communications, Harjono Nimpuno, also commented on the fact that development in Papua Barat was being delayed because of poor maritime connections and transport facilities. Meanwhile, the approbation given by various Indonesian spokesmen to the aspirations for self-determination of the people of eastern New Guinea, on the occasion of a visit by members of the House of Assembly of the Territory of Papua-New Guinea in March 1971, has only caused exiled West New Guinea Papuan nationalists to intensify their own efforts for an independant Irian. Whether Suharto's *Orba* will be able to neutralize continuing Papuan discontent remains very much to be seen.

CHAPTER SEVEN

Problems of Economic Rehabilitation

SHORTLY before the 30 September 1965 coup, President Sukarno during an address on National Peasant's Day, noted how he recently had "issued a challenge to the Supreme Advisory Council": "My challenge was: 'Anyone among you capable of lowering prices in a short period ... I will make a cabinet minister in charge of prices.'" Sukarno added that he also had threatened jail to anyone who took up his challenge but failed. "Nobody dared to respond to my challenge," Sukarno went on. He then lashed out at the "colonialists" and "neo-colonialists" who, he said, were inciting the Indonesian people "to rebel against the Government by confusing our prices".

These remarks of Sukarno, as the authoritative *Quarterly Economic Review* (October 1965) of The Economist Intelligence Unit of London rightly noted, marked the "complete bankruptcy" of his economic policy. And, indeed, particularly in the four or five years before the *Gestapu* affair, the stagnation and chaos of the Indonesian economy seemed daily to become more apparent, as Sukarno by his own admission deliberately neglected economic problems in order to develop what he termed Indonesia's "thunderous revolutionary spirit". "There can be little doubt", as Dr J. Panglaykim, one of Indonesia's leading economists, wrote in June 1966, "that the economy has been brought to its present desperate straits by the lack of realism of the previous rulers of Indonesia who had the unfortunate habit of subordinating the needs of the nation's economy to their political ambitions." Amidst risky foreign adventures, like the confrontation campaigns against Dutch-held West New Guinea and later against Malaysia, and an announced revolutionary expansionism in Southeast Asia in tandem with Peking, domestic economic stabilization and development efforts virtually went by the board. Meanwhile public attention was diverted by such unrealistic schemes as the Eight-Year National Development Plan, submitted to Sukarno in

August 1960, and by Sukarno's own, largely rhetorical Economic Declaration (*Deklarasi Ekonomi—Dekon*) of March 1963.

The true facts of the Indonesian economy however lay in the rapidly mounting price spiral, mainly prompted by ever larger annual budget deficits (in 1954 the budget deficit was Rp.3.6 billion, in 1958 Rp.9.7 billion, and in 1962 over Rp.16 billion, after which deficit figures began to assume an almost astronomic quality). The price index of nineteen basic food-stuffs on the Djakarta market (taking 1953 as 100) jumped from 177 in 1957 to 760 in 1961. As the population kept growing at a rate of at least 2.3 per cent per annum and by the end of 1962 passed the 100 million mark, food production, meanwhile, except for cassava, appeared to be declining. For example, production of rice (in stalk) according to the 1967 annual supplement on Indonesia of the earlier-named Economist Intelligence Unit, stood at 13,347,000 metric tons in the crop year 1962-3, but at only 12,628,000 metric tons in the crop year 1964-5; annual rice imports in excess of 600,000 tons were rapidly becoming the norm in this period. With the exception of petroleum — which had seemed to become virtually the principal steady foreign exchange earner for the Indonesian Government — almost all major exports had begun to slip. Rubber production, for example, after its 1951 high of 814,406 long tons during the Korean War dropped to 629,808 long tons in 1960, while sugar production, as late as 1959, stood at 665,684 tons, or less than half of the pre-World War II production total of 1,606,598 tons in 1940.

Foreign trade generally was declining. In 1960 Indonesian exports totalled US$840 million in value, in 1963 only US$696 million, with imports (c.i.f.) also falling from US$574 million to US$502 million in the same period. Despite the contraction of imports, however, there were "large deficits on current accounts in the balance of payments owing to heavy invisible imports (especially transport costs and oil company profits)", as the June 1965 issue of the *Bulletin of Indonesian Economic Studies* of the Australian National University pointed out. These deficits were met largely by drawing on reserves and by borrowing, and the mounting cost of servicing the foreign debt was to be one of *Orba's* major rehabilitation problems. The above-mentioned bulletin also notes the steady deterioration of Indonesia's transportation and communication system in the last few years of Sukarno's guided democracy:

> Railroad capacity is said to be barely '15-16 per cent of the total demand for freight'. The cost of necessary road repair in South Sumatra is estimated to be Rp.9 billion, while the budget provides

only Rp.180 million. In Surabaja, one firm operates only 3 of its 23 buses, another 3 out of 30 buses, a third 1 out of 6. Probably, the worst transport bottleneck of all is shipping. Rice and maize surpluses accumulate in Makassar for want of shipping to Java. Thousands of tons of gaplek (dried cassava) in Java cannot be exported. Storage facilities at many ports experience congestion.

Rationalizing the foreign debt, halting the inflation, liberalizing foreign trade and attracting development capital — these have been some of the avowed economic and financial policy targets since Sultan Hamengku Buwono became Minister for Economic Affairs in 1966. The immediate problems confronting him and the Suharto regime generally were spotlighted by Derek Davies in the 16 June 1966 issue of the *Far Eastern Economic Review*:

Estimated export earnings for 1966	US$ 475 million
Present foreign exchange reserves	US$ 8 million
Total foreign exchange available for 1966	US$ 483 million
Total debts payable in 1966	US$ 530 million
Other expenditures (essential spare parts, rice, raw materials purchases, upkeep of embassies, etc.)	US$ 615 million
Total outgoings	US$1,145 million
Total deficit	US$ 662 million

Bringing inflation under control has been a staggering problem. The following table suggests something of the dimensions of the inflationary pressures before as well as after Suharto assumed leadership:

TABLE I

Cost of Living Index, Djakarta
(1957 = 100)

December 1963	2,226
December 1964	5,234
December 1965	37,500
December 1966	267,276
December 1967	567,088

Source: Central Bureau of Statistics, Djakarta

During 1966 monthly increases in the cost of living index were becoming notably smaller, although from January 1968 to January 1969, the cost of living index in Djakarta (now operating with a new base, that is, September 1966 = 100) rose from 395 to 535. During November 1969, however, the price of rice, according to an Antara despatch of 4 December 1969, remained stable at Rp.35 per litre, as did the price of salt at Rp.15 per briquette and of batik at Rp.435 per sheet. According to the Central Bureau of Statistics, the price index of nine essential commodities in Djakarta even declined by 0.9 per cent during the first week of December 1969. Though increased stability in foreign exchange prices and active government trading in essential commodities, like rice, sugar, cooking oil, fish, soap and so on, assisted in slowing down the rising cost of living, the money supply meanwhile continued to show an alarming upward trend:

TABLE II

Money Supply in Indonesia
1959-67
(in thousand million rupiahs)

End of Year	Total Money Supply	Percentage increase*
1959	34.9	18.6
1960	47.8	37.1
1961	67.6	41.4
1962	135.9	101.0
1963	263.4	93.8
1964	675.1	194.2
1965	2,582.0	282.4
1966	21,024.4	714.2
1967 (January)	22,391.0	6.5
1967 (August)	38,133.0	4.27

* as compared with previous year or month
Source: *Far Eastern Economic Review, 1968 Year Book;* Bank Negara Indonesia, Unit I

A more recent calculation of money supply growth, appearing in the March 1969 issue of the earlier-named *Bulletin of Indonesian Economic Studies,* notes an increase in the money in circulation, from about Rp.23 billion in January 1967 to Rp.113.7 billion in December 1968, while, according to an Antara despatch from Djakarta on 26 November 1969, the total Indonesian money supply in October 1969 had risen to Rp.168.6 billion. Thus while, percentage-wise, the increases might have been slowed somewhat, there is no question that they had not (as yet?) been slowed enough for a significant stabilization programme.

Certainly in 1966-7 the severe increases in living costs could be attributed in part to the steady growth in the money supply. A few illustrations must suffice. The price of a litre of rice jumped from Rp.7.92 in January 1967 to Rp.27 by the end of

159

December of that same year, a brick of salt in the same period went from Rp.2.68 to Rp.7.50, kerosene (per bottle) from Rp.1.38 to Rp.3.85, a bar of washing soap (Sunlight B29) from Rp.14.51 to Rp.21.93, and low-grade textile (per metre) from Rp.24.85 to Rp.43.57.

During the Sukarno era reports of cases of severe malnutrition and hunger edema regularly broke through the official censorship. In the Suharto era, with censorship somewhat mitigated, similar reports have continued. For example, on the island of Lombok, as one perceptive American journalist, Peter Kann, writing in *The Wall Street Journal*, 25 August 1969, recently discovered, hunger and near starvation are daily worries in a rodent-infested, plague-ridden society. And on 30 November 1969 *The New York Times* reported a growing threat of famine and physical debilitation among the population on the island of Flores, where recent crop failures led people to eating poisonous *katela* plants. On 26 November 1969 Antara reported corroboration by the provincial police commander of North Sumatra of a long-existing practice of the sale of women, including young girls, from North Sumatra to undisclosed "localities abroad". This practice stems, at least in part, from the poverty of the local population. It is reports like these which suggest the distance which economic "rehabilitation" still has to go in Indonesia today.

Certainly in the first few months after the abortive *Gestapu* coup, as Sukarno clung to power and the PKI was still attempting to ride out the political storm, there was little indication that meaningful economic reforms were to get underway. On 25 November 1965 Chairul Saleh, as Third Deputy Premier, proclaimed a new national economic policy for the following year, and presidential decree no. 26/1965 envisaged a balanced budget, new attempts to increase production, institution of new rationalized budgeting procedures, and so on. Whatever the good intent of this programme, it was soon nullified in a whirlwind of conflicting economic directives, bureaucratic strangulation, rapidly rising prices, and by the poorly prepared introduction of a new rupiah at a rate of one to 1,000 old rupiahs. The last measure, though expected to enhance the Government's supervisory powers over the money supply, shortly had, in effect, the opposite result, and the ensuing financial chaos in the early months of 1966 was undoubtedly a factor in accelerating Sukarno's slide from power (see chapter II).

The new Ampera Cabinet, which began its work on 25 July 1966, initiated yet another new policy departure, adumbrated earlier in the policy statements of 4 April and 12 April 1966 of the new Vice-Premier for Economic and Financial Affairs, Sultan

Hamengku Buwono. The Sultan's sober and modest policy formulations ("We decline to make promises which may arouse unrealistic hopes among the people," he said on 12 April, adding, "The only promise we give is that we will do our best honestly to meet the challenge.") were in marked contrast to the more sweeping pronouncements of some of his predecessors in office, as well as of Sukarno. The Ampera Cabinet's general economic policies included a liberation, as much as possible, of all productive forces in the economy shackled too long by bureaucratic control and administrative inefficiency; a hospitality to foreign private capital; establishment of a more realistic and simpler exchange rate system in order to bring sanity in the money market and in overseas trade; operational rationalization and enhanced efficiency in the State enterprises to be achieved also by permitting some selected private enterprises to compete with them; and the institution of a balanced budget and of improvements in credit and banking services. By its decision no. 23/1966 the MPRS, the country's highest policy-making body, in effect legitimized these policies, but placed stress on the immediate demands of the people in terms of "economic democracy", that is the need for a sharp reining in of the galloping inflation, and for meeting food and clothing requirements, as well as emphasis on a long-term rehabilitation of agriculture, transport and communication, industry and mining.

According to the 1968 year-book of the *Far Eastern Economic Review*, a three-stage stabilization programme now commenced, beginning with the issuance of a raft of directives and regulations by the Government on 3 October 1966. These measures included not only incisive alterations in budgetary procedures, including new and serious efforts to balance the budget in order to curtail inflation, but also

(1) a freeing of much of the external trade sector through the institution of a new floating exchange rate and a reform of the BE (export bonus certificate) system;

(2) initial negotiations to bring in more foreign capital;

(3) some modest efforts at reform in the overblown government bureaucracy; and

(4) institution of new credit policies to channel bank credits more efficiently.

Perhaps the reforms brought about in the external trade sector by these 3 October regulations were most important . For example, the new regulations also eliminated the import sector's "notorious quota and licensing system which was one of the important sources for various types of corruption by the bureaucracy", as Panglaykim and K. D. Thomas have pointed out.

A second phase of stabilization began on 10 February 1967 when some price discrepancies were removed, marketing procedures of both State and private enterprises were simplified, and business concerns generally were permitted to negotiate with and buy directly from their own assets what they required for their production, instead of having to follow the previous, cumbersome and inefficient government control procedures. The third stabilization effort began on 28 July 1967, much of it again involving the export sector. The whole foreign trade procedural and licensing system was greatly simplified so as to give importers and exporters additional further control over their own transactions and credit allocations. Export taxes were reduced and customs duties and sales taxes were considerably revised. As the *Far Eastern Economic Review* 1968 annual points out, by foregoing some of its income from these taxes and duties the Government anticipated an upswing in trade and productivity — a hope that was only partly realized however.

Meanwhile, though, the variable rates of the rupiah still tended to prolong the nightmarish impression made by the Indonesian economy generally. As the *Far Eastern Economic Review* 1967 annual noted, as of early October 1966, an American dollar in Indonesia could variously be worth

(1) Rp.45, the "basic rate" initiated on 25 August 1959, and used in the compilation by some agencies of national import-export statistics during the next few years;

(2) Rp.250, the "transaction rate" (NTR) introduced on 27 March 1964, and used in much of the import-export business;

(3) Rp.10,000, according to new Rp.10 denominations introduced on 21 December 1965, and reflecting a new "transaction rate" of Rp.250 plus Rp.9,750 export premium (or equivalent "Contribution for Import Retribution for Transfer");

(4) Rp.(new)57, a rate used only in determining import duties beginning 3 October 1966 and subject to a three-month review;

(5) Rp.(new)100, a BE (export bonus certificate) rate, announced by the Bank Negara pending determination of rates by the BE exchange, and also used in import calculations involving BEs, ADO or automatic foreign exchange allocations for the outer provinces, and BLLD or foreign exchange obtained from the Foreign Exchange Fund;

(6) Rp.(new)100, used by the Hotel Indonesia in converting dollars into rupiah, but only when payment for hotel accommodation is being made;

(7) again Rp.(new)100, the tourist exchange rate, reduced to Rp.79 in the middle of October 1966;

(8) varying rates, "applicable to various foreign exchange earning

162

sectors which receive different percentages paid in DPA" (supplementary foreign exchange rates), or which concern, for example, the foreign oil companies, which receive Rp.0.52 to the US dollar.

The Alice-in-Wonderland quality of Indonesian currency convertibility policies, whatever limited short-term advantages it may bring in selected aspects of foreign trade, remains one of the surest indices of the economy's continuing ill health.

Perhaps the most significant long-run stabilization effort made by the Suharto Government so far has been in rationalizing Indonesia's foreign debt. As indicated earlier, in 1966 Indonesia faced debt payments of US$530 million for that year alone, while total foreign exchange available amounted to only US$483 million. Indonesia's total foreign indebtedness, shortly after the *Gestapu* coup, is indicated by Table III.

The required projected payments on this huge indebtedness were originally calculated as follows: US$530 million in 1966, US$270 million in 1967, US$275 million in 1968, US$198 million in 1969, US$184 million in 1970, US$145 million in 1971, US$124 million in 1972, US$107 million in 1973, and US$96 million in 1974 — sums obviously beyond Indonesia's capacity to meet. Rescheduling of the debt would mean allowing creditors something of a say in the development of the economy generally. By the middle of 1966 Indonesia had agreed to deal with an international consortium, composed of her principal creditors, in order not only to reschedule her obligations but also to acquire yet additional credits for the planned rehabilitation of her economy. There is evidence of considerable reluctance in some Indonesian business and political circles to such an agreement, but Suharto's and Sultan Hamengku Buwono's economic advisers prevailed.

In Tokyo, in September 1966, some of Indonesia's principal non-Communist creditors, including the US, UK, West Germany, Italy, Japan, France and the Netherlands, met and accepted in principle a rescheduling of Indonesia's obligations toward them, though no new credits were as yet agreed to on that occasion (bilaterally, new credit arrangements were already being discussed, however). Most important, perhaps, for Indonesia's long-term rehabilitation was the fact that the participants in the Tokyo meeting, in effect, formally constituted themselves into a consortium with potentially enormous resources available for subsequent Indonesian stabilization efforts. The Inter-Governmental Group on Indonesia (IGGI) thus formed met again in Paris in December 1966, in Amsterdam in February 1967, in Scheveningen, Holland, in June 1967, again in Paris in October 1967, in Rotterdam in April 1968, again in Scheveningen in April 1969, again in Amsterdam in

TABLE III

Indonesia's Foreign Debt
on 31 December 1965*
(in million US dollars)

Communist Countries

USSR	990
Yugoslavia	115
Poland	100
Czechoslovakia	77
East Germany	72
Hungary	19
Rumania	16
People's China	13
Others	2
Total	1,404

Non-Communist West

USA	179
West Germany	122
France	115
Italy	91
UK (incl. Hong Kong)	42
Holland	28
Switzerland	3
Others	7
Total	587

Asian Countries

Japan	231
Pakistan	20
India	10
Total	261

African Countries

UAR	4

International Agencies

IMF	102

Grand Total	2,358

* Total excludes $110 million owed Shell Oil Company and compensation to be paid to foreign estate owners.
Source: J. Panglaykim and H. W. Arndt, *The Indonesian Economy: Facing a New Era?*

December 1969, again in Paris and Rotterdam in April 1970, and so on. Results of these, and also of direct bilateral conferences between Indonesia and individual creditors were slowly and cumulatively beneficial to the Indonesian economy. A debt moratorium was agreed to initially for 1967 and later extended to 1971 after the USSR, in a November 1966 protocol, also agreed to a moratorium until April 1969, with payments then to be stretched out until 1981. In May 1967, however, Indonesia unilaterally postponed payment on its Soviet debt until April 1970 and shortly was to seek a still further postponement. In the latter half of 1969 Indonesia began developing a German proposal, to be presented to the IGGI later that year, suggesting a conversion of its debt into interest-free liabilities over a thirty-year period. Some IGGI members at their December 1969 meeting meanwhile agreed to permit Indonesia to postpone payment on the US$80 million due in 1970, pending achievement of a long-term debt rescheduling system (announced in April 1970).

Meanwhile the Suharto Government's 3 October 1966 external trade regulations, noted earlier, the enactment of a new Foreign Investment Law in January 1967, and evidence of a new spirit of financial rationalism and realism in the Government's announced policies, also had a sufficiently favourable impact on IGGI members so as to loosen new credit commitments to Indonesia. Thus for 1967 the USA pledged US$65 million in new credits, Japan US$60 million, the Netherlands US$30 million, West Germany US$29 million and other countries, including Australia, the UK, and India together, some US$12 million. The noteworthy new readiness in Dutch financial and commercial circles to invest in or make new loans available to Indonesia was spurred particularly by an Indonesian agreement in 1966 to pay about US$165 million in compensation for Dutch firms and estates taken over during 1957 and 1958. In November 1967 members of IGGI agreed to make a credit of US$325 million available to Indonesia for 1968, US$250 million of which would be extended through the BE system for balance of payment support in the purchase of raw materials, rice, and technical equipment, including spare parts, while the remainder would be applied to the implementation of various State development programmes, including the fishing industry. These new credit grants seemed to be but a prelude to steady annual credit requests by Indonesia at successive IGGI meetings. Shortly after the Rotterdam meeting of the IGGI in April 1968, the Indonesian Government declared that a total of US$270 million in new foreign aid had been pledged (including US$110 million by the US, US$80 million by Japan, US$26.2 million by Holland and US$22.5 million by West Germany, with lesser sums coming from Australia, France, the UK and so on). Additional grants raised IGGI aid for 1968 to US$325 million.

Then, in Scheveningen, in April 1969, some US$490 million was promised for 1969, the US and Japan again contributing the lion's share with US$207 million and US$120 million respectively. But at the IGGI meeting in Amsterdam in December, Indonesia requested its largest annual credit' allocation yet: US$600 million for 1970 and for the first three months of 1971. Included in this figure was a US$140 million food aid request to the US, although most of the desired funds were to be used for the implementation of Indonesia's new Five-Year Development Plan, to be discussed presently. It seemed doubtful at first that by 1971 the US$600 million would have been provided, but it was (President Suharto, on 3 December 1969, after a meeting with US Ambassador Francis Galbraith, publicly expressed the hope that the US would "stand by" in the event that the entire US$600 million aid request was not met). Thus Indonesia has had little cause for complaint. In Paris, on 24 April 1970, Indonesia's principal non-Communist creditor nations in the IGGI group in effect agreed to a repayment scheme, initially drafted by the German financial expert Dr Hermann Abs, providing for an interest-free repayment of an estimated US$900 million in debts over a thirty-year period, beginning in 1972. Shortly before, at the conclusion of the eighth IGGI meeting in Rotterdam, Indonesia's creditors had emphasized their rising confidence in the rupiah, and praised the simplification of foreign exchange, trade and monetary regulations in the country. New and definite aid commitments were also received, ranging from US$140 million pledged by Japan to US$2 million from Belgium. One is bound to observe that presently Indonesia appears to be acquiring foreign financial, commodity and technical assistance — including new credit obligations — at a rate equal to if not faster than in the most irresponsible years of Sukarno's *ekonomi terpimpin* (guided economy). There is also some concern abroad that despite regulatory controls the aid obtained from Western countries may be used, in one way or another, to make payments on Indonesia's huge debt to the USSR.

This Soviet obligation became particularly pressing because, as indicated earlier, the Russians in November 1966 had agreed to a moratorium on Indonesian debt payments, until April 1969. Late in August 1969, a Soviet delegation, headed by V. A. Sergeyev, Deputy Minister for Development and Foreign Economic Relations, arrived in Djakarta to discuss financial problems between the two countries. Though Soviet-Indonesian diplomatic intercourse has not sunk to the nadir to which relations between Peking and Djakarta have now fallen (see chapter VIII), Moscow's relations with the Suharto regime remain somewhat chilly. During the Djakarta talks Indonesia made it clear that it could not begin paying off its Soviet debt and that it not only needed more time but, indeed, would be appreciative of new Soviet credits. The Russians were unenthusiastic and demanded stiff concessions in return, including free entry of Soviet fishing trawlers into Indonesian waters, a proposal which the Indonesians rejected. The talks ended with little accomplished, and the Soviets remained adamant in their refusal to grant significant new credits until an agreement was implemented on Indonesia's repayment of its old debts. Somewhat haphazardly, discussions continued throughout 1970 with the Soviets gradually mellowing.

The diversification of the Indonesian economy — which means in the first instance a development away from the heavy reliance on just a few foreign exchange earners like rubber and petroleum — may well be retarded in the light of continuing foreign investment concentration in primary and extractive production sectors. Disregarding oil for the moment, more than forty-five per cent of Indonesia's export earnings are derived from rubber, for example. But what with the problem of over-aged rubber trees and inadequate replanting, and the competition from synthetics, the country's rubber economy is in a bad way, and rubber exports have fallen from 737,088 tons in 1955 to 663,066 tons in 1966, while receipts have dropped by more than fifty per cent to about US$223 million in the latter year.

Industrial development, though slowly acquiring firmer foundations, was unquestionably harmed at first by the Suharto Government's rigid, anti-inflationary, credit-curbing and stabilization policies. Few up-to-date and accurate statistics are available for the industrial sector, but the following data, culled from the 1968 annual supplement on Indonesia of the Economist Intelligence Unit, and the 1968 year-book of the *Far Eastern Economic Review* are perhaps suggestive. By the end of 1967 many industries were, and had been for several years, working at only from thirty to ten per cent of capacity and sometimes at even less: "Out of 86 pharmaceutical factories, 40 per cent were operating in August 1967 at 10 per cent to 20 per cent of their capacities, 25 per cent had stopped producing, while 35 per cent had closed down completely. No less than 60 per cent of textile industries in the country had stopped operation by October 1967 because imported products retailed cheaper." Foreign exchange shortages for the purchase of required raw materials and spare parts or new equipment, inadequate transport or electric power, and the continuing diversion of domestic capital into more speculative but also more profitable trading ventures, impeded a balanced industrial development, so that "Large and small industry in Indonesia accounts for less than 10 per cent of the national product".

Thus far one cannot be sure whether the influx of private foreign capital since 1966 will in the near future begin to give a significant impetus to industrial development, although in the long run — if present stabilization efforts continue — it is bound to do so. In January 1967 a new foreign capital investment law took effect, detailing the position of foreign corporations, cooperation between national and foreign capital, taxes, resources use (including land), compensation for nationalization and so on. Distinctions are drawn in the law between State capital, native Indonesian (that is national) capital, the capital of co-operatives and foreign capital, and priorities are assigned to each. For example, communications or the armament industry are the exclusive preserve of State capital, while cottage and other small industries are assigned to the co-operative capital sector. Selected areas of mining, estate and other forms of export agriculture, exploitation of forest resources and — in conjunction with national capital — many areas of large industry are typically open to foreign investors. But the strong preference is for joint ventures with national capital, or for production sharing, management sharing, or similar arrangements in which, from the start, domestic resources and Indonesian nationals function in some kind of partnership with the foreign manager/investor. Foreign companies are obliged to "Indonesianize" their personnel as much as possible, and to make personnel upgrading procedures and advanced training available to Indonesian employees. There are special tax benefits, for example exemption from certain company and dividend taxes on profits for the foreign enterprises, at least in the initial stages, and capital transfers abroad in the original foreign currencies are permitted.

On 24 March 1969, *The Djakarta Times* reported that a total of 106 foreign investment projects, with a committed capital outlay of US$365 million, had now been approved (how much of this sum actually has been invested thus far, however, is a matter of speculation). Investments in the oil industry, including exploration expenditures, came to an additional US$200 million. The US$365 million figure did not include the initial capital input of some fifteen foreign banks, but did include a US$158 million commitment of three mining companies: Freeport Sulphur (US), engaged in copper exploration in West Irian; Billiton N.V. (Holland), concerned with tin exploitation in the Riau islands; and

International Nickel Company of Canada, which is mining nickel in Malili, Sulawesi. *Inter alia* it might be mentioned that Indonesia is fast catching up with Canada, the world's biggest nickel producer, in the mining of this mineral. Indonesian nickel production rose from 45,528 tons (pure nickel) in 1963 to 240,725 tons in 1968. Canada's production in the same period went from 219,941 tons to 265,000 tons. Some twenty foreign companies with a total capital investment of US$86 million were reportedly engaged in forest exploitation in Sulawesi and Kalimantan, while manufacturing industries, involving some forty-seven projects, accounted for a combined investment of about US$72 million. Apart from mining, oil and banking investments, US firms provided the largest investment commitment (US$42 million), followed by Japan (US$20 million), the Netherlands and Hong Kong (both US$17 million).

On 6 July 1970, Antara reported from Djakarta that the amount of intended foreign investment in Indonesia had, by the middle of 1970, reached over US$1 billion, but that the actual amount of disbursed investment was only 10 per cent of the planned figure thus far. There were but few foreign investment projects that had already spent more than US$10 or US$15 million, and most projects continued to be in mining, forestry and some processing industry.

The Indonesian Government has been comparatively swift in reaching decisions about foreign capital investment applications: forty-three out of sixty applications were accepted in 1967 alone, for example. But there remain problems with the leasing of land for industrial sites (land cannot be bought by a foreign investor and the chaos in cadastral records and surveys greatly delays a clear determination of land rights and titles), with the acquisition of local work permits, and with time-consuming, bureaucratic assessments of the relative impact which a foreign venture may or may not have on local industry and manpower. Some Western industrialists, unused to Indonesian ways, quickly become disgusted with the widely accepted practices of bribes, "key-money", and other gratuities expected of almost any would-be foreign investor. Even so, there have been significant long-term investment plans by foreign capital, for examples, the US$48 million South Korean forest exploitation projects and the US$257 million Japanese land development project for the production of rice and corn in Lampung district of South Sumatra. But again, only fractions of these sums have been invested thus far, however, and hence their totals are not included in the earlier-mentioned US$365 million figure. It remains to be seen whether current foreign investment regulations in Indonesia are doing enough to encourage the influx of capital into other than primary and raw material development projects.

Meanwhile, Indonesia is on the threshold of an oil boom. The major foreign-owned producers — Stanvac, Shell and Caltex — are presently reaching new production heights. Pertamina, the Indonesian State petroleum company, through which most new exploration ventures must be channelled, has entered into off-shore exploration agreements with Refican (Refining Associate of Canada), IIAPCO (Independent Indonesian American Petroleum Company), Japex (Japanese Petroleum Exploration), and others. In 1969 alone new oil investments in Indonesia exceeded US$100 million, while US$130 million and US$160 million are expected to be invested in 1970 and 1971 respectively. Huge off-shore "blocks" of oil reserves, comprising in effect much of the Java Sea between Kalimantan and Java, as well as the waters between Kalimantan and Sumatra, are said to be ready for exploitation. But exploitation costs are likely to be very high. And the production-sharing contracts between Pertamina and the foreign companies, providing for a sixty-five to thirty-five per cent division of profits in Pertamina's favour, and containing a clause which reserves management of operations to Pertamina, are considered by some to be too risky, at least for the time being. Continuing successful strikes may well alter this reluctance on the part of some foreign concerns, however. Off the North Sumatran coast, where Japex has been exploring, a recent well tested out at a yield of more than 5,000 barrels a day. Late in November 1969, two American companies, Union Oil and Jeny Oil, were reportedly ready to start exploring off Sumatra's west coast, around Nias and the Mentawei islands, as the oil-boom fever meanwhile began to spread. Oil production averages are generally showing steady gains, as the following data suggest.

TABLE IV

Crude Petroleum Production
in Indonesia
1964-9
(monthly averages in thousand metric tons)

First Quarter 1964	1,865
,, ,, 1965	1,994
,, ,, 1966	1,968
,, ,, 1967	2,068
,, ,, 1968	2,293
,, ,, 1969	2,782

Source: *Quarterly Economic Reviews* on Indo-nesia of the Economist Intelligence Unit

In July 1970, Pertamina's director, Ibnu Sutowo, in a reference to the fruitful partnership between Pertamina and foreign oil concerns, made particular mention of the Far East Oil Trading Company of Tokyo. Ibnu Sutowo declared that since their co-operation Indonesian crude oil exports to Japan had risen from 122,000 kilolitres in 1965 to 4.1 million kilolitres in 1969, and was estimated to reach 7 million kilolitres in 1970. Sinclair/Atlantic Richfield Company, meanwhile, in their Java Sea operations have brought in four wells, one of which is producing 900,000 cubic feet of gas a day, while the other three range from 1,914 to 4,582 barrels a day. Pertamina seems always ready for relatively unique and individually adjusted exploration and production agreements (one source of the continuous criticism of Ibnu Sutowo's management). Thus, in February 1970, the American oil magnate Wendell Phillips revealed a multi-million-dollar agreement with Pertamina. Phillips who, reportedly, had already paid half a million dollars for "technical information", has agreed to pay a "bonus" of one million dollars when his wells produce 50,000 barrels a day, another million-dollar "bonus" when they start producing 75,000 barrels a day, and a two-million-dollar "bonus" when daily production reaches 100,000. He has also committed himself to a US$17.5 million development expenditure on production projects and has agreed to consider the building of schools, hospitals and other welfare facilities for Indonesian workers. What returns Philips expects is not known, but his agreement with Pertamina suggests something of the scope of present contracts.

On 31 December 1968, the Indonesian Cabinet approved the *Rentjana Pembangunan Lima Tahun* 1969-70/1973-74, or Five-Year Development Plan, usually called *Repelita* by acronym-minded Indonesians. On 1 April 1969, at the same time as the start of the new fiscal year, implementation of the new plan formally began. Drafted by *Bappenas,* Indonesia's National Planning Board, *Repelita* concentrates on the development of three critically important areas — agriculture (particularly food production) infrastructure (that is power, communications and transport), and mining and industry. Some of the principal production targets of the plan are set forth in Table V.

In the communications sector *Repelita* envisages reconstruction of some 11,000 kilometres of roads throughout the country, as well as the improvement of an additional 6,000 kilometres, and extensive construction and repair of the railway network. About 40 million cubic metres is to be dredged out of ports and rivers. Extensive modernization is also envisaged in domestic air traffic and air terminals. Information campaigns on behalf of

TABLE V

Some Production Targets of the Five-Year Development Plan

	1969-70	1973-4	% increase
Rice			
million tons	10.52	15.42	46.5
Rubber			
thousand tons	104	132	27
Petroleum			
million bbls	293	440	50.1
Tin			
metric tons	16.16	19.4	19.9
Copra (Government estates)			
thousand tons	1.1	1.5	36
Sugar (estates)			
thousand tons	677	907	35
Bauxite			
thousand tons	1,000	1,200	20
Corn			
million tons	3.4	4.2	26
Textiles			
million metres	450	900	100
Phosphates			
thousand tons	18 (1971)	168	833
Electricity			
thousand kw	659	1,084	64
Paper			
thousand tons	16	167	940
Cement			
thousand tons	600	1,650	175
Fertilizer			
thousand tons	65	572	790

Source: Bappenas, Five-Year Development Plan

family planning are to be intensified, and 1,200 family planning clinics are to be established by 1974. A new campaign, which is to be initiated in Java, to eradicate malaria has also begun, and public health centres throughout the country are to be expanded.

Total planned expenditures of *Repelita* are Rp.1,420 billion. Principal allocations of this sum under the plan are as follows (end of 1968 prices):

Agriculture and Irrigation	Rp.395 billion
Mining and Industry	Rp.380 billion
Electric power	Rp.100 billion
Communications and Tourism	Rp.265 billion

Rural Development	Rp.50 billion
Health and Social Welfare	Rp.172 billion
Defence and Security	Rp.28 billion
Miscellaneous projects	Rp.30 billion

Bappenas chairman Professor Widjojo Nitisastro declared at the close of December 1968 that with *Repelita* Indonesia would see the end of rice imports and that at the successful conclusion of the plan Indonesia's export market would be worth some US$800 million.

It is evident that meeting *Repelita*'s costs depends heavily on massive financing from abroad. Foreign aid of all categories is expected to provide Rp.833 billion or nearly 59 per cent of the total Rp.1,420 billion to be expended under the plan, while anticipated foreign investments of Rp.200 billion comprise an additional 14.1 per cent. Total domestic Indonesian sources thus amount to only Rp.387 billion (including a projected Rp.66 billion in domestic investments) or 27.3 per cent of the needed funds. For 1969-70 an income of only Rp.161 billion is expected for the benefit of the plan, but this will hopefully increase to Rp.404 billion by 1973-4, *Repelita*'s last year (above data are all at 1968 prices). As the plan itself accelerates, domestic bank savings and direct investments may well increase with growing public confidence. But even so the magnitude of the sums expected from foreign quarters raises as much of a question about the plan's realism as do some of its production targets, for example, the projected 27 per cent increase in Indonesia's rubber output.

By the end of 1969, with *Repelita* only half a year old, the Indonesian press seemed to have already told more than its normal quota of problem stories about the plan's implementation. As early as the close of July 1969 President Suharto took note of public criticisms that the plan was failing. According to *Indonesia Raya* of 28 July 1969, Suharto conceded that there had been delays in getting *Repelita* started, but he added: "How is it possible to say the plan has failed while development has been taking place for only three months and there is still a period of four years and nine months ahead?" Complaints of bureaucratic bottlenecks in processing fund authorizations for development projects have continued undiminished, however, in subsequent months. On 3 September 1969, *Angkatan Bersendjata* complained editorially that "Too much paper has been used already to explain the meaning of the Five-Year Development Plan", and yet, the paper argued, popular ignorance was preventing efficacious implementation of the plan as much as bureaucratic bungling and arbitrariness.

There are other obstacles. Surely one of the most serious remains official corruption and the public's thousand-and-one ways in evading the law. The American correspondent, Robert Keatley, has given one telling illustration in *The Wall Street Journal* of 21 June 1969:

> Bad management upsets economic policies in many ways. For example, in the nearby city-state of Singapore, a special water-front section has been fenced off for Indonesian traders, whose motor vessels chug in daily with cargo holds bulging. For the return haul they load such freight as cement, refrigerators, or old American newspapers which shopkeepers use to wrap rice. Small sailing boats also cross the straits from Indonesia, bartering their loads of scrap iron or fresh fish for watches and radios that fetch fancy prices back home.
>
> The two-way trade is brisk and organized; some $350 million worth took place last year, according to Singapore authorities, and the volume is rising. But from Indonesia's viewpoint, it is highly distressing: these traders are all smugglers who sneak goods in and out by bribing officials to protect them from the perils of law enforcement.
>
> This illegal trade costs Indonesia about $50 million yearly in export taxes (equal to this year's expected budget deficit) and probably more in import duties. It keeps scarce foreign exchange out of the central banking system ... And the high payoffs involved prevent General Suharto's subordinates from taking reforms seriously, however much it might help the national economy.

Writing in the March 1970 issue of the *Bulletin of Indonesian Economic Studies*, C. G. F. Simkin estimated that between 1958 and 1962 smuggled rubber averaged to about 76,000 tons a year, or more than a tenth of officially recorded shipments. Differential exchange rates for different types of imports and exports, as well as differential tax rates on what is traded, the old Bonus Export scheme, and bureaucratic mismanagement no less than inflation, all kept incentives to smuggling at a high peak. A reversal of the trend is some considerable distance away.

The structural difficulties in the Indonesian economy are not likely to be overcome by *Repelita*. Are targeted increases in food production likely to bring much benefit, for example, so long as the tenancy and/or land fragmentation problems, and their train of peasant indebtedness and thinly disguised feudal dependence in rural social relationships, especially in Central and West Java, remain unsolved? Is Suharto likely to press for land redistribution under the "basic agrarian law" of September 1960? It seems improbable. Yet "land reform" remains in many respects an even more pressing problem than production. Land tenure in particular shows ominous concentrations. Recent surveys have revealed conditions such as the village of Gelung (Paron district, East Java province) where 2.2 per cent of the population, the principal landowners, control 27 per cent of the village land area, while 62 per cent of the population, described as labourers, hold no land at all. In Tjibodas village, West Java, another survey has shown that 1.5 per cent of the population controls nearly half of the arable village land, while 44 per cent of all Tjibodas families hold no land at all. In Tjaruj (Sidaredja district, Central Java province) landlord families, who account for only 0.25 per cent of the total population, reportedly possess 4.3 per cent of the total village land area, having average holdings of 32.1 hectares of land, while 44 per cent of the total population consists of village labourers without any land. The significance of Java's rural problems in the PKI's recent resurgence has already been noted (see chapter V).

Agrarian legislation in 1960 authorized the Government to redistribute land held in excess of certain maxima and upon proper compensation to landowners. The size of permitted land-holdings was made dependent on prevailing population density. For example in areas with a density of over 400 persons per square kilometre, maximum family holdings were 5 hectares of *sawah* (irrigated land) and 6 hectares of unflooded fields, while in regions with a density of 50 persons per square kilometre or less, holdings of 15 hectares of *sawah* and 20 hectares of dry fields would be permitted. Implementation of this land reform legislation occurred but slowly, partly because of cadastral confusion, effective resistance of landlords, and partisan political manoeuvring. The Indonesian Communist Party's drive to unilaterally redistribute land during 1964-5 created widespread opposition and gave the entire land reform programme a bad name. With the rise of *Orba*, many landlords, especially in Central and East Java, were often successful in re-acquiring previously distributed lands through various legal and extra-legal means. Special "land reform courts" ceased to function. Even so, one authoritative estimate, made by Professor E. Utrecht, notes that between 1962 and 1968 probably a million hectares of land were redistributed to some one million families through the land reform programme. Whether this average of one additional hectare of land made available to each family is a significant step in the structural improvement of Indonesian peasant agriculture, or will, for example, have an important effect on the output of staple crops, must remain doubtful. Meanwhile, there is marked concern in the Suharto Government to raise estate agricultural production by maximizing efficiency, introduction of new scientific cultivation and management methods, and reorganization of leadership. As a result of this concern, for example, Agriculture Minister Tojob Hadiwidjaja announced in July 1970 that the number of State-owned plantation companies had been reduced from 102 to only 28. Increasingly, foreign operational control is permitted again in the estate agricultural field, as part of the new hospitality to foreign capital investment — but with what effect on food production?

Is a really drastic reform in the over-bureaucratized structure of government services, and their numerous impediments to a more free and more efficient deployment of enterprise, foreseeable? Few who know Indonesia would say yes, though it cannot be denied that there is some tinkering around the edges of the problem. At government estates, in the Garuda airline, and in other public services, there has been some personnel retrenchment, some of it prompted ostensibly by a desire to remove *Gestapu*/PKI sympathizers. In some cases significant pensions and severance payments were granted. D. H. Penny and Dahlan Thalib, writing in the March 1969 *Bulletin of Indonesian Economic Studies*, note, for example, the recent case of some 4,000 dismissals in the State plantation system, involving a total severance expenditure on the part of the Government of no less than Rp.700 million, with individual payments ranging from about Rp.30,000 to as high as Rp.2 million per employee! "With interest rates in the private capital market at 9 per cent per month or more, ex-employees receiving payments of Rp.100,000 or more could for a time live as rentiers," Penny and Thalib remark. "For a time", perhaps, yes — but it seems improbable that the Indonesian Government will long continue to tackle its personnel redundancy problem with such generosity, even if it had the funds.

Meanwhile, Indonesia's excess manpower problem threatens to become more, not less, acute. The Economist Intelligence Unit in one of its quarterly report (1969, no. 1) on Indonesia, points to the prediction of the Indonesian Government's own manpower department that in spite of the Five-Year Development Plan unemployment will rise during 1969-73 to approximately 12 per cent of the labour force of 44.6 million, and that over 11 million will be semi-employed. By 1973, and the time of *Repelita*'s end, Indonesia's labour force will have grown to 48.4 million, but employment will have grown by only 2.5-2.9 per cent. So that, relatively, unemployment and underemployment will have increased at the close of the Five-Year Plan period! Even by 1973 only 12 per cent of the whole Indonesian labour force is likely to be employed in industry.

In this connection one must note that dysfunction in the Indonesian educational system also continue. Despite the current government stress on the importance of middle-level technical-vocational training orientated toward development, preference for more traditional academic programmes, strongly related to white-collar employment expectations, persists unabated. Anomalies abound. For example, on the one hand, there is a surfeit of employable graduates of teacher training institutions: in January 1969 alone about 12,000 such graduates were unable to find jobs in the public school system because of insufficient provisions in the government budget for school expansion, while by December 1969 hundreds of teachers were reported unemployed from the Sulawesi area alone. In May 1970, Hidayat, chairman of the association of teacher training colleges, declared that a total of 20,000 teacher training college graduates were unemployed. On 21 May 1970 Antara also reported that 21 to 30 per cent of the Indonesian people were still illiterate, although in 1964 the Government had declared that illiteracy had been wiped out. Inadequate budgets clearly impede further schooling for many. Education Minister Mashuri declared in early January 1970 that the 204 billion rupiahs earmarked in the 1969-70 national budget for education was deficient by more than 50 per cent considering the needs of school expansion and rehabilitation. Some 75 per cent of all elementary school graduates in Indonesia "are forced to drop out" of further schooling and find themselves jobs "because of a lack of secondary schools", according to the Elementary Education Directorate of the Education and Cultural Affairs Department in April 1970. As Indonesian teachers' federations have pointed out, in 1968 there were 11.8 million pupils in school and under the care of only 320,569 primary school teachers; this meant that more than 4.5 million children of primary school age were without regular formal education due to lack of teachers and facilities. In 1959, one might add, there were 7.4 million primary pupils, with 182,425 teachers, leaving at least 2.5 million children untaught. University graduates, also in such fields as medicine, veterinary medicine, and engineering, are increasingly experiencing employment difficulties — in large part because of government service preferences. In some respects the problem of university graduate unemployment in Indonesia is as serious — also in its unstabilizing political and social effects — as that encountered in India and the Philippines. Of the more than 18,000 who in 1968 graduated from Indonesia's public and private universities (including 5,500 in technical and scientific fields), not more than 35 per cent can now expect to find work commensurate with their training. Yet in 1969 there were nearly 115,000 students in all areas of higher education, and the pressure here continues to grow as it does in all types of secondary school with their nearly 1.6 million students.

The principal, long-term dynamics of Indonesia's economy is the country's rapid population growth:

TABLE VI

Growth of Population in Indonesia
1920-70
(in thousands)

Year	Java and Madura	Total Indonesia
1920	34,977	49,344
1930	41,718	60,727
1940	48,416	70,476
1950	50,456	77,207
1960	60,976	94,576
1970 (est.)	72,000	113,000

Source: Central Bureau of Statistics.
N.B. In 1870 the population of Java and Madura was estimated at 16.2 million, Indonesia's total population at 23 million.

There is evidence that the rate of growth of the population is accelerating. Before 1950, estimated growth rates were usually under 2 per cent per annum, but in the following two decades annual rates of 2.3-2.8 per cent came to be more commonly accepted. Since the middle nineteen-sixties, some informed estimates have risen to 3 per cent and even higher. The growth rate is not uniform; in Java, where around 65 per cent of the population is concentrated, it is probably significantly higher than in portions of eastern Indonesia. Still, the growth prospect is a frightening one. Some demographic experts on Indonesia have pointed out, for example, that in a century and a half Java's population alone, at a growth rate of 2.5 per cent (possibly too low an estimate), will exceed that of the 1966 world population total! Nothing, perhaps, could put the urgency of Indonesia's future economic development in better perspective than this calculation.

Yet, clearly, Indonesia is not and, for years to come, will not be able to achieve a rate of economic growth adequate by itself to meet her population explosion. Two additional measures, therefore, have been commonly proposed — transmigration and extensive family planning. By the former is meant Government-encouraged movements of people, from the more densely populated rice-growing sectors of Java to colonization areas on the other Indonesian islands, particularly the Lampung districts and the other parts of South Sumatra. Despite initial, spectacular

178

increases in the number of migrants, and notwithstanding various grandiose migration schemes especially after World War II, transmigration cannot be considered as meeting even remotely Java's population problem. From 1933, when there were 751 migrants, through 1940 (52,208 migrants), 1959 (46,096), 1964 (24,390), to 1968 (25,000 — estimated), it is unlikely that the total number of those who annually left Java under the auspices of the Government's Transmigration Service exceeded 500,000 — but Java's population in that same period grew by more than fifty times that number! Other schemes of the Transmigration Service to transport some two million people between 1956 and 1960, and yet another plan to transport some 390,000 families, an estimated 1.5 million people, between 1961 and 1968 (the period of Indonesia's largely still-born Eight-Year Development Plan), have remained illusory.

While the present *Repelita* makes provision for continued transmigration, it is clear that Indonesia's economic planners do not set great store by it as a significant answer to the country's development problems. The cost and technical difficulties of recruitment and transportation of the migrants, and of the preparation of new colonization reception areas, as well as the cultural and psychological problems in persuading the needed large numbers of Javanese to move permanently to a non-Javanese environment, have all been impediments. Then, too, the voluntary influx of people (an estimated four million between 1950 and 1965 alone) from other islands to Java has been considerable, while voluntary, unsponsored emigration of Javanese in that period is about half that figure. Increasing emphasis in official policies since 1965 on self-help and self-reliance among migrants (*transmigrasi swakarja*), both among those already settled and among new arrivals, has thus far had but ambivalent success: reported initial increases in the number of migrants have been offset again by later declines.

Since 1957 there has been a family planning organization in Indonesia, in which, before *Gestapu,* Mrs Subandrio, wife of the former Minister, played a leading role. Though birth control information and an assortment of contraceptive equipment were quietly made available, in a number of clinics and hospitals, usually in the larger cities, to those desiring them, in much of the Sukarno era birth control was not greatly in favour. For one thing, Muslim opinion was (and still is) sharply divided about the matter, while influential minorities, like the Catholics, were opposed to all but the rhythm method of contraception. At first, Sukarno himself was at various times quoted as implying, or saying, that birth control, having contributed to immorality in the West, would also harm the "unspoiled" Indonesian people, and that the solution to the country's population problem lay not in family planning but in greater productivity of the land. In 1963, however, Sukarno appeared to have become somewhat more flexible. Additional clinics were made available to the Indonesian family planning organization through aid from international bodies, and between 1963 and 1968, according to a 15 March 1968 Reuter's despatch from Djakarta, some 50,000 people had been given information and/or treated in about 75 clinics, while the association claimed that "several thousand" intra-uterine "loop" devices had been made use of.

The Suharto Government has moved slowly but deliberately forward in the family planning field, and, as already indicated, the number of family planning clinics is to be increased under *Repelita* to 1,200. Already in 1967 the Indonesian Planned Parenthood Association, succeeding previous organizational efforts in this field, had been formally established and by the end of that year training of health workers had been greatly accelerated. In 1968 a Government National Family Planning Institute was created and a year later the Health Ministry provided additional personnel, funds and further co-ordination to operating clinics throughout the country. By the end of 1970 the Government planned to have more than 800 clinics functioning in the country and to have at least three million people engaged in family planning. The Suharto Government, mindful of Orthodox Muslim and Roman Catholic opposition, continues to move cautiously, however. On 29 June 1970, when installing a new advisory council and co-ordinating chairman for the national family planning campaign, President Suharto stressed that planned parenthood was not being enforced, but had to arise naturally "from the consciousness of the community itself" for the benefit of future generations. On the other hand, Islamic modernism in Indonesia has been hospitable to the idea of birth control, and members of the PMI, the new Muslim party, have urged in Parliament that, according to Islamic authoritative writ, man has a religious obligation to ameliorate his life and that family planning can assist him in doing so. Time will also obviously be needed in persuading both the urban and rural poor, among whom family planning is particularly needed, to avail themselves of the facilities of the new planned parenthood clinics. There is evidence that in the larger towns growing numbers of the poor are in fact beginning to make use of these facilities. But few demographers expect a significant down-turn in the possibly 3 per cent (and up) current growth rate of the Indonesian population before the end of the nineteen-seventies, if then. Production meanwhile simply is not keeping pace with population growth. According to *Warta Harian*, 2 March 1970, the Central Bureau of Statistics recently calculated that the average per capita increase in gross domestic product of Indonesia during the period 1960-68 was only 0.2 per cent!

During 1970-71 Indonesia seemed to be increasingly caught between the potentially revitalizing effects of huge capital injections and the drag of steady population growth and structural economic impediments. At the tenth IGGI conference in Amsterdam, in April 1971, Indonesia received a new US$640 million credit for the 1971-72 year. The new credits pushed total Indonesian indebtedness incurred during the post-Sukarno era well beyond the obligation of more than US$2 billion acquired in Sukarno's term of office. The tangible benefits of this rapidly mounting new burden of debts remained visible to only a relative few, although there is no denying that inflationary pressures continued to be effectively contained (taking September 1966 as the equivalent of 100, the Djakarta cost of living index, including food, fuel, and textiles, rose from 535 in January 1969 to 607 in May 1970, and to 622 by end November 1970) compared to the last years of the Sukarno presidency. Huge imports of rice continued to be necessary, however, and at the close of December 1970, the US agreed to ship another 110,000 metric tons of rice to Indonesia, under the US food aid programme. The long-term political implications of the investment race in Indonesia began to give growing concern. The daily *Suluh Marhaen* pointed out on 8 February 1971 that six US oil companies, contracting to work with Pertamina, now control oil-producing regions in Indonesia aggregating an area of 192,200 square kilometres. Characteristically, the concern over foreign economic domination assumed, during 1970-71, an increasingly anti-Chinese character. This was the so-called *tjukong* issue (the system of entrepreneurial backing by "foreign" money, that is silent Chinese business partners), and despite Government warnings against anti-Chinese sentiment, the role of "alien domestic" (largely Chinese) capital in the *Orba* economy seemed to be becoming increasingly a nationalist question, reviving the bitterness of the nineteen-fifties.

A growing realization of the long-term implications of the Suharto regime's investment and credit policies, coupled with the small evidence of significant improvements in the living conditions of the mass of Indonesians, may well prove to be decisive in determining *Orba*'s future.

CHAPTER EIGHT

Old Principles and New Directions in Foreign Policy

SINCE the fall of Sukarno, Indonesian diplomacy has undergone some radical changes but it also has repeatedly affirmed pre-*Gestapu* policy principles. Generally, the concept of an "active and independent foreign policy", which during most of the Sukarno era guided Indonesia's international relations, has been retained in the *Orba* period. Relations with People's China have deteriorated just short of a formal rupture of diplomatic ties, but this has not meant significant movement toward a recognition of the Chinese Government on Taiwan. Formal diplomatic relations with the Democratic Republic of Vietnam in Hanoi continue, but there has been a distinct chill. The confrontation of Malaysia dramatically ended by the middle of 1966, as did the PKI-encouraged Sukarnoist rhetoric about Indonesia's "revolutionary role" throughout Southeast Asia. But in milder terms Indonesia remains committed to decolonization throughout the world and to the principle of "Asian solutions for Asian problems". Djakarta has also participated in and strongly encourages new patterns of Southeast Asian regional co-operation, such as ASEAN (Association of Southeast Asian Nations, founded in Bangkok in 1967 and comprising Thailand, Malaysia, Singapore, Indonesia and the Philippines). But it has resisted the notion that ASEAN should be transformed into a formal collective security system. In general, Indonesia is also firmly opposed to the concluding of military alliances with powers outside the region, although it has been prepared to develop a framework of limited military co-operation with its Malaysian neighbour in combating border insurgents in Kalimantan. Quite dramatic since the advent of Suharto has been Indonesia's hospitality to private British, Dutch, American and Belgian foreign investors, in sharp contrast to the period 1959-65. But, again, this new accommodation of Western capital is not unqualified, and in influential Indonesian business and political circles today the return of "the age of investment", as Sukarno used to call it contemptuously, continues to raise fundamental questions about the future character of the Indonesian economy.

Of all course alterations in Indonesian foreign policy since Sukarno's slide from power the rapid transformation of Sino-Indonesian friendship into bitter hostility has perhaps been the most noteworthy. Particularly since early 1963 and the confrontation of Malaysia, Indonesia and People's China had appeared to be moving steadily toward closer co-operation, as meanwhile the Peking-orientated PKI rapidly rose in influence on the domestic Indonesian scene. Indonesia's formal relinquishing of its membership in the United Nations, in early January 1965, was part of this new *rapprochement* with People's China, and it was followed on 28 January 1965 by a wide-ranging agreement signed in Peking by the two Governments. In this agreement the Communist Chinese and Indonesian Governments declared that they shared the view of a polarization of the political forces in the world between the "imperialist" or "old established" forces (*Oldefo* in Sukarnoist vocabularly) on the one hand, and the "anti-imperialist", or "revolutionary", and "new emerging" forces (*Nefo*) on the other. No "peaceful co-existence" between these two camps was held to be possible. Malaysia was described as a "tool for the suppression of the revolutionary movements of the people of Malaya, Singapore, Sarawak and Sabah", as well as "a military base which poses a direct threat to Indonesia, a military base for aggression in Southeast Asia". Peking expressed "resolute support" both for the Indonesians and for "other Southeast Asian countries" in their "revolutionary struggle against US and British imperialists".

During much of 1963-5 Indonesia had also begun to act as a kind of front man for the Chinese Communist diplomatic and political offensive in the African-Asian world as a whole. This was particularly apparent at the African-Asian Conference in Moshi, Tanganyika, in February 1963, and at the Afro-Asian People's Solidarity Organization Conference in Nicosia, Cyprus, in September 1963, where Indonesian delegates informally served as articulators or amplifiers of Chinese Communist policy interests. From 1963 on, until the *Gestapu* affair, Indonesia and People's China also seemed to be collaborating toward the creation of a number of African-Asian special interest groups, like the African-Asian Journalists' Association, which functioned as so many megaphones for the Maoist ideology and strategy in the developing countries. There is, in retrospect, also little doubt that Peking was well aware of the PKI's plans for the *Gestapu* coup and that it secretly sent quantities of arms to the Indonesian Communists in the weeks before Untung attempted to seize power.

Under the circumstances it was probably inevitable that Indonesian anger over the *Gestapu* plot should also be directed toward People's China and toward the Chinese community in Indonesia generally. Popular rumours and official reports of continuing Chinese subversive burrowing in Indonesia fanned such anger ever higher throughout 1966-7. Early in March 1966, for example, student demonstrators, ransacking the Foreign Ministry offices in Djakarta, reportedly discovered documents revealing an agreement between Subandrio (then still Foreign Minister) and Chinese Premier Chou En-lai, signed at an unspecified time well after the *Gestapu* affair. According to this agreement, a new attempt would be made by Indonesian "progressives" to eliminate anti-Communist military leaders in Indonesia, while in return Peking would continue to give support to Sukarno's favourite project, the Conference of New Emerging Forces, which he hoped would rival the United Nations.

The Indonesian press, in the second half of 1966, also began to carry a steady stream of reports describing how Peking had been giving refuge to and was in fact fast becoming the centre of dissident Indonesians who were said to be plotting and training for a new Communist drive in Indonesia. Prominent in this group were Djawoto, former Indonesian Ambassador to Peking, who shortly emerged as the secretary-general of the Peking-based African-Asian Journalists' Association; Sukrisno former Indonesian Ambassador to Hanoi; and Muhammad Ali Hanafiah, former Indonesian Ambassador to Ceylon. By November 1966 Antara claimed that "an estimated 700 *Gestapu*/PKI fugitives from Indonesia are now gathered in Peking and directing a political guerilla warfare against the New Order in their home country". Among these 700 were such prominent PKI Politburo figures as Jusuf Adjitorop, who in 1969 was to become identified in the Peking media as the "Leader of the Delegation of the Central Committee of the Indonesian Communist Party". Among them were also Indonesian students, some of whom had managed to find their way to Communist China from the USSR and Soviet bloc countries. Inflammatory anti-*Orba* statements were soon being issued by the publications of an Indonesian Students' Organization in China (*Persatuan Peladjar Indonesia di Tiongkok*). "The presence of Chinese at nearly all the arrests of Communist-*Gestapu* leaders", Antara reported in January 1967, "gives the evidence that Communist China is still launching its acts of intervention in Indonesian internal affairs." In March and May 1967, Indonesian Foreign Minister Adam Malik charged Peking with providing military training to "hundreds of Indonesians staying in China", for the purpose of launching a campaign of political and economic sabotage when they returned to Indonesia.

Amidst the arrests of dozens of Indonesian Chinese on charges of having financed underground PKI activity, *Angkatan Bersendjata*, the chief armed forces newspaper, stated on 17 April 1967 that the Chinese in Indonesia wanted the PKI to come back to power. On 22 August 1967 Antara reported that Communist Chinese agents were infiltrating into Indonesia through Sulawesi and even via Tandjong Priok harbour. The accelerating guerilla insurgency of the PGRS and the increasing suspicion of the Chinese in Western Kalimantan during this period (see chapter V) further amplified for the Indonesian public the apparent danger to national security presented by Peking.

Meanwhile the campaign of relatively minor abuse, insults and brutality against the three million Chinese in Indonesia (about half of whom are considered Indonesian citizens), during the latter weeks of 1965 and early months of 1966, erupted in subsequent months, and particularly in the first half of 1967, into violent anti-Chinese harassment, pogroms, rioting, looting and destruction of Chinese dwellings and business establishments, principally in Java and Sumatra. Scores of Chinese were killed in these incidents, and Indonesian police or Army troops often seemed unable or unwilling to contain the depradations of rampaging Indonesian mobs (especially youths). Under the pretext of searching for hidden weapons or prohibited Communist literature, gangs of Indonesian youths in several areas in Java during April and May 1967 broke into the homes and shops of Chinese. The Sino-Indonesian Dual Nationality Treaty originally signed in 1955 (exchange of letters of ratification did not occur until 1960), which had given the Chinese in Indonesia a citizenship option, to all intents and purposes, had become a dead letter by November 1966, and early in November 1968, the Suharto Government introduced a bill into the Indonesian Parliament formally repealing this treaty. Perhaps as many as half a million Chinese who had not yet completed their formal naturalization (also because of endless bureaucratic delays) found themselves virtually stateless persons in an environment of hostile suspicion and official arbitrariness and brutality.

Toward the close of 1967 the anti-Chinese pogrom began to taper off, however, as at the same time new citizenship and "mass civic assimilation" procedures — marked by "Indonesianization" of Chinese names — began to open new avenues of legitimization. But as late as November 1967 Indonesian authorities announced the arrest of several members of a new underground PKI military

185

force, "established with the assistance of the People's Republic of China", and in chapter V attention has already been called to repeated charges by Indonesian Army spokesmen that Chinese in Central and East Java were financing the reorganization of the PKI during 1968.

Well before this time, diplomatic relations between Peking and Djakarta had already been strained to the breaking point. In early October 1965, the Chinese refusal to fly their embassy flag in Djakarta at half mast in mourning for the six Indonesian generals, who had been killed by the *Gestapu* plotters, had heightened tensions. In countering Indonesian protests the Chinese said that they only flew their embassy flags at half mast when a head of state or prominent local Communist party leader died. On 18 October 1965 the New China News Agency charged that Indonesian military had broken into and sacked a Chinese Government commercial centre in Djakarta, and on 4 November 1965 there was issued the first of a long row of official Chinese diplomatic protests, complaining of hostile acts against Chinese nationals, destruction of Chinese properties, insults to the Chinese flag and diplomatic personnel, and so on. The Chinese news media commenced their ceaseless barrage of reports and comments on the humiliations being endured by Indonesian Chinese, on the spreading anti-Communist pogrom and on the rapid deterioration in Sino-Indonesian relations. Already by 4 December 1965 Indonesian authorities announced that the last remaining Chinese Communist technicians had been withdrawn and that Peking had stopped delivery of spare parts and other equipment in connection with the construction of a cotton spinning mill in West Java. By March 1966, the Djakarta office of the New China News Agency was closed, and after a mob had stormed into the Chinese Embassy in a mass demonstration on 12 April 1966, Peking warned that "the Indonesian Government is pushing relations between the two countries to the verge of a complete split".

Whether this warning had its effect, or whether other domestic problems, including continuing efforts to demote Sukarno and to bring his close collaborators to trial, pre-occupied *Orba*'s leaders is hard to say; in any case there was something of a lull in the Sino-Indonesian verbal war during the latter half of 1966, even though the anti-Chinese pogrom in the country continued without let-up. In the United Nations' General Assembly, Indonesian representative Ruslan Abdulgani found it possible to say in December 1966 that Indonesia, while deploring People's China's "change of attitude" toward her, would nevertheless continue to support the seating of the Communist Chinese in the UN. However, in some military as well as political circles increasingly open hostility toward Peking was reflected in demands (like the one made in February 1967 by Husein Kartasasmita, chairman of the Indonesian Parliament's defence and foreign affairs commission) for an Indonesian adhesion to a new regional Southeast Asian defence pact "to curb Communist invasion from People's China". Still, despite reciprocal expulsion of a few members of Chinese and Indonesian Embassies early in 1967, Indonesia's Foreign Minister Malik insisted that Indonesia would preserve her diplomatic relations with People's China "unless the Chinese desire the opposite".

The continuing campaign in the Chinese media against the "naked Fascist dictatorship" of Suharto, spurred by the plight of Chinese nationals, was having its effect on Indonesian parliamentary opinion, however. In the middle of June 1967, the Indonesian Parliament passed a resolution urging that "firm and positive steps" be taken concerning Sino-Indonesian diplomatic relations, including, if necessary, the severance of diplomatic ties. Malik replied that "the Government would try hard to meet the wish of the people", but pleaded that time was needed. In his message to the nation on the occasion of the 17 August 1967 Independence Day, Suharto accused Peking of complicity in *Gestapu* and of continuing subversion in Indonesia, but also counselled patience and in effect requested "understanding" on the part of those seeking an end to diplomatic ties with Peking. Such requests seem to fall on deaf ears, however.

Already on 5 August another Djakarta mob had again attacked the Chinese Embassy, setting fire to furnishings and attacking embassy personnel. An attempt to tear down the Chinese flag failed, according to Peking media, because "Chinese embassy members, armed with Mao Tse-tung's thought, put up a valiant fight in defence of the flag". This attack provoked vehement new demonstrations before the Indonesian Embassy in Peking, and among participants here were reported to be "revolutionary members of the Indonesian student association in China", wearing armbands of the "Red Flag Revolutionary Brigade Safeguarding Mao Tse-tung's Thought". On 24 August Djakarta announced that it was recalling all its diplomatic staff from Peking, but the Chinese reportedly obstructed their departure and it was not until 14 September that the Chinese interim Chargé D'affaires in Djakarta also left his post.

A complete break now seemed imminent, particularly after another mob stormed the Chinese Embassy in Djakarta in the early morning hours of 1 October, and a mob of some 100 Indonesian youths attacked a camp in Medan, North Sumatra, inhabited by Chinese awaiting repatriation to China. At an emergency

187

cabinet meeting on 9 October 1967, it was decided to suspend Indonesia's diplomatic relations with China, and two days later Djakarta radio announced that such relations had in fact been "frozen". On 27 October Peking announced the closing of its own Embassy in Djakarta and four days later a Chinese plane brought the last remaining seven Indonesian diplomatic officials from Peking, thereupon returning with about twenty Chinese.

Since that time Indonesian trade connections with Taiwan have become significantly firmer but there is no likelihood of a formal recognition. In the United Nations meanwhile, Indonesia managed to be absent both in 1968 and 1969 when the critical votes on the question of People's China's admission were cast. (In 1967, to the dismay of Taiwan, Indonesia had again voted in favour of seating People's China in the UN.) But, as in the case of Malaysia, where government spokesmen also habitually attack People's China's alleged subversion throughout Southeast Asia and particularly in their own country, so Indonesia has managed to maintain significant commercial connections via Hong Kong. Both Peking and Djakarta find the current "freeze" in their relations operationally useful. Except for periodic disclosures by the Indonesian Army that local Indonesian Chinese are involved in financing PKI subversion, anti-Chinese sentiments have since the middle of 1968 decreased, although there still are outbursts. On 29 June 1969, Indonesian Foreign Minister Malik, commenting on reports that Sino-Indonesian relations were becoming warmer again, said that any move to normalize relations between his country and the People's Chinese Government "should come from Peking", and that in any case China should "show goodwill and stop her hostility to Indonesia". The latter undoubtedly was a reference to the continuing stream of anti-Suharto comment in the Chinese Communist news media. Denunciations of the Suharto "Fascist gang", now said to be working in collusion with both the American "imperialists" and "Soviet revisionists", continue to be the stock-in-trade of those media to the present day, although there has been a lessening during 1971.

Meanwhile "assimilation" continues to be the Suharto Government's lodestar for Indonesia's Chinese residents. On 7 June 1967, the Suharto Government issued an "instruction" concerning foreigners of Chinese nationality which opened the way to a new legitimization of citizenship in return for extensive assimilation, including the virtual disappearance of private Chinese schools and political organizations of Chinese aliens in Indonesia. On 6 December 1967, the assimilation procedures were further extended, particularly with regard to required adoption of Indonesian names and guarantees of equal treatment in society and under the law.

On 25 January 1968, however, bloody anti-Chinese riots again erupted in Djakarta, possibly as an unintended consequence of student demonstrations against high prices. In retaliation for the alleged beating of an Indonesian soldier by some Chinese, Indonesian troops had gone on a rampage in Djakarta's Chinatown section, beating and stabbing at least 150 persons. An Army spokesman subsequently indicated that the incident was "not serious" and that no punishment was planned for the troops involved. Throughout 1968 and 1969 Indonesian Chinese, sometimes in mass meetings and ceremonies, and after appropriate application, adopted Indonesian names. On 29 January 1969, for example, Antara reported that some 13,700 out of 30,000 Indonesian Chinese in Pontianak, West Kalimantan, had adopted Indonesian names. But complications continued for those Indonesian Chinese wishing to return to the Chinese mainland, in part because of delays by the Peking Government to send the requisite vessels. Naturalization procedures for Chinese in Indonesia, though again simplified in February 1968, also continued to operate but slowly, while local military commanders in North Sumatra as well as East Java frequently accused Indonesian Chinese of "commercial manipulation" and "subversion". Quite apart from the changing nuances in the state of diplomatic relations between Djakarta, Peking and Taipeh, the position of the Indonesian Chinese has remained precarious.

Although Soviet-Indonesian relations did not fall to the freezing point of those now existing between Djakarta and Peking, here too there were notable, though less severe and more transient, strains. The Soviet readiness in November 1966 to accept a moratorium on Indonesia's huge debt did not end periodic charges in the Indonesian press that the Soviets were covertly supporting the PKI and that a Soviet spy network continued to flourish in Indonesia. Criticism in the Soviet press of the "mass repressions and acts of terrorism" being perpetrated by the "Indonesian reaction" (*Pravda*, 28 May 1967) brought equally sharp Indonesian press and political comment. On 24 August 1968 some 200 Indonesian students stormed into the compound of the Soviet Embassy in Djakarta to protest the Russian invasion of Czechoslovakia, and later the same mob hauled down the flag at the Polish Embassy. This incident occurred at a time of notable new sharpness in Soviet press comment on Indonesia, probably occasioned in turn by the intensified operations of the Suharto Government against the PKI underground in Central and East Java (see chapter V).

The wave of arrests in Indonesia and reports of the deplorable conditions in the camps of political prisoners led the Soviet news agency Tass, on 19 June 1968, to call for an international investigation into the living conditions of the detainees in Indonesia. Charges of inhuman treatment of the prisoners also frequently appeared in other Russian media. Despite appeals by the Central Committee of the Soviet Communist Party and by President Nikolai Podgorny, on 29 October 1968 PKI leaders Njono, Sudisman and Wirjomartono were hanged, and, in its comment on this event on 30 October 1968, *Pravda* declared that "Indonesian reaction has evidently set itself the task of the physical annihilation and political suppression of all patriots and anti-imperialists" in Indonesia. Throughout the first half of 1969 the Soviet press campaign began to subside again, however, and on 28 August 1969 a new Soviet Ambassador, Mikhail Volkov, presented his credentials, expressing his Government's assurances that the USSR did not intend to "interfere with the internal affairs of any other country" and emphasizing that peaceful co-existence was his country's foreign policy objective. A few days earlier there had arrived in Djakarta a Soviet mission, led by V. A. Sergeyev, Deputy Minister for Foreign Economic Affairs and Development, for the purpose of discussing outstanding financial problems between the two countries.

According to the 30 September 1969 issue of the Djakarta daily *Sinar Harapan*, as well as other Indonesian sources, the Indonesians wanted the discussions confined to new Soviet credits and completion of Soviet aid projects agreed to earlier. The Russians, reportedly, wanted to talk about the repayment procedure of Indonesia's debts. On 29 September 1969 the talks formally ended, but they had reached a stalemate long before. The failure of the talks, and the general attitude of inflexibility conveyed by the Russians, led to a renewed though brief upsurge of anti-Soviet feeling in Indonesia. But it is clear today that neither side wants to drive tensions to the diplomatic breaking point. Indonesia is well aware that no matter how distasteful it may be, it must come to some sort of acceptable debt repayment schedule with the Russians, particularly if it wishes new Soviet credits. Receipt of these new credits, in turn, is essential if Indonesia's "active and independent" foreign policy is to be more than a sham. President Suharto, in his Address of State on 16 August 1969, on the eve of Indonesia's independence anniversary, tried to convey his interest in maintaining Indonesia's freedom in matters of foreign aid:

> In receiving foreign aid and economic co-operation we frankly state that no aid would be accepted if political strings were attached to it. This principle is equally applied to the Western as well as the Eastern blocs. It is a fact that at present we are receiving a great deal of concrete aid from the Western bloc; but this should

not be taken to mean that we have closed the door to aid from the Eastern bloc. For the time being development projects with credits from the Socialist countries are being continued and their co-operation is still needed. The completion of some of the delayed projects which happen to be aided by Socialist countries is not based on political considerations, but solely reflects adjustment to the priorities of the current Development Plan and subsequent financing capacity.

The 'Tonasa' cement factory was finished last year with a credit aid from the Czechoslovakian Government. The Citronella factory in Solo and the Electric Motor Project are being completed with a credit from Bulgaria. The spinning mill in Palembang has been completed with a credit from East Germany, and so on. We have excellent relations with Yugoslavia....

On 11 February 1970, when receiving the credentials of the new Ambassador of the Mongolian People's Republic to Indonesia, Suharto declared that Indonesia was "steadfastly maintaining a free and active foreign policy", directed against "colonialism and imperialism in all their forms", but (perhaps paradoxically also) looking toward establishment of friendly relations with all countries "irrespective of their social systems".

It is precisely professions of this kind (whatever the realities of Indonesian "independence" in foreign policy) which continue to ensure Soviet interest. In December 1968, several weeks after the campaign in the Soviet media protesting recent anti-Communist purges and the execution of Njono, *et al.* had reached its peak, the authoritative Soviet journal *International Affairs* published an article on Indonesia which, while continuing to deplore the allegedly repressive policies of the Suharto Government, declared that "An analysis of concrete facts shows" that "despite the pressure", Indonesia "has until recently remained largely true to her traditional foreign policy of non-alignment". And on 14 May 1969, one commentator on Radio Moscow, G. Afrin, denied that Soviet policy toward Indonesia had changed. Allegations in the Indonesian press that a change had occurred were untrue, Afrin said. He went on to describe Soviet policy as being founded on firm Leninist principles, not on shifting considerations, and he noted that the USSR had provided Indonesia with over a billion US dollars in foreign aid and had agreed to a rescheduling of Indonesia's debt repayment. Afrin concluded by admitting that a "rather critical" situation presently prevailed in Indonesia, but added that the Soviet people were confident that "temporary difficulties will be overcome" and that Indonesia would once more move ahead on the road to independence.

Soviet professions of friendship for Indonesia increased in September and October 1969 during, as well as in the aftermath of, the fruitless Sergeyev mission to Djakarta. The reasons

191

probably lie in the Russians' new strategy in the Indian Ocean and Southeast Asian areas. Since the latter half of 1968 a Soviet naval squadron of from twelve to fourteen vessels, including a guided missile destroyer and several submarines, has become relatively a fixture of the Indian Ocean, and in October 1969 there was pronounced Soviet interest in the possible development of a Soviet naval installation on the Saint Brandon islands, some 250 miles north of Mauritius, to which these small islands belong. On 7 June 1969 Soviet party leader, Leonid Brezhnev, in his address to the International Conference of Communist and Workers' Parties in Moscow, had said: "We are also of the opinion that the course of events is also bringing to the fore the need to create a collective security system in Asia". Brezhnev's words aroused much speculation throughout the Far East in subsequent months, and from India (mindful of Sino-Pakistani pressures), and even Australia (where the Gorton Government was cautiously developing a new strategic flexibility), there came responses that could only be interpreted as sympathetic.

Publicly, Indonesia expressed polite interest in Brezhnev's words but nothing more — indeed, privately, Indonesian foreign-policy makers were probably quite apprehensive. For already months before the Brezhnev speech Indonesian Foreign Minister Malik had vented his concern in capitals around the Indian Ocean about a possible Soviet military build-up in the Indian Ocean area. For example, early in March 1969, during an interview in India with a reporter of the Madras daily *Indian Express,* Malik urged the big powers, and specifically the US, the USSR and People's China, to keep their hands off the Indian Ocean after the final planned British military withdrawal east of Suez. The Indian Ocean should be a "preserved area of peace", Malik said, looked after only by the nations of the region itself, namely, India, Pakistan, Ceylon, Indonesia, Malaysia, Singapore and Thailand. Late in April 1969, Malik had a conversation in Djakarta with the Australian External Affairs Minister Gordon Freeth. According to the *Sydney Morning Herald* of 1 May 1969, Freeth revealed that behind this conversation lay Malik's fears that the mutual antagonism beween India and Pakistan and their respective orientations toward the USSR and People's China might provoke increased Communist interest in the Indian Ocean area, presenting new threats to surrounding countries. By the middle of June 1969 Malaysia's then Deputy Premier and Defence Minister Razak said he would welcome a "security arrangement" with countries surrounding the Indian Ocean, adding that the idea of such a "security arrangement" had been suggested by Malik. Was Malik now in fact attempting to head off a Soviet-sponsored regional collective security pact?

In subsequent weeks Antara claimed that the Soviets were assiduously "courting Indonesia" to participate in the formation of Brezhnev's security system, particularly at the United Nations where Soviet Foreign Minister Andrei Gromyko had reiterated Brezhnev's proposal. Antara also took good note of the comments of radio commentator Lev Alnasov over Radio Moscow in early October 1969, who described the Brezhnev-Gromyko proposals as closely coinciding with Indonesia's own interests. Other Radio Moscow comments at this time similarly seemed to be conveying the Soviet Government's desire for friendly relations with Indonesia. Behind the scenes, meanwhile, there was some Soviet diplomatic activity in other Southeast Asian capitals. But all this apparently did the Russians little good. The Brezhnev proposal, for the time being, has remained just that, a proposal and nothing more, and in many political-diplomatic circles in the region a Soviet-backed collective security idea was considered interesting but premature. On 22 October 1969 an Indonesian Foreign Office spokesman was reported by Antara as having said that Indonesia was still "paying attention" to the Soviet collective security proposal, but that "it is still uncertain what is actually meant by the Soviet Union". Somewhat earlier, on 16 October 1969, *The Straits Times* quoted Malik as saying, in response to a question about the Brezhnev suggestion, that Indonesia would endorse a collective security system which was supported by all major nations of the world, but that the Brezhnev idea itself was far from clear and therefore he could not comment on it. By the middle of March 1970, Malik seemed to be sounding the death knell of the Brezhnev proposal. During a stop-over in Singapore the Indonesian Foreign Minister declared that all Asian countries had now rejected the Soviet Union's idea of regional security for Southeast Asia. Malik managed to sound somewhat disillusioned. "All the Russians want", he was quoted as saying, "is to sell the idea and if given the backing of Asian countries they will think of something for the continent. But Asia has turned down their offer because all Asian countries believe that they must solve their own problems."

To some commentators Indonesia's apparent aloofness to the Brezhnev proposal was but an expression of well-established Indonesian policy, however. In August 1968, Malik had said that while Indonesia should not completely neglect "what is known as the US nuclear umbrella", a strong economy and ideology were ultimately of far greater importance in the national defence policies for the countries of Southeast Asia. Declaring that the intended

British military withdrawal from Asia by the end of 1971 would have no direct impact on Indonesia, Malik added, however, that Southeast Asian nations might well wish to consolidate their "national endurance" through various regional and sub-regional organizations. But whether or not such organizations would include a collective security arrangement Malik left unexplained. In November 1968, Malik said Indonesia would not take an active part in combating international Communism if the US left Vietnam because Indonesia was too busy with its own internal problems.

In January 1969, President Suharto in a press interview stressed that there was no need for military pacts among the members of the Association of Southeast Asian Nations (ASEAN). Suharto added that the preservation of security and freedom were and should remain the principal responsibilities of each individual Southeast Asian country, on the basis of a strong economy and ideology, and an efficient armed forces establishment. On 16 March 1969, in an interview with Syed Zainal Abidin, general manager of Malaysia's national news agency Bernama, Suharto declared again that Indonesia would not enter into any defence arrangements in Southeast Asia after the supposed British withdrawal in 1971, but that it would concentrate instead on regional co-operation in the social and economic fields. Suharto added that mutual co-operation in Asia could be directed towards a common market in similar agricultural and mineral products, such as rubber, copra and tin. Suharto also said, however, that he had no objection to Australia and New Zealand retaining their forces in Malaysia and Singapore after the British withdrawal. The stationing of ANZAC (Australian and New Zealand Army Corps) forces in Malaysia and Singapore, the Indonesian President declared, "can be well understood as long as Malaysia and Singapore feel the need for their presence".

Despite assertions opposing a regional collective security system, however, the growing Soviet penetration into the Indian Ocean area was apparently causing Indonesia a good deal of disquiet. Being opposed to this rising Soviet influence, Indonesia was equally loath to abandon its continuously proclaimed position that no Southeast Asian security system was necessary. Malik's quandary was revealed in his earlier-cited conversation at the end of April 1969 with Australia's External Affairs Minister Gordon Freeth. Though having expressed his concern to the Australian about possibly rising Communist influence in the Indian Ocean area, Malik, according to a Djakarta Reuter's despatch of 25 April 1969, declared on the one hand that he saw "no urgency" at present to arrange a military pact in Southeast Asia, while on the other hand he was quoted as saying: "We may agree to co-operate in some sort of security arrangement to neutralize the area." As indicated earlier, Malaysia's then Defence Minister Razak subsequently also understood Malik to be interested in promoting a "security arrangement" for Southeast Asia. What the difference between such an "arrangement" and a formal military or collective security pact would be Malik has thus far not elucidated, and with the decreasing likelihood of the Brezhnev proposal reaching fruition, Indonesia's Foreign Minister will probably prefer not to go into the matter unless compelled to do so. But the episode does suggest that Indonesia's professed policy of "non-alignment" is capable of some refinement in response to regional threats that are felt.

In his 16 August 1969 Address of State, President Suharto declared again that Indonesia rejected "any form of military alliance". "Military pacts", said Suharto, "evidently are not an effective form of defence for they may weaken national defence and identity. Aside from that, military pacts will only provoke other sides to strengthen their armament and form counter militar pacts." During a visit to Malaysia in the middle of March 1970, Suharto asserted that the "only answer" to expansionist and subversive threats directed at Southeast Asia lay in the development of "national endurance", based on deployment of "national identity" and "national potential", as well as a social unity in the nation reflecting a sense of "common fate and mutual respect". There may be wisdom in these assertions. But the point surely is that — apart from the strategic pressures which Malik's ambivalent policy statements have revealed — Indonesia's rigid domestic anti-Communism, and her hospitality to private Western capital, rightly or wrongly gives ground for some suspicion that militarily too she may not be altogether a neutral. In the middle of 1968 there was speculation, for example, in the press of a number of Southeast Asian countries that within ASEAN there now existed a "Defence Liaison Group" which, backed by and linked to the American military establishment, was developing a network of military installations throughout the region. On 24 July 1968, Antara reported that Malik had formally denied (1) that such a Defence Liaison Group existed within ASEAN, (2) that there had been an attempt to turn ASEAN into a military alliance, and (3) that three US military bases were being built in Indonesia, respectively, at Sabang, off the northern tip of Sumatra, at Tjilatjap, on Java's southern coast, and at Bitung, North Sulawesi. Reports that the alleged Sabang base would be linked to military installations in Thailand, that the base in Tjilatjap would be connected with Australia, and the base in Bitung with the Philippines, were also denied.

Despite Malik's denials, however, rumours persisted that the US had a strong military interest in ASEAN, that it had its own Defence Liaison Group for this purpose, and that Indonesia was accommodating American military interests. On 12 December 1968, the weekly of the Maoist faction of the Australian Communist Party, *The Vanguard*, partly citing Antara and the Indonesian armed forces paper *Angkatan Bersendjata* in support, said that recently two high-ranking US Defence Department officials had visited Indonesia in order to inspect a number of military projects being built in Indonesia under the auspices of a "US Defence Liaison Group" (USDLG). In February 1971, a US Congressional staff report declared that the new US$18 million American assistance programme for Indonesia was in fact being administered by a twenty-man USDLG in Indonesia, as "part of the American effort to retain a 'low profile' on the Indonesian scene".

On 30 December 1969, Antara also announced from Canberra that during 1970 "Australia will continue bilateral co-operation in the military sector with Indonesia". This "co-operation", in the first instance, is directed toward the modernization of the Indonesian armed forces with the aid of Australian service specialists, as well as of small quantities of military hardware. Some eventual pattern of regular "joint manoeuvres" was also envisaged and an Australian military mission was shortly to leave for Djakarta. Many details of this Australian-Indonesian military co-operative venture are not publicly available. But enough has leaked out to suggest a possible far-reaching and long-term pattern of defence assistance, and eventually even of co-ordination, that might make Indonesia in the end a silent partner in the five-power Commonwealth security system in Southeast Asia.

In the light of all this, some observers of the Indonesian scene have asked themselves if *Orba*'s anti-Communism is likely to remain confined to Indonesia's national boundaries, particularly if the military's position should become further threatened by domestic parliamentary and partisan political forces after the national elections. Would the Suharto regime, despite its professed disinclination to lead an anti-Communist crusade abroad, revive the Sukarnoist tactic of proclaiming an alleged external threat, this time of the Communist rather than of the "neo-colonialist" variety, so that political conformity can more easily be demanded at home?

In an interview with R. L. Michael, editor of Ceylon's *Daily Mirror*, in December 1968, Suharto stressed the persisting danger coming to Southeast Asia from People's China. Suharto spoke in terms usually employed by then Malaysian Premier Tunku Abdul

Rahman. Accusing Peking of "already employing subversive tactics in undermining the stability of certain nations with the idea of spreading its philosophy", Suharto, in reply to Michael's question, "If and when the British and American forces pull out do you think China will attempt any military expansion in this region?", also said, "Yes, probably", and "In fact I do not put it past them". In early February 1969, Suharto warned that the ending of the Vietnam war "will give the Communists bigger scope for infiltration and subversion of the region", though he again rejected military pacts as a means of meeting this potentially larger Communist threat. While since early 1969 the publicity surrounding the domestic anti-Communist campaign in Indonesia has somewhat slackened, there is no indication that the Suharto Government has changed its basic policy conviction that Communist subversion continues to menace Indonesians, both at home and in their region of the world.

This basic policy conviction, along with the pressures within its military establishment, may, then, yet push Indonesia farther and farther away from its stance of strict "non-alignment". Still another illustration of the point is afforded by Djakarta's recent attitude toward the Asian Pacific Council (ASPAC). Founded in 1966 in order to further the financial and technical-economic co-operation of the Asian Pacific region, ASPAC includes Australia, New Zealand, the Philippines, Malaysia, Thailand, South Korea, South Vietnam, the Republic of China on Taiwan, and Japan. Neither Singapore, Burma nor Indonesia joined ASPAC when it was formed, and for the same reason: the majority of ASPAC's members are militarily allied with the US and have been among its principal international diplomatic supporters. As late as March 1969, President Suharto, in the earlier-mentioned interview with Syed Zainal Abidin of Bernama, rejected the likelihood of Indonesia joining ASPAC, "in consideration of her independent and active foreign policy" (as Suharto put it). But at the ASPAC ministerial conference in Kawana, Japan, in early June 1969, an Indonesian "guest representative" appeared for the first time, leading to increasing speculation that despite denials Indonesia would eventually accept membership. It was evidently in deference to Japan's repeated entreaties that Djakarta had decided to send a representative to Kawana. Unquestionably, ASPAC's rejection of an American proposal made in September 1968, that ASPAC transform itself into an Asian regional collective security alliance, may have made the Indonesians more amenable to attending the Kawana conference. And at the opening meeting of that conference Japanese Foreign Minister Aichi pointedly noted that "a clear and positive agreement now exists among the member countries that ASPAC is not intended to be a military alliance". Indonesian attendance at ASPAC meetings has continued.

Support for Indonesian participation in ASPAC has been growing in Indonesia itself. On 3 March 1969, for example, Imron Rosjadi, chairman of the foreign affairs committee of the Indonesian Parliament, suggested that Indonesia join ASPAC as it would benefit her relations with other Asian countries. In some top-ranking Army circles, where interest in an Indonesian adhesion to some kind of anti-Communist collective security system in Southeast Asia has always been strong, there are similar sentiments.

According to Foreign Minister Malik, however, "The primary reason for regional co-operation is the necessity for modernization [as he wrote in the January 1968 issue of the influential American quarterly, *Foreign Affairs*].... Especially in our region the question of war or peace is not the only problem. There is a desperate struggle too, against poverty, disease, illiteracy and many other ills." The major forum of that kind of regional co-operation, for the present, is ASEAN. The second ASEAN ministerial conference held in Djakarta in August 1968 had no difficulty in listing five priority areas of regional co-operation: food production, communications, civil aviation, shipping and tourism, and in adopting a modest working programme in each area. The ASEAN ministerial conference at Cameron Highlands, Malaya, in December 1969, similarly approved committee recommendations for some ninety-eight inexpensive projects for economic and technical co-operation.

But, significantly, it was not the economic aspect of this conference that attracted attention, but rather its political concerns. The presence of "observers" from Laos and South Vietnam, notwithstanding Singapore's pointed opposition to ASEAN membership for the latter at this time, served to accentuate the fact that a conference on prospects of purely regional economic co-operation has become something of an impossibility in the Southeast Asia of today. Indeed, though the second ASEAN ministerial conference apparently had agreed that membership in ASEAN would be restricted to Southeast Asian countries, when he arrived at the Cameron Highlands meeting the next year, Malik suggested that membership be expanded. Not just Laos and South Vietnam, but also Burma, Cambodia, North Vietnam and "the Vietcong", as Antara reported from Djakarta on 19 December 1969, were said to be favoured by the Indonesian Government to attend the ASEAN meeting. This proposal ran directly counter to the views of Singapore's Foreign Minister S. Rajaratnam, who argued before the conference began that ASEAN first should prove its present viability before taking on any additional members. Malaysia, too, opposed the presence of North Vietnamese and Vietcong delegates, although it favoured attendance by delegates from Vientiane and Saigon. In the end, the question of expansion of ASEAN membership was left off the formal agenda of the Cameron Highlands conference. But it was evident that Indonesia did not intend to let the matter rest.

It is not altogether clear why Indonesia desires an expanded ASEAN (even Australia and New Zealand have been suggested as possible members by some Indonesian parliamentary leaders), but one reason surely is Djakarta's persistent interest in some kind of a new "security arrangement" for Southeast Asia outside a formal collective security pact. Conceivably, through such a broadened ASEAN the organization might perhaps also play a more useful role in a Vietnam settlement. By broadening ASEAN's membership, and by making as many individual countries become involved with the interests of the region as a whole, possibly nearly the same thing can ultimately be achieved as by a conventional collective security pact, namely the fostering of a sense of mutual responsibility and continuous concern, without the threatening overtones of a military alliance.

If this is, in fact, the Indonesian objective it would probably also go quite a way toward relieving the latent concern which Indonesia herself continues to arouse among her neighbours. This concern is particularly apparent in Australia, Malaysia and Singapore, and in reduced measure also in the Philippines. Given her size and burgeoning population, her simmering political instability and regional discontent, most of Indonesia's problems have a tendency to become those of the nations in her immediate vicinity as well. After Suharto, what? — this is the question that most often serves as the matrix for worried speculations among the nations in Indonesia's vicinity. Reports such as those circulating in Djakarta in December 1969 about recent arrests of two Army generals and the impending arrest of three more, all on charges of having attempted to bring former President Sukarno back to power, have a way of underscoring concern that yet another Indonesian government might eventually emerge, ready to resume more adventurist and confrontation-style policies. The death of Sukarno does not alter the basic problem. For if the charge of an attempted Sukarno restoration was but a pretext, as it probably was, the evident dissension in the top levels of Army leadership is hardly a source of comfort for Indonesia's neighbours.

In Australia, and particularly in the Territory of Papua-New Guinea under Canberra's control, the question of the future of

New Guinea island, and the interaction between the two halves of that island, continues to arouse apprehension. Will West Irian eventually become a base for expansionist interests toward eastern New Guinea, possibly with the help of frustrated Papuan nationalism in the Territory of Papua-New Guinea? Or will Indonesian neglect and repression in West Irian — so very evident in the past — encourage Pan Papuan sentiments in the eastern part of the island, especially as the latter steadily moves toward greater autonomy? And where will this leave Australia and its carefully constructed new *rapprochement* with Suharto's *Orba*?

As for the Philippines, its leaders have not altogether forgotten how in Sukarno's hey-day a huge map hung in the Indonesian presidential Merdeka Palace, showing the southern and Muslim part of the Philippine islands as belonging to the national territory of *Indonesia Raya* (Greater Indonesia), which also included Malaysia, and indeed reached all the way into southern Thailand. Before *Gestapu*, Indonesian Communist infiltration into the southern Philippines — amplifying local Muslim secessionist undercurrents there — had greatly assisted the revival, under Sukarno, of the historic concept and mystique of *Indonesia Raya*. Today, as Suharto's *Orba* begins to fall short of public expectations, the possibility that the Sukarno era may eventually acquire a new attraction and may perhaps bring a return of Sukarnoist policies gives good grounds for alarm among those of Indonesia's neighbours who were once the particular targets of those policies. Malik's idea of a broad-based, regional though non-military association, with emphasis on growing mutual responsibility and co-operation, may not only be useful in containing future power plays and diplomatic pressures whose source is external to Southeast Asia. But in the long run such an association could aid also in containing aggressive impulses internal to the region as well, for example those that may one day again be coming from Indonesia herself.

At the same time, however, Indonesia is of course also affected — and rightly alarmed — by the instability of her neighbours. An example is Malaysia. One reason sometimes given by Indonesians for their erstwhile official opposition to the creation of the Malaysian Federation was that such a federation would have no future owing to the communal antagonism between Malays and Chinese and that this animosity would also accentuate Chinese loyalties toward Peking in a manner threatening Indonesia's own security. Former Indonesian Vice-President Mohammad Hatta, for example, took such a position. Hence, it was argued, the new Federation would represent a danger located directly on Indonesia's doorstep and Djakarta had no choice but to oppose Malaysia's formation. Whatever the merits of this argument may have been in 1963 — if Indonesia really feared Peking's influence it remains to be explained why, precisely, in the period of Djakarta's anti-Malaysia confrontation campaign Sino-Indonesian relations became ever warmer — today there is no doubt about Indonesian concern over Malay-Chinese racial tensions in the Federation. In the aftermath of the bloody communal riots in Kuala Lumpur in May 1969 Djakarta is known to have urged then Malaysian Prime Minister Tunku Abdul Rahman to restrain his security measures to the utmost and avoid further provocation. In turn, Indonesia has consistently refused to provide a haven for agents of the Malay-chauvinist and anti-Chinese Pan Malayan Islamic Party (PMIP) at odds with the Rahman Government. In the closing days of Sukarno's guided democracy PMIP representatives, some of them long-time ideological supporters of the *Indonesia Raya* notion (which would encourage incorporation of Malaya into Indonesian national territory), had been given sanctuary in Indonesia. But those days are gone. And the Suharto Government, mindful especially of the ties of blood, religion, language and commerce that bind many Sumatrans to the Malays across the Straits of Malacca, has quietly given strong indications that it does not wish to be dragged into a racial war on the Malay peninsula.

Still, those who recall the asperity of Malaysian-Indonesian relations not so long ago cannot but be surprised by an Antara report, of 29 December 1969 from Djakarta, that Indonesian Foreign Minister Malik, arriving home from the third ASEAN ministerial conference in Malaysia, should be compelled to counter speculation that Indonesia and Malaysia were considering forming a confederation! And even then, Malik was careful not to close the door on such an idea altogether, but merely said that "it is impossible to form a confederation without careful preparations because this concerns the people of both Malaysia and Indonesia". It is unlikely that such a Malaysian-Indonesian confederation would materialize in the near future, notwithstanding the modest strides that have been taken toward greater unity between the two countries, for example in such areas as standardization of spelling of the Malay language and the *bahasa Indonesia*. Yet, the mere fact that confederation can even be considered, little more than three years after the end of confrontation, suggests something of how rapidly national interests and needs in Southeast Asia are realigning themselves.

Much of the same ambivalence is apparent in Indonesia's relations with Singapore. The latter remains an Indonesian smuggler's haven, the informal control centre, too, for much illegal financial activity throughout Indonesia. Indonesian attempts to persuade Singapore authorities to be a little less accommodating to smugglers and financial manipulators have had little effect. Singapore's Israeli-style posture of trenchant self-reliance, of compelling her bigger neighbours to respect her — it almost seems — regardless of cost, may sooner or later bring her into a severe collision with Djakarta. On 15 October 1968, for example, the Singapore Government rejected President Suharto's appeal for clemency on behalf of two Indonesian terrorists, caught in 1965 during the confrontation. Two days later the two terrorists were executed and subsequently their bodies were reburied and given a hero's funeral in Indonesia. The Indonesian Parliament formally condemned the executions and the Singapore Embassy in Djakarta was attacked by a mob of youths, while the Singapore Ambassador went into hiding. Anti-Singapore demonstrations in Surabaya, on 21 October 1968, led to the outbreak of several fires, while in Djambi, South Sumatra, a similar mass protest quickly turned into an anti-Chinese riot.

Anti-Singapore (read anti-Chinese) sentiment ran so high in several places that, for example, in various sections of the capital the Army was ordered to patrol in front of Chinese business establishments and President Suharto had to threaten demonstrators with severe punishment. Several branch organizations of parties and youth groups in Djakarta urged the Government to break off diplomatic relations. At the close of a cabinet meeting on 24 October 1968 it was announced that the Government would begin curtailing the nation's Singapore trade, and the Economic Stabilization Board said new measures were being planned to end smuggling. As the days went by, however, and tempers cooled (Foreign Minister Malik and his Singapore counterpart S. Rajaratnam all along had urged calm) it became only too obvious that rechannelling the Singapore commerce or halting all smuggling was easier said than done. On 3 November 1968, Communications Minister Frans Seda, in effect, dealt the entire boycott proposal the death blow when he remarked that Indonesian vessels would continue to frequent Singapore because of the importance of existing trade connections between the two nations.

The whole incident, however, did spoil potential benefits from the useful talks held between Rajaratnam and Malik in Singapore in March 1968, in which the Indonesian Foreign Minister had indicated a readiness to enter into a bilateral security arrangement with Singapore, and even to defend it against Communist attack, while urging that the smuggling problem be more firmly taken in hand. Since the October incident Singapore has been less interested than ever in a bilateral security arrangement with Indonesia, or for that matter in doing much about the smuggling problem. Singapore's independent, "poison shrimp" stance, however, may well eventually find her with decreasing assets of popularity and goodwill among her neighbours, so that another incident could well drive simmering Indonesian resentment quickly to the boiling point.

A "Billy-be-damned" truculence certainly does not characterize the dealings of another Asian power with which Indonesia has ever more to do these days, namely Japan. The story of Japanese-Indonesian relations since *Gestapu* is largely one of a steadily growing sheaf of Antara and other news items describing the entry of Japanese mineral, lumber, land development and a host of other enterprises into the Indonesian islands, interspersed by reports on debt rescheduling and on the granting of or negotiations for still more development credits. Since 1966 Japan's trade with Indonesia has shown an increasing deficit for the former, mainly due to sharp increases in Japan's imports of Indonesian oil. During 1969 Japan's imports from Indonesia rose to US$352 million, against only US$213 million in exports. The US$352 million figure, it might be noted, represented no less than a fifty-seven per cent jump over 1968 imports. (By way of further comparison, one might observe that trade between the two countries was about balanced at US$15 million in 1949.) Textiles, which once comprised as much as eighty per cent of Japan's exports to Indonesia, have dropped to about half that amount today, while chemicals and machinery now top the list. Apart from mining and banking investments, Japan's US$30 million represents the second-largest foreign investment component in Indonesia and it is growing rapidly.

But it is not, of course, Japan's economic role alone in Southeast Asia that concerns Indonesia and her neighbours. To be sure, at the ASEAN ministerial conference at Cameron Highlands in December 1969, the concensus of the participants was, according to Antara, that Japan should restrict its activities in Southeast Asia "to the economic field only and avoid controversial military involvements". According to Antara it was specifically Indonesian Foreign Minister Malik who, with the concurrence of then Malaysian Deputy Premier Razak, laid down this "guide-line" for Japan at the conference. Japan's reaction, if any, to this report is now known, but certainly the ASEAN ministers must have been aware for several years now that Japanese rearmament is well on its way. Over the past decade Japan has been spending only slightly less than one per cent of its gross national product on defence; even so that amounted to around US$1,300 million in 1969. And by the time Japan's third long-term defence plan ends in 1971, authorized ground forces will have risen to 180,000, while 280 new medium-sized tanks will have been obtained, fourteen destroyers (including some with ship-to-air missile facilities) and five 800-ton submarines will have been constructed, two additional ground-to-air missile battalions will have been formed, and the nation's jet fighter force will have been significantly strengthened by the new Mitsubishi F-4E-J aircraft. All this within the limits or — depending on one's point of view — in contravention of the famous Article Nine of the Japanese Constitution which prohibits Japan from having any war-making potential, though "self defence" forces are presumably permitted.

The point is not just that the growth of Japan's military power is accelerating, but rather that it is accelerating in the context of a rising Japanese nationalism. The American promise to return Okinawa to Japanese control in 1972, a promise which greatly assisted the Sato Government's 1969 election victory, has, however, also permitted the US to continue to make a case for the renewal, in some form or other, of its defence treaty with Japan in the near future. In short, by continuing to extend formal military protection to Japan, the US is not only in a position to limit Japanese rearmament interests but also to determine policy — a circumstance which for many Japanese across the country's political spectrum reinforces a sense of humiliating dependence. For Southeast Asian countries, with fresh memories of the Japanese Occupation during World War II, the spectre of a militarized and more nationalist Japan in the future is a fearful one indeed. Yet, despite Malik's "guide-line" for Japan, there is also an Indonesian realization that in the Nixon era Japan, like other Asian countries, must undertake more to ensure its security on its own or, as the US would prefer it, in tandem with its Asian neighbours. Like Indonesia, Japan is not sure, however, what the new framework of that security should be. On 29 September 1968, during the closing days of the Johnson administration, US Defence Secretary Clark Clifford suggested that Australia, India and Japan should work together with Southeast Asian powers to develop a new Asian regional security system, with the US assisting in a limited, and principally economic, way. Somewhat earlier, the US was reported to have been trying to persuade the Japanese to transform ASPAC into a military alliance. And, on 19 October 1968, during his campaign for the presidency, Richard Nixon also suggested to Asian nations that they develop regional pacts as "buffers" between the greater powers, stressing also that, in future, Asian nations would be expected to make the initial response to "any new aggression in their area" and that the US would not unilaterally fight the wars of Asians for them. Much of the underlying rationale of this statement by candidate Nixon was reiterated the next year in the so-called Guam Doctrine enunciated by then recently elected President Nixon.

In India the notion of such regional defence pacts was quickly rejected. Australia, relatively secure in the protection of the ANZUS pact (Australia-New Zealand-United States Security Treaty), might be interested, but could hardly, by herself, overcome a negative Indian reaction. Japan's reservations about a militarization of ASPAC have already been noted earlier. Nevertheless, Japanese nationalism and American pressure may yet combine so as to bring about not a formal regional military pact, but a strengthened and broadened ASPAC, which, though remaining primarily economic-financial in nature, nevertheless can muster significant political and diplomatic force. Such a development might well correspond to Malik's own search for a new "security arrangement" short of a complete military alliance, and Indonesian hestitations about ASPAC might under such circumstances vanish entirely. At the same time a politically and economically aggressive Japan — and such an image is rapidly building in Indonesian business circles — is likely to arouse as much resentment and fear as a militarized Japan. Japanese leadership in Asia in the seventies will not come without some demurrers from Djakarta. According to *Warta Harian*, on 1 December 1969, Malik, upon his return to Djakarta after a visit to several Asian countries, neither denied nor amplified his recently expressed opinion (which had caused some consternation) that in future Japan could make its relations with Indonesia "more difficult". Official Indonesian apprehensions about the new Japan are unmistakable.

Making possible Japanese leadership in Asia more acceptable to Indonesia will require all the diplomatic resources which a "retractionist" US can muster. A broad display of friendship Washington now clearly deems indispensable after the diplomatic strains of the Sukarno era. "We want to be with you, want to assist you in any way that you think is appropriate," President Richard Nixon said to Suharto on 27 July 1969 during Nixon's brief visit to Indonesia. Nixon generally was fulsome in his praise of Indonesia during his visit, declaring at his departure that Indonesia's "chances for a great economic breakthrough" were "better than ever before" and that he left "confident that the future of this country is in good hands". Like the history of Japanese-Indonesian relations since Sukarno, that of American-Indonesian relations, too, is essentially a matter of increasing investment, food allocations and credit transactions. But there is no question that, officially at least, the US enjoys a much more favourable position since Suharto assumed control, and there has come an end to the steady round of anti-American demonstrations and the pillaging of US diplomatic and information service offices and facilities that especially characterized the 1964-5 period.

The new atmosphere is also well illustrated by Indonesian attitudes toward the Vietnam war. In the hey-day of the Sukarno era, Hanoi was considered a vital link in the Asian chain of "new emerging forces" along with Peking, Pyongyang and, with some reservation, Phnom Penh, while Sukarno left no doubt of his sympathies for the struggle of the National Liberation Front in South .Vietnam. Today, though formal diplomatic relations between Djakarta and Hanoi continue, and though no official contact exists with Saigon, the Suharto Government studiously avoids the Vietnam problem beyond vague expressions of hope for its peaceful solution. Official policy often appears to be one of deliberately creating seemingly contradictory impressions which, hopefully, will be considered acceptable to all parties. For example, on 26 March 1968 *The Djakarta Times* noted that Foreign Minister Malik had "strongly" denied reports attributed by Antara to a Cambodian paper that he had congratulated the "Vietcong representatives" in Djakarta upon their military successes during the previous month. Malik added that ending the bombing of North Vietnam "might pave the way to a peaceful solution of the Vietnam war", and also said that he had "always" supported a peaceful solution of the war "through the 1954 Geneva agreement". Malik, on the same occasion, did not deny, however, another recent Antara report that Suharto had asked Nugroho, the Indonesian Ambassador in Hanoi, to convince President Ho Chi Minh of Indonesian support for the struggle of the Vietnamese people against "American aggression". Malik also "explained" that Indonesia believed that the fate of Vietnam must be determined by the Vietnamese themselves without intervention from any foreign powers — a formulation which in its unqualified blandness could not but be acceptable to all sides. In early February 1970, Malik simultaneously announced that Indonesia would establish a trade office in Saigon (the first time that an Indonesian mission would be lodged in the South Vietnamese capital since 1964, when diplomatic relations between Djakarta and Saigon were severed), and that Indonesia continued to prefer "negotiations" as a means of solving the Vietnam problem. A withdrawal of American forces, provided that this move was arrived at through negotiations, would mean that "no one would lose face" — the path which Malik apparently prefers. It is of such relatively inoffensive and euphonious generalities that Djakarta's official Vietnam policy is presently constituted.

Venturing beyond such generalities has, thus far, brought Indonesia but small gain. An example was the largely still-born effort to mitigate the Cambodian crisis. The overthrow of the Sihanouk regime in Cambodia in mid-March 1970 initially produced a random series of Indonesian reactions, including hints by Malik that Indonesia would be prepared to help save Cambodian neutrality; a denial that Indonesia had agreed in principle to to supply the Lon Nol Government with military aid; and a formal demand at the "Asia Assembly" in Manila on 15 April that all foreign troops be withdrawn from Cambodia and the Geneva Conference be reconvened. Possibly with American encouragement, Malik by the middle of April was already sounding out other ASEAN powers, as well as non-ASEAN nations, Australia, New Zealand, People's China and the Democratic Republic of Vietnam in Hanoi, on the desirability of a broad-based conference to discuss the Cambodian crisis. Peking and Hanoi quickly rejected the idea, as did North Korea, while in Japan there were doubts (reportedly Tokyo favoured a much smaller and more informal parley), and in India and Pakistan there was a good deal of reserve (in the end neither attended the conference). Although Malik, virtually simultaneously with President Nixon's announcement, on 30 April 1970, that American and South Vietnamese forces were moving into Cambodia, requested the US not to make the planned conference on Cambodia "difficult" by any military intervention, and although he sharply criticized the South Vietnamese presence on Cambodian soil, few in Asia or elsewhere saw Malik's conference call as reflecting genuinely independent Indonesian policy initiatives. Of the twelve states that ultimately attended the conference on Cambodia (that is Indonesia, Japan, Laos, Malaysia, Australia, New Zealand, South Korea, South Vietnam, Thailand, the Philippines, Singapore, and Cambodia which had the status of "informant"), begun in Djakarta on 16 May 1970, all but Singapore are militarily directly involved with or dependent on the US. The conference communique, calling for respect of Cambodia's territorial integrity, an end to all hostilities, and withdrawal of all foreign troops from Cambodian soil, seemed but a *pro forma* document, having little bearing on the realities of the Cambodian or, for that matter, the South Vietnamese situation. In the Djakarta press, however, and among political leaders, the mere fact that the conference had been held at all was seen as a not insignificant demonstration of the concept of "Asian solutions to Asian problems", and of the increased diplomatic initiative among Southeast Asian nations called for by Nixon's Guam Doctrine. Malik's behind-the-scenes efforts to mobilize regional political interests on behalf of a multilateral solution to the Cambodian problem continued after the Djakarta conference, but with little result thus far. Shortly after the conference, Malik was especially bitter over Soviet failure to support the conference, saying that if the Russians had been more sympathetic "the USA and South Vietnam would not have gone beyond the Cambodian border". Subsequently Malik also threw cold water on the notion of a Thai-South Vietnamese-Cambodian military alliance, saying that it afforded no solution to regional problems, although, he said, Indonesia would not formally oppose such an alliance.

Apart from US financial assistance the Suharto Government has also sought to benefit politically from the obvious US approval of post-Sukarno developments in Indonesia. Nixon's praise of the Suharto regime during his July 1969 visit was quickly used to rebut the regime's critics. In a commentary on the Nixon visit, Radio Djakarta declared on 28 July 1969:

> President Nixon's remark that the Indonesian Government under President Suharto's leadership is a truly democratic government has refuted allegations of the existence of so-called militarism in Indonesia. These allegations have been launched by certain elements and countries abroad who like to defend the PKI and the *Gestapu* movement. From President Nixon's remarks, we get the impression that the United States has really come to realize and understand the ideals, aspirations, and struggle of the Indonesian people under the leadership of President Suharto.

But Suharto also took care to remind his American guest of the chasm that yawns between their two countries. The Indonesian President, in conversations with Nixon, questioned the value of the recent Apollo-11 moon landing when so many problems remain on earth: this achievement, said Suharto, referring to Apollo-11's journey, "has not taken place in this world of ours". It was the first and only public criticism of the moon landing that Nixon heard on his 1969 trip, and it served notice that America's public endorsement of *Orba* is expected to produce more than mere words. In effect, Djakarta has made it clear that it looks to the US for an increasing share of the long-term development aid which it requires and that, together with Japan, American leadership in the IGGI is anticipated to yield a steady flow of credits from other quarters as well. Will the US eventually replace the USSR as Indonesia's biggest single creditor nation and will this not accentuate still further — as critics of Suharto already allege — *Orba*'s general character as an American militarist client state of a type already too prevalent in the Third World? Observers of Suharto's policies may well regard the Indonesian President as too intelligent, and the countervailing pressures coming from parties and interest groups in Indonesia as too powerful, to permit this to happen. But as the domestic development problem makes its heavy financial needs increasingly felt in the next few years, and as a military-civilian polarization in political life deepens, the options open to Suharto and his staunchest supporters may well narrow drastically. Washington, though attempting to loom much smaller on the Asian horizon in the aftermath of the Vietnam war, may find itself yet as ultimate guarantor of *Orba* or its acceptable successor. Such a development would not be a novelty in recent US relations with the new countries of the world. It must be admitted, however, that verbally, at least, Suharto is at pains to make clear that he has not become an American cat's paw. During his visit to Washington late in May 1970 Suharto pointedly noted that there were "differences of outlook with regard to various world problems" between the US and Indonesia, and expressed his conviction in the necessity of "peaceful co-existence" among states. As for Indonesia, Suharto said to Asian-African representatives at the United Nations, an "active, non-aligned and independent foreign policy" remained a matter of principle.

This may be so. But not a few would argue that Indonesian "neutralism" currently has more room for friendship with the US in it than at any time since the early nineteen-fifties. Nuances in this area are sometimes subtle, but not insignificant. An example came at the session of the standing committee of the Non-Aligned Nations in Lusaka, Zambia, on 26 July 1970. At this session the Indonesian delegation opposed the seating at the forthcoming plenary conference of the Non-Aligned Nations in September of "representatives of governments in exile" or of other than "legal members of the United Nations". It was as clear a slap at Prince Norodom Sihanouk's exiled regime in Peking as at the Democratic Republic of Vietnam in Hanoi or, for that matter, at People's China. However, Malik said that while Indonesia would not object if an invitation to Peking was extended, the Communists had already indicated that they did not wish to come. Indonesia, however, would not herself extend an invitation.

There is little question that it is Djakarta's caution, and particularly Malik's penchant for behind-the-scenes diplomatic manoeuvring, both in such sharp contrast to Sukarno's more expansive and flamboyant style, that greatly endears Suharto's Indonesia to Nixon's America. Her new national priorities of economic stabilization and development require that Indonesia (like the US) also assume a less grandiose posture on the Asian or even the world scene: for Indonesia too this is an era not of confrontation but of deflation.

Consequently, beyond her immediate Asian environment, and disregarding permanent concerns with such super-powers as the US and USSR, Djakarta's diplomatic interests and initiatives have become notably fewer. Diplomatic posts and personnel, particularly in Europe, Africa, and Latin America, have been reduced. With nations like the Netherlands and the Federal German Republic financial and economic interest dictates close ties. But significant has been the lessening of concern with the Arab-Muslim community. Suharto himself was reported to be "unable" to attend the 1969 Muslim powers' summit conference in Rabat, though Indonesia was eventually represented by a prominent Islamic figure, and there were considerable delays in granting the Al Fatah Palestine Liberation Movement the right to open an office in Djakarta. On 23 December 1969, the Indonesian Ambassador to Saudi Arabia announced that the Indonesian Government had not only extended such permission to Al Fatah but also to "other similar Palestine Liberation organizations", some of which, one might add, are Al Fatah's bitter rivals. In the United Nations Indonesia votes with the Arab states on matters relating to Israel, but Djakarta's anti-Israelism has a formal and somewhat perfunctory character that is not lost on the Arab states. Moreover, Malik's pronouncements on the Middle East crisis — like those in his interview with the Indonesian dailies, *Pedoman*, *Kompas* and *Indonesia Raya*, on 29 December 1969 — have been markedly conciliatory, even implying, at one point, that Israel's desire for national and territorial recognition by the Arabs must be respected. Malik's remarks were not well received in the Indonesian Islamic community, and, perhaps to make amends, after personally attending the Jeddah Islamic Conference in March 1970, the Indonesian Foreign Minister made it a point to note that the conference had "steadied the joint struggle against Israel". During the subsequent state visit of King Feisal of Saudi Arabia to Indonesia, in June 1970, Suharto also firmly declared support for the "lawful" Arab struggle against Israeli "aggression". But this Indonesian support is likely to remain largely of the moral type.

In the same 29 December 1969 interview Malik also reiterated that "If China no longer sends agents to Indonesia for carrying out subversive activities or keeps accusing Indonesian leaders, there is no reason why relations between the two countries cannot be restored". At the close of July 1970, Malik said that abusive, anti-Indonesian programmes, of late, had been less frequent in Radio Peking, and added that, since there were indications that People's China was changing its attitude by seeking better relations "with the outside world", he had the Rumanian Government "to sound out People's China's policy" toward Djakarta. Clearly, Malik sounded quite conciliatory. But on 20 November 1970, Indonesia was listed as "present but not voting" when the UN General Assembly again rejected an attempt to seat People's China, and, on 15 April 1971, Malik said he did not observe a change in Peking's attitude toward Indonesia and "subversive activities by Chinese Communist; in Indonesia" have not subsided as yet. It would be surprising however, if the new rush to establish diplomatic relations with People's China visible in the world today would leave Indonesian policy unaffected.

By mid-September 1970 Malik was able to announce to Parliament that agreement finally had been reach on 27 August 1970 with the USSR on debts to Russia. Like the April 1970 agreement between Indonesia and her principal Western creditors (see chapter VI), the Soviet-Indonesian debt repayment agreement involves a thirty-year repayment period, with interest to be paid during the last fifteen years, and with certain rights of deferment of instalment payments. Sizeable Soviet purchases of Indonesian rubber and coffee, a Soviet promise to resume assistance to the Tjilegon steel plant construction, and new Soviet readiness to sell spare parts for Soviet-built Indonesian naval vessels and planes, all suggest Moscow's willingness to turn over a new leaf in relations with Djakarta. Concurrently, Foreign Minister Malik said in early March 1971, in a Djakarta press interview, that Indonesia, along with other ASEAN states, should not fear the presence of the Soviet or other big power fleets in the Indian Ocean. This surely heralded a rather remarkable shift in Malik's reported position on the future problems of the Indian Ocean area.

On 20 March 1971 Malik also announced that Indonesia would shortly appoint a new ambassador to Hanoi and earlier, in February, the Indonesian Government formally had urged that Laotian sovereignty and neutrality be respected, and that all foreign forces in Laos be withdrawn. To those who might see in these developments a genuine concern for a preservation of traditional Indonesian "independence" and "neutralism" in foreign policy, it should also be pointed out that since December 1970 Indonesia has been providing training to an undisclosed number of Cambodian military; that in early May 1971 Djakarta and Tokyo agreed "to exchange military experiences" (not further identified); and that, following Suharto's May 1970 visit to Washington, the US has agreed to expand its military assistance programme for training and weapons to Indonesia to a total of US$18 million for the fiscal year 1971. Clearly Indonesia intends to keep her options open, and a pragmatic flexibility is likely to remain the lodestar of Indonesian foreign policy for some time to come.

CHAPTER NINE

Conclusion: The Elections and Beyond

ON 10 SEPTEMBER 1969, General A. H. Nasution, MPRS chairman
and *Orba's* senior statesman, in an address to the Indonesian Air
Force Staff College at Lembang, West Java, said that Indonesia
should carry out the general elections by July 1971, as decided
earlier. The holding of the elections, Nasution declared, "will
support the people's sovereignty and constitutional life", and he
added that the urgency to hold the poll was not "diminished"
because there were "technical difficulties" in arranging it. The
General's words were widely interpreted as a warning to parties,
parliamentary representatives, as well as to some military circles,
which all during the previous year had remained deadlocked on
crucial bills governing the 1971 elections. In the middle of July
1969, the Indonesian Parliament had gone into recess without
passing the needed elections' legislation, and the representatives of
some parties on a special parliamentary committee that had been
studying the election bills gave it out that the major stumbling
block was the Suharto Government's insistence that it be given
the right to appoint a major segment of the membership of the
national and regional legislatures.

Other observers noted, however, that parties themselves were
divided over the old issue of proportional representation and over
the candidacy or participation of members of the former *Masjumi*
and Socialist parties, as well as of the PNI. The *Partai Katolik*
and the *Murba* party counselled postponement of the elections
altogether, on the grounds that there first had to be an improvement in the social and economic life of the nation. This sentiment
also appeared to find some favour with President Suharto who,
on 15 October 1969, only hours before he was to meet again with
representatives from the major parties in another attempt to break
the stalemate, was quoted in an address to a governors' conference
as saying that "solid political and economic stability" was required
in Indonesia before the poll could be held. Suharto further

declared that the elections "should not deviate from the *Pantja Sila*" (that is the official five principles of the Indonesian State, including belief in God, nationalism, democracy, social justice and humanitarianism), nor "from the constitution"; nor should they be permitted "to obstruct the Five-Year National Development Plan". These conditions seemed sufficiently broad so as to allow Government intervention in, or to justify postponement of, the elections for almost any reason, and by the end of October the concensus among many knowledgeable Djakartanese was that Indonesia was not likely to see a national poll before 1972. Nor was postponement of the elections seen by everyone as necessarily undesirable. For example, *Indonesia Raya*, frequently *Orba*'s voice of reason, declared editorially that considering the present arrangement of the political parties "The election would produce only the same people — those who were once Sukarno's yes-men and who once accepted the *nasakom* idea which we deplore". A similar view was also voiced by *Harian Kami* and by many student radicals.

Yet all these pessimistic utterances had a tendency to obscure the fact that gradually, and under consistent prodding of cabinet- and sub-cabinet-level officials, a weary and resigned agreement on the elections was nevertheless beginning to emerge in principal political circles. Already on 25 June 1969, for example, the daily *Kompas* reported that while a decision had not as yet been reached on the number of appointed members in regional legislative bodies there was now agreement on such previously divisive questions as the number of delegates from the regions in the future People's Consultative Assembly (MPR), on the appointment of governors, and on guarantees for organizations defeated in the general elections. It was also becoming clear that while many military leaders had the gravest misgivings about the potential effects of the electoral strength of orthodox and conservative Muslim groups, they realized too that a postponement of the poll because of a well-publicized fear of organized Islam would be a cure worse than the disease. Certainly Nasution, looked on by a number of Muslim factions as their champion in the military-political arena, reportedly left little undone to persuade a reluctant Suharto and other Army commanders that elections were necessary. The argument that *Orba* and Indonesia's post-Sukarno reconstruction could not survive a Muslim-military confrontation, and that the only way to head off a clash would be through the national poll, thus became more and more decisive.

On 10 October 1969, K. H. A. Sjaichu, the second chairman of the *Nahdatul Ulama* (NU) party — the group where distrust of Suharto and *Orba* modernism is quite strong — denied recent allegations by a Dutch daily that the party had reached a secret understanding with the military to postpone elections until 1974. In subsequent days Suharto intensified his search for a compromise with parliamentary leaders, and by mid-November Antara reported that an agreement had finally been achieved on the number of Government-appointed members in the provincial and regency legislative councils. To the end, the minor Muslim party PSII (*Partai Sharikat Islam Indonesia* — United Indonesian Islamic Party) had tried to hold out for a ten per cent appointed membership, but the Government refused to settle for anything less than twenty per cent allocation. At last, on 22 November, as the Government announced that general elections would definitely be held on 5 July 1971, the House approved most of the essential *Undang-Undang Pemilihan Umum* (General Elections Act) in a near-empty chamber.

According to this measure — actually consisting of several separate bills linked together — the new House will have a total of 460 members, 360 of whom are to be elected and 100 appointed by the President. As Antara put it in its 24 November commentary on the election legislation, "the number of members elected during the General Elections must be in proportion to the number of the population of each area", but the means of determining proportional representation are poorly described in the new law. Members of parliament will come from twenty-six electoral regions, and each member of parliament is to represent 400,000 voters, each member of a provincial legislative council 200,000 voters, and each member of a regency legislative council 10,000. The 100 appointed members of the House will come from the armed forces (upon the recommendation of the Minister of Defence), and from their own *golkar* (from *golongan karja*) or functional groups (upon recommendations of their own organizations or at the President's initiative), in approximately a three-to-one proportion. Other *golkar* candidates competed against party candidates in the election. The ruling (no. 12/December 1969) of Home Affairs Minister Amir Mahmud barring *golkar* candidates from formal party affiliation stirred up much controversy.

The new People's Consultative Assembly (MPR), the nation's highest policy-making body, is to have 920 members, and is to include the members of the new House as well as representatives of the regions, functional and other special interest groups, including the military, parties, and so on. One-third of the MPR is to be appointed, and one of its major responsibilities will come in 1973 when it is to elect the President of Indonesia. One-fifth of the membership of provincial legislative councils is to be appointed by the Government from among the armed forces and functional groups. The regency legislative councils will have a similar composition. Special conditions are imposed by the Elections Act on members of the armed forces, in view of the latter's "dual function as defenders of the *Pantja Sila* and the 1945 Constitution, and as citizens". Also "in order to prevent dissent", members of the armed forces will neither vote, nor stand for or be elected to any office (their relatives can do so, however). Civil servants, according to a government regulation (no.6/1970), were at first barred from such political activities which were "not in accordance" with their employment. But this was not a blanket ban on membership in political parties. Those barred from political organizations and/or political activity included members of the armed forces, all judges, and other top public servants, but there appeared to be many qualifications of the rule in practice. A presidential decision on 26 October 1970 officially permitted civil servants to become candidates for seats in Parliament. If elected and willing to take his seat, the civil servant must resign his government post. There was never any question that civil servants were entitled to vote.

Perhaps the most controversial feature of the General Elections Act has been the first section of Article 2, which stipulates that Indonesians who have been members of the PKI, or other mass organizations which have been involved "directly or indirectly" in the *Gestapu* movement, or who have been members of "other banned organizations", will not be permitted to vote and cannot be elected. Those who consciously participated in and/or planned the *Gestapu* affair, or who had knowledge of *Gestapu* plans but failed to report them to the authorities, are considered to have been "directly" involved; those who by word and deed showed that they approved of the *Gestapu* movement, or who consciously opposed *Gestapu*'s extermination, are considered "indirectly" involved. Considering the possible nuances in knowledge of the attempted coup or in conscious opposition to the eradication of the *Gestapu* movement, such an interpretation, as some Indonesian legal experts have pointed out, opened the door wide to possible disenfranchisement. For example, how could the electoral eligibility be determined of the 50,000 or so political prisoners in the "C" or "D" classification, that is those said to be least culpable in connection with *Gestapu*, or those whose culpability is not really known but who have been arrested on various unsupported suspicions? Prisoners in these categories have increasingly been released — usually without trial or other formal adjudication of their cases. In a regulation in January 1970, the Government announced that political prisoners in the "A", "B" and "C" categories would not be permitted to take part in the elections. But what, particularly, of *released* "C" category detainees? Would they be permitted to vote? Judging from the storm of controversy which met the remark of Lieutenant-General Sumitro, deputy for the Security and Order Command, on 30 November 1969, that released Communist prisoners would be allowed to participate in the elections, it seemed perilous to answer that question.

It was, however, less the issue of the electoral eligibility of *Gestapu* suspects and more the eligibility problem of the one-time members of the former Socialist (PSI) and *Masjumi* parties that provoked the sharpest discussions. In August 1969, Sukarno had ordered the two parties to dissolve themselves within one month or face a formal ban, on grounds that they still had not dissociated themselves from their leaders involved in the regional rebellions in Sumatra and Sulawesi in the fifties. The parties duly complied. At first, on 24 November 1969, shortly after the passage of the major election legislation, Minister of Justice Oemar Senoadjie was quoted as saying in Djakarta that the Government had made "no mention" of either the *Masjumi* or the Socialist parties as organizations whose members were ineligible for participation in the elections. But the next day the Minister denied that he had made any mention of the *Masjumi* and PSI twenty-four hours before, and soon the controversy became general. Bustaman, a member of parliament who had sat in the special committee on the elections legislation, declared that during the House discussions on Article 2 of the General Elections Act the "*Masjumi* and PSI had never been mentioned", while a former PSI leader, Subadio Sastrosatomo, gave it as his view that Article 2 did not refer to the PSI or its former members since the PSI had never been formally banned, having dissolved itself within the one-month period as laid down by Sukarno. The same argument was also advanced on 22 December 1969 by Lukman Harun of the new Muslim party *Parmusi* or PMI (*Partai Muslimin Indonesia*). It should be noted, however, that, according to the then PMI general chairman Djarnawi Hadikusumo, in a statement reported by Antara on 30 December 1969, "no less than 99 per cent of former *Masjumi* members and cadres have become members of the *Partai Muslimin Indonesia*".

In the controversy the Government steered a seemingly uncertain course. Information Minister Budiardjo at first declared on 5 December 1969 that the Government would not become involved in the dispute over the "banned political parties", but instead would concentrate on the job of organizing the elections. However, Home Affairs Minister Amir Mahmud shortly thereafter added to the confusion by a statement in Semarang on 30 December in which he said first that "only" members of the PKI "and other outlawed political parties" would not be permitted to participate in elections. But when pressed by newsmen to explain if his words "other outlawed political parties" referred to the *Masjumi* and PSI, Mahmud declined, and when asked whether former *Masjumi* and PSI members were also prohibited from taking part in the elections he replied, "Should rebels also be elected?" — an answer taken by some to mean "yes". On 17 January 1970 President Suharto declared that any political restructuring should be accomplished "democratically" through general elections. But then he went on to stress that the outcome of the poll "should unequivocally reaffirm the *Pantja Sila* as the nation's ideology". What would happen if the elections "democratically" resulted in a desire for a change from the *Pantja Sila* Suharto did not elucidate and may seem, in any case, a rhetorical question were it not for the fact that support for the *Pantja Sila* as the State ideology has come to be inextricably interwoven with the earlier-mentioned problem of the Djakarta Charter (see chapter III). Knowing the Army's fear of a possible Islamic political ascendancy, did Suharto's demand that the elections result in adhesion to the *Pantja Sila* constitute a veiled warning to NU, PSII and other Muslim organizations restive under *Orba* "secularism"? Some observers thought so. Others, however, opined that it was merely a general warning to the PKI underground, *as well as* to former rebels of the *Masjumi* and PSI, not to attempt to use existing parties and the forthcoming elections for a new attempt at subversion.

On 13 January 1970, Antara reported the substance of two new government regulations on the general elections, one of which (no.1/1970) declared that all former PKI members or members of Communist-affiliated organizations, or political prisoners in the "A", "B" and "C" categories, would be barred from participating in the elections but that "Members of formerly outlawed political parties or organizations who have been pardoned are entitled to take part". The latter provision was a particular boon to a number of *Masjumi* and PSI members who had joined in the Sumatran rebellion of 1958, and to participants in the Muslim extremist insurgencies of Kartosuwirjo in West Java and their allies in North Sumatra, South Kalimantan and South Sulawesi, and who had been given a pardon in 1961 when they "returned to the lap of the Republic" (that is ceased their rebellion). But it did not really help an indeterminate number of former *Masjumi* and PSI members who did not openly participate in the regional rebellion in Sumatra and South Sulawesi in the late fifties, and who therefore did not seek a formal pardon. Were they still excluded from participation in the elections as non-pardoned former members of "banned" organizations? The regulation also raised again the troublesome question of released "C"and"D" category *Gestapu* political prisoners—did their release automatically mean a pardon, or could they participate in the elections anyway?

In subsequent months new government regulations and announcements attempted to answer some of these questions. But often it seemed that the thicket of legal and political complications surrounding the *Pemilihan Umum* was steadily growing. In the middle of March 1970, Home Affairs Minister Mahmud announced that some 2,500 former members of the *Masjumi* and PSI parties would not be permitted to participate in the elections; these presumably were "hardcore" leaders of the regional rebellions of the nineteen-fifties. Other former members of the two banned organizations however would retain "their rights to elect and be elected", the Minister said. Former *Masjumi* stalwart Mohammad Roem, now a prominent executive in the PMI, announced that he would "sue the Government" if even one former member of *Masjumi* was barred from full participation in the forthcoming elections. Among other PMI members too there was dissatisfaction over Mahmud's announcement. PMI deputy secretary-general Imrah Kadir however termed Roem's objections unduly provocative, and Home Affairs Minister Mahmud subsequently reiterated that the figure of 2,500 which he had used was "only an example" and that it was really up to the Command for Restoring Security and Public Order (*Kopkamtib*) to determine the eligibility of voters. (Indeed, as early as 23 February 1970, Antara had reported Mahmud as saying that *Kopkamtib* had "exclusive authority" to "screen all candidates in the election".) The legal grounds barring some former *Masjumi* and PSI members and not others came increasingly under attack after the middle of 1970, and the Government had no ready answer to critics who argued that evidently there had been an *ex post facto* modification of the pardons extended by the Government to former participants in the rebellions of the fifties. Mahmud's explanation, to some, suggested that the 2,500 excluded were but a token figure anyway — a concession to critics who were wont to contrast the allegedly greater leniency with which *Orba*'s leaders handled former *Masjumi* and PSI members as compared to PKI followers or suspects.

On 6 July 1970 Antara reported that the secretary-general of the General Elections Institute in Djakarta, Sunadar Prijosudarmo, had said that a "total of 1,730,799 Indonesian nationals" had up to that point been declared ineligible to participate in the elections. These were described as individuals who had been "directly or indirectly" involved in the *Gestapu* affair. Reporters wanted to know whether any released "C" and "D" categories of *Gestapu* political prisoners were in this 1,730,799 group. But no certain answer came from any government agency to this question. Prijosudarmo said that all candidates in the elections would have to pass a screening by "a special committee", and would then be given a "clearance certificate" by the General Elections Institute. But a subsequent explanation seemed to limit this again to candidates who were former members of the *Masjumi* and PSI parties. This explanation was again denied, however, and the exclusive screening authority of *Kopkamtib* was reaffirmed, and thus the matter went on. All the while Mahmud's utterances only seemed to augment the legal confusion. Thus, speaking in Ambon, in the Moluccas in April 1970, for example, the Home Affairs Minister was reported to have "taken note of attempts at nominating former rebels in the coming General Elections". "It would be ironical indeed if the people chose those as parliamentary deputies who betrayed the *Pantja Sila*," Mahmud said, adding that members of "Leftist parties like the *Partindo*" would have no right to be elected. Mahmud's reference to *Partindo*, the former Communist fellow-traveller and offshoot of the PNI, was seen in the context of the then impending trial (on grounds of complicity in *Gestapu*) of *Partindo*'s general secretary, Adi Sumarto. And his statement raised new questions also: were all *Partindo* members excluded automatically from being elected, that is was there to be no "screening or pardon" procedure for them? Did exclusion from being elected also mean exclusion from voting?

Concern also grew over *Kopkamtib*'s "screening" powers. In July 1970, members of parliament complained that in various regencies of East Java *Kopkamtib* had been distributing, through the heads of the regencies, questionnaries to future voters "to determine the mental attitude of the people in political matters". It was charged that the questionnaries were in fact an attempt to determine the nature of prevailing political attitudes which *Kopkamtib* deemed undesirable, in short a "screening" of voters.

These developments may well give rise to questions about the fairness with which the elections have been held. But then, too. difficult technical-administrative problems must be considered. For example, early in April 1970, Home Affairs Minister Mahmud announced that registration for the forthcoming elections would start on 5 July 1970 and that a "population census will be held at the same time". Whether both a census and an election registration should, in fact, be held simultaneously, troubled some party leaders. Mahmud already seemed to have an idea of the registration results: 55 per cent of the people in Indonesia had franchise, he said. Voters and candidates had to be seventeen years old, or be married, or have been married once, if they were not at least seventeen. Proof of age, however, was quite a problem in many areas (as it was in the 1955 general elections). Perhaps one index to Indonesia's manifold problems is that the administration of public records today is, despite and probably because of bureaucratic growth, little if at all better than it was a decade and a half ago.

It was already apparent early in 1970 that *Orba*'s political antagonisms had a way of crossing the elections provisions. To some it has seemed that the Government, and especially the military, managed to manoeuvre matters in such a way that some of the Government's principal actual or potential supporters, not just such former PSI stalwarts like Sumitro Djojohadikusumo (Minister of Trade) and Sudjatmoko (Ambassador in Washington), but also the *Masjumi* and Socialist parties' rank and file, have been politically legitimized, while at the same time *Orba*'s potential opponents, often far less culpable of actual acts of rebellion than the former *Masjumi*-PSI leadership, have seemed doomed to remain in a political limbo. The reference here is not to the PKI but to the PNI. On 20 December 1969, the daily *Suluh Marhaen* first reported that the Home Affairs Ministry had revoked and annulled regulations of the South Sumatra provincial government prohibiting PNI members in that province from voting and being elected. The paper noted that on a number of occasions in the recent past South Sumatran provincial authorities had cancelled the outcome of local elections in the province because PNI members had won office in them. However, the revocation of the anti-PNI regulations by the Home Affairs Ministry, *Suluh Marhaen* predicted, would open the way to a "more democratic way of life" and to a firmer establishment of the rule of law in South Sumatra.

This prediction soon proved to be false. On 15 January 1970 Antara reported from Palembang that police authorities in South Sumatra were prohibiting the PNI and its organizational affiliates from putting up signboards and posters in their election campaign. The PNI had filed for a police permit to display its posters on 15 January but it was rejected. For the time being, at least, the revocation of earlier anti-PNI regulations by the Home Affairs Ministry appeared not to be having much effect, even though Home Affairs Minister Mahmud shortly was quoted to have termed the whole matter a "misunderstanding" and to have instructed South Sumatran authorities to permit PNI political activity. But South Sumatran PNI leaders continued to complain of official obstruction and "negative pressures". No doubt in subsequent months PNI complaints resulted in further moderation of present opposition to the party's election activity. But the incident was illustrative of the unabated tensions that are *Gestapu's* legacy and that unquestionably affected the 1971 general poll. President Suharto and some of his military advisers reportedly have overcome some of their earlier suspicions of the PNI, if for no other reason than that they see the party as yet another convenient electoral barrier against dissident conservative Islamic groups. But it is evident that the President will have to move cautiously in dealing with anti-PNI sentiment among local military and security agencies, as well as among anti-Sukarno and Muslim youth groups, not just in South Sumatra but in the remainder of that island as well. In February 1970, PNI leaders in Acheh complained again that officials blocked party activity. The impression that the PNI still had not wholly divested itself of all Sukarnoist influence seemed to remain widespread despite the PNI's own protestations. And opponents of the PNI repeatedly cited Information Minister Budiardjo's warning, made in a press interview in Medan, North Sumatra, at the close of December 1969, that the 1971 elections "should not give an opportunity to Dr Sukarno to come to power again, and therefore the Indonesian people must remain vigilant".

Meanwhile other military commanders and spokesmen kept on stressing the danger of a PKI come-back through the elections. Major-General Witono, Siliwangi military territorial commander, according to *Angkatan Bersendjata* on 11 August 1969, declared that "many political groups and mass organizations are watering at the mouth for former PKI members, in order to be able to add them in the coming general elections". He said that even some "religious" organizations were hoping for such PKI support, thus giving substance to current, mostly unverified reports of underground Communist penetration into some Muslim mass organizations. Attempting to fuse Islam and the PKI into a common enemy of the military is a hazardous tactic indeed, and assertions or implications that such a fusion is, in fact, occurring may well polarize already dangerous civilian-military political antagonisms even after the campaigning for the election has ended. Consciously or not, some military spokesmen seem to do all in their power to deepen such a polarization. In an address to the House in November 1969, on the subject of the new election legislation, a spokesman of the military parliamentary faction, Sujono, asserted, for example, that the active participation of the military in the forthcoming national poll was not "absolutely necessary" in order to guarantee the safety of the Constitution and *Pantja Sila*, but he also warned the political parties against any "violent and noisy" campaigning which would be exploited by the Communists. The implication seemed to be that the parties simply could not be trusted in the elections. Sujono also said that the continued presence of the military in the Government was justified by the historical record of the armed forces' defence of the country against past "Leftist" as well as "Rightist" take-over attempts. Sujono's words were interpreted by many as an indication that the Army would not hesitate to intervene even in the conduct of parties during the elections, if it deemed it desirable. Was Sujono merely indulging in the rhetoric of the military-man-turned-politician, and only raising chimeras whose realization Suharto would never permit? Who, looking at the pattern of the Army's political powers in the country, could confidently say yes to such questions?

Throughout most of 1970 the controversy over the General Elections Act showed no signs of abating. Already in the middle of January the earlier-mentioned regulation (no.12/December 1969) of the Home Affairs Ministry, denying representatives of *golkar*, or functional groups, the right to have party affiliation, was bitterly criticized in Parliament amidst demands for its revocation. NU's Central Java branches threatened to boycott local provincial and regency legislative councils if the regulation was not revoked. By early March 1970 the principal PNI leaders had also condemned the measure, and, at about the same time, PMI leader Mohammad Roem charged that it had already cost the loss of eleven representatives of his party in local legislative councils in South Kalimantan. These protests were to no avail, however. Suharto and his military advisers were adamant that the *Golkar* would not become part of the existing political party system. Instead they saw the *Golkar* as their own political force, a stabilizing element in and supporter of *Orba*, to balance the parties.

Beginning in February 1970 and throughout subsequent weeks Home Affairs Minister Mahmud proceeded with the implementation of his regulation no.12/December 1969. By early April Mahmud declared implementation to have been "virtually" completed throughout Indonesia. *Golkar* members of provincial and regency legislative bodies who were considered partisan (that is belonging to labour, women's, peasant, youth, entrepreneurs' and other groups affiliated with one of the political parties) were dismissed. Critics, especially in East Java, alleged that their places were frequently taken by overt or covert members of the military, or by civilians close to local military commanders. Defenders of Mahmud's measure have asserted that the *Golkar* component is now much more "independent" and "technically specialized", presumably meaning that it is closer to the actual needs of the functional group in question. Just the same, the regulation no.12/December 1969 significantly augmented the influence of the armed forces in the sphere of local government, at a time when two-thirds of the heads of local governments (provinces and regencies) already come from the military, and when the pattern of public services at the urban and rice-roots level similarly shows no sign of increased "civilianization".

In the weeks after the passage of the Elections Act, criticism was often voiced that the elections were not likely to bring a significant change in the quality of the membership of the House, or even in the relative strength of the parties, and hence it was said that the nation would benefit but little from the expenses of a national poll at this time. Questions were also raised about the complexity of the elections procedure. Some fifty-five million voters would be expected to take part, according to Information Minister Budiardjo, and each would be expected to vote for a candidate for the House of Representatives, for a candidate for the provincial legislative council, and for a candidate for the regency legislative council — presumably involving choices a good deal more complicated than those presented by the parliamentary elections of 1955.

There were also those who wondered whether the elections would really contribute much to a solution for persisting constitutional problems, such as the place of the Djakarta Charter and the role of Islamic law in the Indonesian State (see chapter III). In the event — not altogether improbable — that the group of principal Islamic parties, including NU, PMI, PSII, and *Perti*, would win a large block of seats in the elections, and that the demand for a formal constitutional legitimization of the Djakarta Charter would be raised with new force, would the Suharto Government yield? In early September 1969, just a few weeks before the passage of the election legislation in the House, A. Hafiluddin, secretary-general of the Government's Department of Religious Affairs, in a lecture to departmental officials from West Sumatra, declared that it was not necessary for the Islamic community in Indonesia to raise a new controversy over the Djakarta Charter. The Charter, according to Hafiluddin, "merely" states that "the obligation to practice the laws of Islam is binding for the adherent of that religion" — and this obligation already exists for each and every Muslim in the country as a matter of course, so that there was really no need to make an issue about the matter. To critics Hafiluddin's argument seemed rather disingenuous, considering the psychological and political importance of a constitutionalization of the Djakarta Charter for many Indonesian Muslims. And, in any case, one could obviously retort that if nothing out of the way was to be found in the Charter, there should be no reason then to prevent its inclusion in the fundamental law of the land. But Hafiluddin's statement was significant just the same for an appreciation of the Suharto Government's policy. Meanwhile, a general acknowledgement of "belief in God" — the first pillar of the *Pantja Sila* — is as far as Suharto is apparently prepared to go in recognizing Muslim religio-legal demands.

Under these circumstances the antagonisms between the Suharto regime and the Muslim community are hardly likely to lessen, even after holding of the elections — in fact, the results of the elections suggest new patterns of political polarization and a sharpening of the controversy. To be sure, the Islamic community is not politically homogeneous and Suharto may continue to benefit from that community's division. Yet, there is a question of whether the PMI — despite the lack of warmth between itself and NU — could go against, or even remain neutral in, a demand for a formal constitutionalization of the Djakarta Charter. Here, precisely, the present lack makes itself felt of a secular non- or anti-Communist, Left-wing political grouping, free, as the PNI is not, from the taint of the *Orla* past. Such a party could more closely reflect the interests of much of Indonesia's intelligentsia and academically trained elite, and because of its informal ties with the *Orba* leadership could perhaps also act constructively in keeping the Suharto Government within democratic bounds. Though the creature of Suharto and the *Orba*, the *Golkar* organizational structure might well eventually assume the role of such a party. In time, however, fears of the Suharto regime being unable to mitigate its autocratic tendencies might well align the *Golkar* with opposition Muslim parties, more so since *Golkar* as a collection of more than 200 groups has never been monolithic.

Suharto himself in the first half of 1970 appeared to be assisting in the formation of a PMI-NU alliance by means of his so-called *naspika* proposal. Already in 1966 Major-General Dharsono, then commander of the West Java-based Siliwangi division, who maintained close connections with some of *Orba*'s leading intellectual supporters (see chapter III), had suggested a "simplification" of Indonesia's multiparty system into a *dwi grup* (two-party) system composed of a "progressive" faction and a more "conservative" faction. Before Dharsono's suggestion, another simplification scheme, involving factional alliances or party fusions into Marxist, religious, and nationalist organizations, had been suggested by former President Sukarno. Neither Sukarno's nor Dharsono's ideas ever acquired much momentum, although early in 1968 the West Java provincial legislative council appeared at one point to have favoured the *dwi grup* concept. By the close of February 1970, after consultations between Suharto and principal political parties, a "concensus" was reported to have emerged according to which a threefold political organizational structure would come into being, composed of "nationalist", "spiritual" and functional groups. The acronym *naspika*, in standard Indonesian fashion, is made up of the first letters of the name of each group and symbolizes the whole system, as Sukarno's term *nasakom* did for the union of nationalist, religious and Communist parties.

Naspika did not come about without some demurrers among the parties themselves however. A complete merger of parties was ruled out; each constituent group would maintain its organizational identity in the larger nationalist group or other rubrics. The spiritual group is entirely Islamic — neither *Parkindo* (the Protestant party) nor the *Partai Katolik* felt comfortable with the Muslim religious parties (or was made welcome by the latter). The two Christian political parties joined the nationalist group composed of the IPKI, the PNI and the "national Communist" *Murba* party. Early in March 1970, the nationalist group's members announced that they had agreed formally to enter into "co-operation" for the "sake of the national interest". A common programme would be announced in the future. On 17 March 1970 Antara announced that NU, PMI, PSII and *Perti*, had formed a "union group" (*kelompok persatuan*) four days previously, thus presumably giving substance to the spiritual group of *naspika*. The functional group segment, through the Joint Secretariat of Functional Groups (usually abbreviated in Indonesian to *Sekber Golkar*), shortly announced its own organizational programme despite the confusion attendant upon its restructuring in conformity with Home Affairs Minister Mahmud's regulation of no.12/ December 1969 noted above. Not a few parties and functional organizations, directly or indirectly, indicated subsequently that the *naspika* notion had been forced on them. Critics wondered what, for example, the *Murba* and Catholic parties could be said to have in common beyond ideological generalities. Others, notably some Central Java PNI spokesman, expressed doubt as to the degree of unity within each group once campaigning for the elections started in earnest. By the end of May 1970, Suharto himself was reported to have had second thoughts about *naspika*. Particularly the difficulty which the Muslim parties were said to have had in forming their spiritual group suggested that creation of political units designed to check or balance the Muslim groups did not seem so compelling after all, as some military commanders once believed. (That *naspika* had been foisted on Suharto by "Javanese" and "Christian" military leaders wishing to neutralize

Muslim political parties was virtually an article of faith in some Islamic circles by the middle of 1970.) Few seasoned observers expected *naspika* to stand up under the rigours of electioneering. Was the whole idea but another instance of not-so-subtle military intervention in national life? Only time would tell.

It cannot be said, however, that Suharto has wholly failed to demonstrate concern over military wilfulness or arbitrariness, whether potential or real. Possibly significant in this connection was the reorganization of the military command structure effected by Suharto in a series of announcements and regulations, beginning last Armed Forces Day, 5 October 1969, continuing on 10 November 1969, and coming completely into force on 1 April 1970. General Maraden Panggabean, the Army commander, was named for the post of Deputy Commander of the Armed Forces, directly under Suharto, who remains Commander of the Armed Forces. Suharto will, for the time being, also retain the post of Minister of Defence and Security. Panggabean, however, will hold the rank of Minister of State, and in this capacity "will represent" Suharto "when the House of Representatives demands explanation", as the Antara commentary put it. The appointment of the 53-year-old Panggabean, a Christian and a Sumatran, was immediately seen, in some quarters, as providing a possible counterweight to the influence of another Sumatran, MPRS chairman General Nasution, who of late has been regarded as *Orba*'s principal spokesman — behind the scenes — for the Muslim community.

Along with the appointment of Panggabean came a restructuring — in effect a demotion — of the top leadership positions in the three main services, the army, navy and air force. The position of Commander-in-Chief in the three services was renamed Chief of Staff, and new appointments were announced in these functions, along with three further appointments to the positions of Chief of Staff of General Affairs, of Departmental Affairs, and of Civic Mission Affairs, respectively, of the Defence and Security Staff. Panggabean now, in fact, heads a much more centralized, Pentagon-style structure of a joint functioning of chiefs of staff, while also holding command of the Command for Restoring Security and Public Order (*Kopkamtib*). The latter is the military's chief agency for domestic security and intelligence, its authority overlapping extensively with that of the police. Prominent casualties of the October shake-up were the naval chief, Admiral Muljadi and the Air Force chief, Marshal Rusmin Nurjadin, who were promised ambassadorial posts. Reports had indicated for some time that Suharto had lost confidence in them.

Not only was the entire command structure of the armed forces establishment greatly centralized and tightened by the

October reforms, and not only did Suharto succeed in filling top posts with his close personal friends, but in the course of the reorganization Suharto also saw to it that henceforth service chiefs of staff and subordinate commanders would no longer be able to move their forces from one area of the country to another without the express approval of the Commander and Deputy Commander of the Armed Forces, that is Suharto and Panggabean. The territorial command structure throughout the country was also reorganized in the October reforms with the introduction of six "regional defence commands" (*kowilham*), comprising Java, Sumatra, Sulawesi, Kalimantan, Nusa Tenggara (the Lesser Sunda Islands), and Maluku-Irian Barat (Moluccas-West New Guinea). The first three are held by the Army, the fourth by the Air Force, and the last two by the Navy. The authority of the new regional defence commanders now appears also a good deal more circumscribed — at least on paper — than that of the previous, often free-wheeling, territorial commanders. To this extent, at least, Suharto met Indonesia's incipient, local "war lord" problem.

Indonesian press and public reaction to the October reforms was quite interesting. Papers basically sympathetic to the Government commented that there were not many among the new countries of the world today where such incisive alterations in the military command structure could occur without incident; the Suharto Government continued to enjoy the support of the nation's leaders, these media contended. But some Muslim circles in particular were apt to be more critical, professing to see in Panggabean's appointment, and in the tighter control to be exercised by the Commander and Deputy Commander of the Armed Forces over the service chiefs and over the individual service branches, additional signs of growing military autocracy. In these circles greater civlian control over the Department of Defence and Security was urged. In KAMI there also was little enthusiasm; here some critics were saying that they suspected the Government was tightening its grip on the military establishment so as to make sure that the forthcoming elections and their results would not prove to be embarrassing to the Suharto regime.

Amidst these and other arguments and speculations one possibility received little attention, and that was that the October reforms were the prelude to a gradual but thorough and badly needed modernization of the Indonesian armed forces, a process to which US Defence Department officials have already contributed significant advice, and to which others — including Australian military experts — would also add their counsel. This modernization process has many aspects, one of which obviously is command reorganization. According to a statement by Brigadier-General

Sajidiman, commander of the Hasanuddin military district, in Makasar, South Sulawesi, and reported by Antara on 1 November 1969, no less than 50,000 Army personnel are to be pensioned off in the 1969-73 period. They will be joining some 5,500 pensioned off during 1967-9. Eliminating over-age, redundant, and inefficient military personnel, and transforming the remainder into a smaller, compact and more effective force, has long been an ambition of many Indonesian military planners over the years and the Suharto Government means to have another try at it — with due regard for the employment problem presented by such personnel re-trenchment. Meanwhile, at the close of November 1969, some of Indonesia's biggest peace-time manoeuvres, involving several thousands of troops, were staged in and around the Tjirebon area of West Java. Observers were quick to note the run-down and obsolete condition of the weapons — some regular Army units used rifles of World War II vintage, including American M 1s, British Lee Enfields, and a few Soviet AKs; local militia had to make do with much older hardware. Such armour as there was appeared badly dilapidated, and tanks remained largely stationary in order, as a Defence Ministry spokesman put it, not to "chew up the roads". There was some artillery but it did not fire a shot. The Defence Ministry also announced that two squadrons of MIG 19s of Korean War vintage would participate, but none did, lending support to rumours that most of the Air Force's MIGs and Ilyushins continued to be grounded for want of spare parts. "Instead," as an Associated Press despatch put it, "three old P 51 Mustangs, with glamorous 'Flying Tiger' teeth on their cowlings, and two lumbering B 26s wheezed into the sky", and presumably provided the illusion to local onlookers that the AURI — the Indonesian Air Force — could still do its bit in repelling a foreign invader. Current Indonesian military planning is said to regard a foreign invasion as unlikely for at least five years, and while there is no question that the Indonesian armed forces could crush local insurgencies and contain guerilla operations, the Tjirebon manoeuvres hardly suggested that a foreign threat would be met effectively.

Modernization will probably also involve a reconsideration of the Army's much-vaunted "civic mission" activities. Building schools, digging irrigation canals and repairing bridges — however they may aid in identifying the Army with the people — have never set well with a significant segment of Army commanders, who view such activities as discipline-destroying and unmilitary, designed solely to "make work". Corruption has, moreover, infected some of the civic mission programmes. In late January 1970, Brigadier-General Sarwo Edhie Wibowo, newly appointed governor of the Military Academy, criticized the civic mission concept, saying that it only seemed to benefit a few individuals. It was disclosed that, under the guise of civic mission, military equipment, from trucks to bulldozers, had been put at the disposal of civilians after they had provided suitable monetary inducements to Army personnel.

The military reorganization initiated in October 1969, also seems to have brought to a head a long-simmering conflict between a few remaining pro-Sukarnoist Army commanders and other military personnel, and the Suharto regime. Judgment on this is difficult because of the secrecy and *Orba*-type rhetoric that surrounds it. But already on 8 October 1969, the paper *Pelopor Baru* reported that five generals of the police had been dishonourably dismissed and arrested because of alleged involvement in the *Gestapu* affair — an involvement which was said to be of the "A" or "heavy" category. It need not be stressed that a charge of *Gestapu* complicity in Indonesia at this juncture may or may not cover a multiplicity of other sins, probably including simple policy differences. And considering the intelligence about the coup available, the question arises why it took so long for these five top-ranking police officers to be apprehended. Despite denials a new wave of arrests apparently also began shortly in other branches of the armed forces, and by the middle of December 1969, Army spokesmen disclosed that "a plot by senior Army officers to restore to power deposed President Sukarno" had been un-covered. Major-General Mursid, former Ambassador to the Phi-lippines and former deputy Army chief, was arrested for allegedly maintaining secret contact with Sukarno, and on 27 December, Major-General Suadi, governor of the National Defence Institute and former Ambassador to Australia and Ethiopia, was appre-hended on a similar charge. *Pelopor Baru*, early in January 1970, predicted the imminent arrest of three more generals, but on 12 January, a spokesman for the *Kopkamtib* denied that additional arrests had taken place. At the new year, however, Antara quoted a Naval Information Centre spokesman to the effect that a naval "purge" was underway also, and that "several men" had been arrested; the spokesman added that "it is not an impossibility that there are men in the Navy who are trying to establish the Old Order".

By this time various estimates of the number of newly arrested among the military ranged from about 50 to over 300 (including a dozen senior officers), and as informed observers increasingly expressed doubt that any or all of these had been engaged either in maintaining covert links with the deposed President, or in a conspiracy to restore the latter to power, Defence Ministry "informants" quoted by the foreign press began to intimate that the real reasons for some, if not most, of the arrests had to do with opposition to the planned military reorganization and with a collision of personal animosities among some officers dating from the pre- and immediate post-*Gestapu* periods. The vagueness of the charges against the accused (Suadi was said to have given "moral and mental support" to Sukarno) certainly suggested to some observers an essentially political motivation. By early February 1970, the concensus in the capital appeared to be that with the new arrests Suharto and his friends simply had wanted to remove some potentially troublesome opponents. This, in turn, not only did not allay public concern about the autocratic course of the Suharto regime, but it may also well have emboldened some critics of the regime to call for a new accounting of some of the Government's policies, particularly in the economic area where the critics were likely to find a maximum of support from the public.

Thus, already in the closing weeks of 1969, much of the Muslim press in the capital had begun to combine its disenchantment over the new elections legislation with ever sharper demands for a "re-ordering of economic priorities" so that "the living standard of the people will not keep on being depressed", as one paper put it. New discoveries of alleged corruption among the military gave such arguments considerable additional force. In an open letter to Suharto in the paper *Indonesia Raya*, on 31 December 1969, the paper's editor, Mochtar Lubis, openly accused some of the President's assistants of malfeasance (they had "done things which are not in line with your policies", Lubis charged). This was something of a culmination of accusations of corruption brought by Lubis against the management of the Government-owned Pertamina oil company in previous weeks. Lubis threatened to publish the names of allegedly corrupt public officials in subsequent issues of his paper, and he proved as good as his word. Very shortly *Indonesia Raya* charged, for example, that a presidential aide, Major-General Surjo, had participated in an alleged embezzlement of some US$700,000 of government funds by a group of Singapore businessmen. On 4 April 1970, Antara announced the arrest of no less than sixty persons, some of whom were government officials, because of alleged complicity in a scheme to swindle government funds which were allocated to rice farmers.

Meanwhile public indignation was mounting — in part by earlier revelations of *Indonesia Raya* — over the free-wheeling policies of Lieutenant-General Ibnu Sutowo, chief director of Pertamina. The importance of oil to the Indonesian economy was underscored again when Ibnu Sutowo declared, around the middle of December 1969, that in 1969 the proceeds of Indonesian petroleum had paid for 30 per cent of the costs of the nation's development projects. A few days earlier Mining Minister Sumantri Brodjonegoro had said that 60 per cent of all the income from crude oil exports was paid directly into the Ministry of Finance. Whether, in view of these significant contributions, the State oil enterprise, and its supervisory ancillaries over foreign oil concerns were being run as honestly and efficiently as they might be, increasingly seemed to some to be becoming an open question. When, therefore, on 6 January 1970 the Government announced a jump of more than 100 per cent in the price of kerosene, still the major source of fuel and lighting in the country, and a 50 per cent increase in the price of gasoline, a public outburst was predictable. Given the disquiet in many circles over the recently passed elections legislation, the Government's announcement that the price rises would be used in part to defray the costs of the forthcoming 1971 elections, appeared to be almost purposely designed to sharpen public animosities.

Before dealing with some of the events following the announcement of the January kerosene and gasoline price increases it should be noted that although inflationary pressures had undoubtedly been mitigated through much of 1968-9 (Trade Minister Sumitro Djojohadikusumo claimed, in November 1969, that the rate of inflation during the previous ten months had averaged "only" 0.82 per cent per month), nevertheless really significant price stability was slow in being achieved. For example, on 12 December 1969, Antara reported that the price index of nine essential commodities in Djakarta, on which the cost of living index is based, fell by 0.92 per cent during the first week of the month, after having shown a continuous rise during the previous three weeks. On 29 January 1970, however, Antara said that owing to recent increases in the prices of rice, frying oil, sugar and soap, the above-mentioned nine commodities' price index had shown an increase of no less than 10.17 per cent compared to the preceding week! By early February 1970, the vice-chairman of the National Planning Board (*Bappenas*), Emil Salim, said that the price of rice had risen steadily since the beginning of the new year and that this was the principal cause of the price increases in other commodities. Although the Government had kept on importing hundreds of thousands of tons of rice during 1968-9, and making them available through local markets or commissaries, by the first week of November 1969, the weekly *Mingguan Chas* (as indicated previously) revealed that there were grave discrepancies between the stock of rice actually

231

available and the much higher amounts listed in official reports; needless to say the question as to what had happened to much of the imported rice soon came to be considered in terms of the Indonesian nation's seemingly endemic problems of official corruption.

It was against this background that the earlier-mentioned Government decision to raise the prices of kerosene and gasoline occurred. On 15 January 1970, Djakarta erupted in a wave of student protest demonstrations numbering from 2,000 to 10,000 participants on various occasions. Carrying a coffin with a sign which read, "The hope of the common people has died", students vowed to keep on demonstrating till prices were lowered, even though Trade Minister Sumitro Djojohadikusumo did his best to explain to them that the increases were unavoidable given the nation's development needs. The students, who shortly included also those of high school age mobilized by KAPPI, continued their marches in the following days, and it was evident that the Government was not just being taken to task by the demonstrators for the jump in prices alone but also for allegedly continuing laxity in combating corruption. The university graduates' action front (KASI) meanwhile issued a statement which said that the 1971 general elections should not be financed by increasing gasoline and kerosene prices, and that an already "undemocratic" General Elections Act had now also turned out to be an added burden to the national budget.

On 22 January 1970 the military's *Kopkamtib* forbade any further public demonstrations without its consent. The order was sporadically defied, however, and meanwhile the student protests spread to Djokjakarta (where cars were plastered with stickers denouncing the price rise and a march was held on the local legislative council), Bandung, and Medan. Indicative of the mounting tension was a report in the daily *Sinar Harapan* that Trade Minister Sumitro, Emil Salim, Widjojo Nitisastro "and a number of other technocrats" had promised demonstrating students that they would resign their government posts if the security forces shot and killed any students. Student protestors now took to "sit-ins" in several government offices, as their leaders kept on issuing sharply worded manifestoes expressing disappointment over the Government's alleged "lack of seriousness" in dealing with the problems of corruption and rising living costs. At the close of January 1970, what was described as a "direct heart-to-heart meeting" between student spokesmen and several cabinet ministers took place. Perhaps the most notable point of this discussion again was the question of the forthcoming elections. Not only did the students assert that the elections were "obviously" too costly and hardly justified the present onerous price rises and those likely to occur in the future, but also that the elections would "turn the public's attention from economic to political activities". The ministers replied that holding general elections was an MPRS mandate and the "democratic wish of the people", hence the people should also pay for the poll's cost. They also took pains to stress that new measures would be taken to combat corruption.

It is doubtful whether the students were satisfied with the Government's assurances and to this day Suharto is clearly continuing to loose support among his nation's younger generation. As mentioned earlier, on 31 January 1970, Suharto announced formation of a new government advisory committee to combat corruption, composed of a group of respected elder statesmen, among them former Premier Wilopo and Catholic party leader I. J. Kasimo. Former Vice-President Mohammad Hatta was to be an adviser both to Suharto and to the committee. The committee was empowered to gather fresh information and propose new measures to combat corruption. In early February 1970, Attorney-General Soegih Arto also submitted a new, more comprehensive "anti-corruption" bill to Parliament, admitting that the existing act (no.24/1960) in this field had proven inadequate. As an earnest of the President's intentions the new anti-corruption committee could not be overlooked. But it would take a good deal more than the creation of yet additional bureaucratic channels to restore waning confidence, especially among the young, that the Government could really clean house. Doubts about the Government's anti-corruption drive rapidly grew with reports that the Wilopo committee had not been given access to all information—especially as regards the operations of State enterprises — which it had requested. On 16 July 1970 the committee was declared dissolved by presidential decision, and Suharto's refusal to make the committee report public (the President promised he would discuss the committee's recommendation in his 16 August 1970 State of the Nation Address to Parliament), followed by an allegedly unauthorized leak of the committee's report to the Djakarta press, all seemed to add but fuel to the flames in the corruption issue. New student protests (including a *malam tirakatan* or meditation night) against seeming Government reluctance to combat corruption persisted in subsequent weeks, as a parliamentary stalemate seemed to develop over the anti-corruption bill. Not until 12 March 1971 was the anti-corruption bill passed, without a provision making its effect retroactive to 1958 (desired by many).

Will Indonesia's new technocrats be able to bring about meaningful stabilization and development, and, above all, bring them about in time? Early in January 1970, Suharto's message

233

to Parliament on the 1970-1 budget, and his review of the past year's economic achievements, seemed to suggest they were doing so. Rice production targets had been achieved, the President said, textile production had reached 415 million metres, total 1969 exports were a little over one billion US dollars in value (an increase of 10 cent over the previous year), and foreign capital investment continued at a high rate. The 10 billion rupiahs earmarked for the forthcoming elections, Suharto said, along with raises in the salaries of civil servants and of members of the armed forces, were among the reasons why routine 1970-1 budget expenditures would significantly exceed those of the previous year. But the Government was carefully controlling costs, Suharto added. The President also said that defence allocations totalled less than 25 per cent of the total budget, but that modernization of the armed services would continue since "We have to possess a strong armed force indeed in order to defend our very extensive territory which has such a strategically significant position".

On the whole the budget message was well received; particularly the claimed increases in production of food and textiles were deemed noteworthy. The press rightly called attention, however, to persistent anomalies in the economy. It was recalled, for example, that on 27 October 1969, Minister of Agriculture Thojib Hadiwidjaja had predicted that the 1969 rice crop would be significantly larger than the 1968 total harvest of 10.5 million tons, due to an average increase in productivity from 1.1 to 1.4 tons of rice per hectare in 1969. Yet, shortly after Thojib's prediction, the Indonesian press reported that some 100,000 people continued to be in immediate danger of starvation on the island of Lombok unless large quantities of food were rushed in. The wide regional disparities in the price of rice also continued to arouse concern. In early February 1970, for example, a litre of first-quality rice costs Rp.30 in Denpasar, Bali, but Rp.55 in Menado, North Sulawesi. There was no question of the flight which domestic industrial development had recently begun to take. Yet, there was also the Antara report of 22 January 1970 that, according to the Government's own Labour Service statistics, not just the number of jobless people in Central Java increased from 12,000 in 1968 to 20,000 in 1969, but, perhaps more important, that in the same period the number described as "under-employed" also rose from four million to six million, that is to more than 25 per cent of the province's total working population! As has already been stressed there is conspicuously inadequate provision for the hordes of educated un- and under-employed in Indonesia today, as meanwhile the school system yearly discharges ever-growing numbers of job-seeking graduates into society. This problem is hardly unique to Indonesia, to be sure. But compared to the Philippines, India, or Japan, which are confronted with similar difficulties and where some significant effort is being made to reorganize the educational system and reorient educational values, Indonesia lags far behind in anticipating the consequences of a burgeoning intellectual *lumpen* proletariat and of a self-radicalizing student community.

The impatience of radical youth, it need hardly be recalled, greatly facilitated the fall of Sukarno, and it may well eventually do the same for Suharto. Yet, the President and his associates too often give the impression of being unable or unwilling to meet the expected thrust of change in the community, or to capture its political imagination with an occasionally bold policy concept or decision. Obviously anxious not to emulate the bombast of Sukarno's political behaviour, *Orba*'s leaders may have gone too far in the other direction: the sobriety and "dullness" of their regime often infuriate many, particularly since there is no end to the old problems of corruption and rising living costs. Over-reaction among the Government's critics seemed sometimes to be the rule, leading inevitably to confrontations which no one wants. For example, at the close of January 1970, Mochtar Lubis suggested that Indonesians use the forthcoming general elections to demonstrate their total rejection of the present political system. Lubis urged that voters turn in blank ballots during the elections, an action which would render the whole poll meaningless and thus presumably open the way to the drafting of a new elections bill that would reflect thorough changes in the political system, including a "simplification" of existing political parties. In view of Lubis's proposals some wondered whether the dissatisfaction with the national elections was now beginning to pass from verbal criticism to sabotage and resistance. House Speaker (and NU leader) K. H. A. Sjaichu, at about the same time, in a press interview warned that co-operation between Parliament and the executive had to improve if "constitutional democracy" was to develop properly in the country. Obviously reflecting lingering parliamentary resentment and frustrations over the way in which the Government had pressured passage of the General Elections Act through the House a few weeks before, Sjaichu dwelled at length on the necessity of "preventing misunderstanding" in the Government, and went on to criticize the Cabinet for raising the prices of petroleum products without prior consultation with the House. If the Government had held such consultations, Sjaichu said, the "recent excesses" (that is the demonstrations) might have been averted. Many observers agreed that if the Government had, in fact, followed Sjaichu's suggestion, and had gone to the House to win its approval for the price increases, it probably would still be waiting for a parliamentary decision by the end of 1970. Even so, Sjaichu's criticism served to underscore again the continuing disharmony between Government and Parliament, and the persistent underlying problem of the conceptual conflict between presidential system and parliamentary system in the country. Equally evident was the absence of any healing political dynamics.

Presidential versus parliamentary system, secular versus Muslim-confessional State ideology, military versus civilians in politics, multiplicity versus simplicity in the parties — these and other unresolved, intractable problems of Indonesia's political style will, then, likely remain in the years ahead, with or without general elections. And socially no less than politically *Bhinneka tunggal ika* (the motto of Indonesia's great seal, meaning "One out of many") is likely to remain an elusive goal. For example, neither in the colonial nor in the guided democracy period have Christian-Muslim relations in Indonesia been as frayed as they are today. Reference has been made earlier to rising Muslim-Christian tensions and attacks on Christian churches in Sumatra and Sulawesi during 1967 and to the mounting opposition of Muslim leaders to the allegedly greater militancy in seeking converts shown by the Indonesian Christian community (see chapter III). At a conference of Christians and Muslims held under Government auspices in November 1967, a spirit of mutual tolerance was often hard to find. Periodic efforts since then to initiate "dialogues" between the two faiths, also in their respective press media, revealed how deep the distrust between the communities was and is. In April, 1969, some 500 Muslim youths attacked and desecrated a recently built Protestant Church in the Slipi section of western Djakarta. Muslims alleged that no permission had been given by the Government for the building of the church (indeed, the mayor's office was specifically said to have opposed it), that Muslims outnumber Christians nearly seventy to one in the area, and that there are five churches in Slipi already, and that hence the building of yet an additional church was clearly "provocative". Christians, appealing to the *Pantja Sila* doctrine, argued that there should be no obstacle to the peaceful practice and dissemination of any recognized religion.

Almost simultaneously with what was quickly dubbed the "Slipi affair", a similar incident occurred at Djatibarang, in the Indramaju area of West Java. Here a Muslim mob also burned down a church and nearly provoked a serious religious riot. Subsequent investigation revealed, according to the Government, that local undercover Communists had provoked the incident by inciting local Muslims. Then, on 23 January 1970, irate Muslims sacked and burned the Roman Catholic Tarakanita Elementary School on the outskirts of Djakarta, because Roman Catholic authorities had refused to suspend work on the expansion of the school building. Such expansion had aroused strong local Muslim opposition and the Djakarta municipality had, in fact, requested that further construction be stopped. After the incident Muslim leaders asked for calm and religious harmony, and Roman Catholic students throughout Djakarta briefly stayed away from classes in protest.

It is evident that all these incidents are not merely of a formal religious nature and that they cannot be prevented by mere appeals to tolerance. At bottom the issue is one of a secular or a religiously (that is Muslim) grounded State. The leadership of the Christian churches in Indonesia is now thoroughly Indonesianized and the Christian community, by virtue of its education and way of life, is a minority but distinctively modern elite in the country, whose present influence in all walks of life is far out of proportion to its numbers. In short, an actively evangelizing Indonesian Christianity is not just a religious but also a political threat to the existing Islamic community. And this threat is felt all the more acutely because of other political antagonisms, for example between *Orba*'s military leaders, fearful of the unsettling pressures coming from orthodox Muslim quarters, and the Muslim parties, especially NU and the PSII. Contributing factors also are the frustrating divisions within the Indonesian *Ummat Islam* (that is the Muslim community), its inability to provide sufficient young and new leadership that can play a united role in national affairs, and to develop a missionizing zeal comparable to that of some of the Christian churches today.

Even more moderate and modern-educated Muslims have sometimes been caught up in these antagonisms. It bodes ill for future religious tolerance in Indonesia that at its 14-19 April 1970 session the executive council of the PMI, meeting in Djakarta, called on the Government to (1) prohibit the construction of a Baptist hospital in Bukittingi, West Sumatra, and declare every Christian missionary in the region *persona non grata*, (2) regulate construction of houses of worship "in proportion to the beliefs professed by the majority of the local population", and (3) stop the inflow of all foreign Christian missionaries. In private conversation PMI spokesmen appear less militant, to be sure, and it is difficult to escape the feeling that the party's demands were frequently dictated by political considerations stemming from the then forthcoming elections and the competition coming from

NU and more conservative Islamic leaders. Even so the channels of communication between the Christian and Muslim communities are becoming ominously clogged.

And, of course, the old racial antagonisms remain. On 6 November 1969 *Warta Harian* reported a statement by a representative of KAPNI, the action front of Indonesian businessmen "who are nationals" (that is autochthonously Indonesian), complaining not only about the present "paralysed condition" of the enterprises of "national" businessmen, but also asserting that present conditions and government policies appeared to favour unduly the enterprises "of Chinese who have been naturalized". KAPNI's representative, in effect, asked parliamentary assistance in curtailing the business operations of naturalized Indonesians of Chinese origin. In a message to the PNI congress on 2 February 1970, MPRS chairman Nasution indirectly seemed to amplify this demand when he noted with apparent approval the call for greater "social control" voiced by "national businessmen" worried about the down-turn in their enterprises. The nature of the "social control" sought was not spelt out, but there is little doubt that these statements reflect the mounting pressure for legislation that would, to all intents and purposes, discriminate against entrepreneurs of Chinese origin, even if naturalized Indonesian citizens. Reference has been made earlier (see chapter VII) to the so-called *tjukong* issue in this connection.

After the *Gestapu* affair, it will be recalled, there were waves of anti-Chinese outbursts and the legal and civic status of thousands of Indonesian Chinese was placed in jeopardy as a result of the temporary halt in naturalization proceedings and the repeal of the Sino-Indonesian Dual Nationality Treaty of 1955-60 (see chapter VIII). On 7 June 1967, it may be recalled, the Suharto Government began to promulgate a new policy for Chinese aliens which, in return for their enforced assimilation, opened the way to new citizenship legitimization. Chinese and "every alien" were now promised protection of life and business, but work permits would not be issued to new Chinese immigrants, special Chinese schools would not be allowed, political organizations of alien Chinese would be forbidden, the celebration of Chinese festivals would henceforth occur "inconspicuously", and Chinese business capital would be carefully regulated. Indonesianization of names and way of life among Chinese was strongly encouraged, and on 6 December 1967 a new government regulation provided that naturalized Chinese would have the same rights and duties as other Indonesian citizens. Special Staffs for Chinese Affairs were organized by the Government throughout the country in order to implement these regulations, as meanwhile the naturalization

238

process was resumed and somewhat simplified and eased. During much of 1968, as Chinese sought to adjust to the pressures of assimilation, it seemed that the new Suharto policies might work, promising new security for and stability in the relations of Chinese with the rest of Indonesian society.

But there was always a question whether more orthodox and extreme Muslims would allow assimilation, and, for that matter, whether traditions of Chinese self-exclusiveness could or would be broken down so easily. Inevitably, as the earlier cited complaint of the KAPNI representative indicates, the economic factor intruded into the problem, quickly exploited by such parties as the PNI and NU where the autochthonous, non-Chinese Indonesian businessman has tended to find political leverage. The old antagonisms between *asli* (autochthonous) and *asing* (non-autochthonous, for example Chinese) economics policies and preferences, already acute in the early nineteen-fifties, now appear to be returning once more despite official policies to the contrary, and the promise of a new assimilated existence for the Indonesian Chinese is again eroding. The elections too have probably further aggravated the Chinese problem. Consider the statement reported by Antara on 2 February 1970 of an Immigration Service spokesman in Pontianak, West Kalimantan, who declared that the 20,000 Chinese refugees in his area would present considerable difficulties to the local authorities at the time of the elections because a majority of them claimed to be Indonesian citizens but said that their citizenship documents had been lost. The refugees in question, it may be remembered (see chapter V), were victims of anti-PGRS operations in West Kalimantan, during which many local Chinese were indiscriminately harassed and maltreated. The above-mentioned Immigration Service official alleged further that difficulties over Chinese voting rights in his area were being compounded by the fact that "the Chinese have up till now failed to adapt their customs and attitudes towards the natives". It is observations of this type which perhaps illustrate *ad oculos* what is wrong with current official interpretations of *Bhinneka tunggal ika* and which cause one to fear for the country's future social stability.

Enough happened before the elections to provide ample grounds to Suharto's enemies for continuous attacks on his regime. It is not altogether unfair to compare the manner in which the Suharto Government sought to control the elections with its tight supervision of West Irian's "act of free choice". Weeks before the polling, government spokesmen made it known that the election results would not be permitted to influence established Government policies. For example, in the middle of April 1971,

Suharto's personal assistant on economic affairs, Brigadier-General Sudjono Humardani declared in Hong Kong that the election outcome would not affect in any way the present "liberalized policy on foreign investments in Indonesia". By the end of March 1971, 555 candidates of parties and functional groups for the elections had been declared ineligible by the General Elections Committee on the grounds of "lack of required personal data", including information on possible involvement in the *Gestapu* affair. The notion that the Government was screening out candidates with political beliefs that it disapproved of was difficult to resist under such circumstances. Such suspicions were were confirmed further by the extensive restrictions on the conduct of the election campaign announced by the Government later in 1970. Candidates were not allowed to criticize President Suharto, the failure of the Government to implement its announced policies or programme, or to do anything that might contribute to a "come-back" of the PKI.

Those associated with the Suharto regime repeatedly and publicly asserted that the *Golkar* would win. Home Minister Mahmud did so, for example, in early February 1971, basing his election prediction on the fact that a number of cabinet members had joined the list of *Golkar* candidates. On 26 April 1971, Army intelligence chief Major-General Ali Murtopo said that the *Golkar* would be victorious because "of the infrastructure available to it". *Golkar,* said Murtopo, who had major responsibility for the elections campaigning of functional group candidates, was able to use government communications facilities, Army transport and other services! *Golkar* candidates also had "unchallenged financial resources". Such statements, while one might admire their frankness, have not been conducive to enhancing respect for the fairness of the elections. Neither has Suharto's interference in a new leadership problem in the PMI (*Parmusi*). When on 23 November 1970 Suharto intervened in the leadership crisis of the PMI, and appointed Muhammad Mintaredja to head the party, there were not just sharp repercussions throughout the party, but also pointed press queries as to the legality and desirability of such presidential intervention. In fairness, one should hasten to add that the conflict over *Parmusi*'s executive is of long standing (see chapter III) and that Suharto had been closely involved in it from the beginning. But the split in the PMI leadership, which matured during 1969-70, involving the formation of rival executive boards, and, reflecting the relative diversity of the party's organizational sub-components, was hardly of the kind which one could hope to settle by means of presidential fiat. Whatever Suharto's good intentions, the decision to intervene in the PMI leadership problem further accentuated an already prominent authoritarian image. It is developments such as these which continue to tarnish *Orba*'s reputation, at home and also abroad.

On 3 July 1971, in Indonesia's first general elections in sixteen years, voters gave *Sekber Golkar* its expected victory at the polls. The *Golkar* won about 60 per cent of the votes cast nationwide, and its strength was particularly impressive in such areas as West Java and Bali where it won 76 per cent and 77.5 per cent, respectively, of all votes. It is clear that along with the 100 seats reserved for the military and their functional associates in Parliament, the Suharto regime, through *Golkar*'s victory, will control at least an additional 250 seats (of the 360 seats up for election) in the new House, providing it with a comfortable working majority — at least in theory. The PNI, NU and *Parmusi* demonstrated their continuing viability, but the future of such parties as *Perti*, *Murba*, PSII and IPKI seems very much in doubt. *Golkar*'s resounding victory is likely to lead to a number of party mergers in the future.

While election day itself was free from major incidents and no instances of fraud in the tabulation of votes have thus far been reported, there is no denying that *Orba*'s heavy hand during the election campaign was widely and bitterly resented. The arrest in May of Hadji T. Hussein, secretary to House Speaker and NU leader Sjaichu; of *Parmusi* leader Suratman, in Central Java, and of another active *Parmusi* campaigner Siregar Pahoe, in Kalimantan; and the arrest in June of PNI leaders Oktavianus Rutasou, in Maluku, and Kosasih Kartawiria, in West Java — all presumably on grounds of "subversive" activity — tended to buttress charges that the Government was seeking to intimidate political opponents. So did the brief ban, just before election day, of the papers *Harian Kami* and NU's *Duta Masjarakat*, and the warning to another daily, *Sinar Harapan*, not to permit circulation of a story dealing with military corruption (*Sinar Harapan*'s editor and his staff took to the streets to recall copies of the paper that had carried the banned story).

In a number of localities election meetings were banned by the military; elsewhere *Golkar* supporters, who had broken up gatherings of rival parties and started fights, went unpunished. Protests by students and particularly by NU leaders over *Golkar*'s strong-arm methods went unheeded until after the elections, when *Golkar* chairman Lieutenant-General S. Sokawati promised an investigation. Public resentment crystallized in such informal groups as the *Golput* (from *Golongan Putih*, literally the "White Organization"), which urged Indonesians *not* to vote, presumably in protest over the unfairness of elections procedures. Like

241

Golput, the Committee for the Support of People's Sovereignty (*Komité Penegak Kedaulatan Rakjat*) was largely organized by Djakarta youth leaders but set itself specifically the task of collecting information on intimidation of candidates and parties during the elections campaign. In a special category fall the so-called *Komando Djihad* (Holy War Commands), groups of extremist Muslims, egged on by fanatical *ulama* (Muslim scholars) urging a "holy war" against all but the most orthodox Muslim candidates. The *Komando*'s "war" turned out to be largely verbal, however, while elsewhere the Government met no opposition in banning *Golput* or the *Komité*. Though there is little doubt of the fairness of the election itself, the Suharto regime's questionable campaign tactics through the *Golkar* organization are not likely to enhance its image, at home or abroad.

For the time being Suharto need not be too greatly concerned about this. But if *Orba* fails to bring significant and tangible material benefits to the mass of Indonesians in the future, its heavy-handed, semi-military character will increasingly become unsupportable. Not just from the surviving major parties and the students but also from within the heterogeneous *Golkar* organization itself the pressures for change are likely to make themselves felt. One must hope that a regime conceived, to some degree at least, as a reaction to one of contemporary Southeast Asia's more prominent political mixtures of authoritarianism and mismanagement will not itself also succumb in the end to the failures and follies of its predecessor.

Bibliographical Note and
Suggestions for Further Reading

THE LITERATURE on modern Indonesia is large and growing. The beginning reader seeking general background information can make his choice from a burgeoning number of volumes, and recommendations are apt to become subjective. A standard reference work, though now somewhat dated, is Ruth T. McVey, editor, *Indonesia*, Yale University Human Relations Area Files, Taplinger, New York, 1963, which contains chapters on most of the country's major concerns and problems written by specialists. Also informative is a more recent compilation by prominent Australian scholars and edited by T. K. Tan, *Sukarno's Guided Indonesia*, The Jacaranda Press, Brisbane, 1967. Among the more popular general surveys that of Leslie Palmier, *Indonesia*, Walker and Company, New York, 1965, can be recommended. For various analyses of Indonesian social institutions and problems see, for example, W. F. Wertheim, *Indonesian Society in Transition*, W. van Hoeve Ltd, The Hague, 1956; Clifford Geertz, *The Religion of Java*, The Free Press, Glencoe, Illinois, 1960; and Koentjaraningrat, editor, *Villages in Indonesia*, Cornell University Press, Ithaca, New York, 1967.

A comprehensive, national history of Indonesia in the English language remains to be written, but J. D. Legge, *Indonesia*, Prentice Hall, Englewood Cliffs, 1964, a publication in Prentice-Hall's series "The Modern Nations in Historical Perspective", and B. H. M. Vlekke, *Nusantara: A History of Indonesia*, revised edition, Quadrangle Books, Chicago, W. van Hoeve Ltd, The Hague and Bandung, 1960, provide useful introductory insights. There is no complete and balanced account of the origins and development of Indonesian nationalism. The pioneering study by George McT. Kahin, *Nationalism and Revolution in Indonesia*, Cornell University Press, Ithaca, New York, 1952, is, however, frequently cited. For the rise of Indonesian nationalism in the first two decades of the present century, Robert van Niel, *The Emergence of the Modern Indonesian Elite*, W. van Hoeve Ltd, The Hague and Bandung, 1960, should also be consulted. Though marred by inaccuracies and often by a lack of realism the study of Herbert Feith, *The Decline of Constitutional Democracy in Indonesia*, Cornell University Press, Ithaca, New York, 1962, remains valuable for a consideration of Indonesian politics in the nineteen-fifties. Stephen A. Douglas, *Political Socialization and Student Activism in Indonesia*, Illinois Studies in the Social Sciences, University of Illinois Press, Urbana, Chicago and London, 1970, is an important contribution to the politics of the student movement.

Indonesia has some two dozen principal dailies and several news weeklies. Chronologies of current events are also provided by the daily bulletin of the Antara news agency and, periodically, also by *Asian Almanac* and *Keesing's Contemporary Archives*. Short synopses of the Indonesian press, topically arranged, and brief surveys of major political and other developments are also regularly carried by the quarterly *Review of Indonesian and Malayan Affairs* of the University of Sydney. The monthly bulletin of the Indonesian Current Affairs Translation Service, published in Djakarta, reproduces excellent translations in English, along with helpful editorial comments, of some of the major articles in Indonesian newspapers and weeklies, and offers a comprehensive chronology of chief happenings in each bulletin issue. Some Indonesian newspapers, like *The Djakarta Times*, periodically also carry columns of summaries of articles and editorials that have appeared in other dailies. All these publications, and in particular the Antara daily news bulletin, the *Review of Indonesian and Malayan Affairs* and the monthly of the Indonesian Current Affairs Translation Service, have throughout the preparation of the present volume directed the author to relevant Indonesian press reports and/or assisted in structuring the description of the chronology of events.

The attempted coup of 30 September 1965 and the subsequent fall of Sukarno are likely to remain among the most controversial issues in Indonesian scholarship for years to come. For some different and essentially synoptic views see John Hughes, *Indonesian Upheaval*, David McKay Company, New York, 1967; Lucien Rey, "Dossier of the Indonesian Drama", *New Left Review*, March-April 1966, pp. 26-40; Nugroho Notosusanto and Ismail Saleh, *The Coup Attempt of the "September 30 Movement" in Indonesia*, P. T. Pembimbing Masa, Djakarta, 1968; Arnold C. Brackman, *The Communist Collapse in Indonesia*, W. W. Norton and Company, New York, 1969; and Robert Shaplen, *Time out of Hand. Revolution and Reaction in Southeast Asia*, Harper and

Row. New York and London, 1969, chapter II, "Indonesia: Sleeping Beauty".

A semi-official biography is that of O. G. Roeder, *The Smiling President*: *President Suharto of Indonesia*, Gunung Agung, Djakarta, 1969. Roeder's brief articles on Indonesia which regularly appear in the *Far Eastern Economic Review*, Hong Kong, are among the more cogent descriptions of current Indonesian events, including the complexities surrounding the recent elections and the role of the military. On relations between Suharto, the parties and Parliament described in chapters III and IV, the author has particularly relied on the informative essays by Herbert Feith, "Suharto's Search for a Political Format", *Indonesia*, Cornell University, October 1968, pp. 88-105 (an earlier version of this article appeared in *Australia's Neighbours*, May-June 1968); Kenneth Ward, "Some Comments on Islamic Reactions to Recent Developments in Indonesia", *Review of Indonesian and Malayan Affairs*, April-June 1968, pp. 37-46; Allan A. Samson, "Islam in Indonesian Politics", *Asian Survey*, December 1968, pp. 1001-17; and Djakarta press comment. See also Donald Hindley, "Dilemmas of Concensus and Division: Indonesia's Search for a Political Format", *Government and Opposition*, vol. 4, 1969, pp. 70-99.

Various aspects of the Indonesian Communist resurgence since 1965 are briefly, but succinctly, dealt with by O. G. Roeder in *Far Eastern Economic Review*, 31 August 1967, and 22 August 1968, and by Jean Contenay, also in *Far Eastern Economic Review*, 23 November 1967, and 11 and 25 January 1968. For the development of Indonesian Communism and the background of recent Communist underground activity see Justus M. van der Kroef, *The Communist Party of Indonesia, its History, Program and Tactics*, University of British Columbia, Vancouver, 1965, and "How Dead is the Indonesian Communist Party?", *Communist Affairs*, University of Southern California, January-February 1967, pp. 3-10. See also Donald Hindley, *The Communist Party of Indonesia 1951-1963*, University of California Press, Berkeley, 1964.

Indispensable for an understanding of the more recent aspects of the West New Guinea problem are the reports of United Nations Secretary-General U Thant, of Dr F. Ortiz Sanz, and of the Indonesian Government on the "act of free choice" and the discussions of these by various UN delegates. A preliminary version of these documents is available (see United Nations General Assembly, 24th session, agenda item 98, A/7723, 6 November 1969, and A/PV. 1810, 13 November 1969, and A/PV. 1812, 19 November 1969). See also N. A. Jaspan, "West Irian: The First

Two Years", *The Australian Quarterly*, June 1965, pp. 9-21, and Peter Hastings, "West Irian— 1969", *New Guinea*, Sydney, September-October 1968, pp. 12-22 For the historic and legal backgrounds of the West New Guinea question generally, see, for example. Robert C. Bone, *The Dynamics of the Western New Guinea (Irian Barat) Problem*, Modern Indonesia Project, second printing, Cornell University Press, Ithaca, New York, 1962; Justus M. van der Kroef, *The West New Guinea Dispute*, Institute of Pacific Relations, New York, 1958; and Rosalyn Higgins, *United Nations Peacekeeping 1946-1967: Documents and Commentary: II Asia*, Oxford University Press, London, 1970, part 2, "United Nations Observers and Security Force (UNSF) in West Irian, 1962-3".

Currently the best-informed analyses of the Indonesian economy, as well as relevant statistical data, appear in the *Bulletin of Indonesian Economic Studies*, published three times a year by the Australian National University Press, Canberra. Equally valuable are the *Quarterly Economic Review* and annual supplements on Indonesia, published by The Economist Intelligence Unit of London. Useful background information on the economic problems and prospects of the Suharto regime is provided by J. Panglaykim and H.W. Arndt, *The Indonesian Economy: Facing a New Era?*, Rotterdam University Press, 1966; K. D. Thomas and J. Panglaykim, *Indonesian Exports: Performance and Prospects 1950-1970*, Rotterdam University Press, 1967; and K. D. Thomas and J. Panglaykim, "Notes on Indonesia's New Five-Year Plan", *Australia's Neighbours*, March-April 1969, pp. 1-7. The last-named essay, and an article by an unnamed "Economist in Indonesia" in the *Bulletin of Indonesian Economic Studies*, July 1969, are particularly useful for summaries of aims and allocations of the Five-Year Plan. Use also has been made of the plan itself, as described in *Rentjana Pembangunan Lima Tahun 1969/70-1973/74* (Djakarta, Departemèn Penerangan, 1969), 5 vols.

There is no comprehensive study of Indonesia's foreign relations in the Suharto or for that matter in any other era. Russell H. Fifield, *The Diplomacy of Southeast Asia 1945-1958*, Harper, New York, 1958, chapter V and *passim*, though dated, can still be consulted for the earlier period. For recent policy changes see Justus M. van der Kroef, "The Sino-Indonesian Rupture", *The China Quarterly*, January-March 1969, and two articles by Peter Howard, "The USSR and Indonesia" and "Moscow, Jakarta and the PKI", both in *Mizan*, London, May-June 1967, pp. 108-17, and March-April 1969, pp. 105-18, respectively. See also V. Viktorov, "Indonesia's Hour of Trial", *International Affairs*, Moscow, December 1968, pp. 42-7.

Index

Garuda, 106
Gasbiindo, 55
General Elections Institute, 218
Gerakan Wanita Indonesia (Gerwani). See Indonesian Women's Movement
Gerakan Mahasiswa Indonesia (Germindo). See Indonesian Students Movement
gerilja politik (gerpol). See political guerilla warfare
Gerakan Tiga Puluh September (Gestapu), 1-19, 22-3, 52, 70, 75, 88, 90, 98, 115, 123, 131, 183-4, 200, 215
golongan karja (golkar). See functional groups
gotong rojong, 46
Guam Doctrine, 208
guided democracy, 33, 46, 48, 51-3, 57, 68, 70-3, 84
guided economy, 78

Hadikusumo, Djarnawai, 216
Hadisubeno, 50
Halim Air Force base, 6-7, 11-3, 18
Hamengku Buwono, 30, 138, 161
Hardi, 50
Harian Kami, 78, 101
Harjono, Anwar, 56
Hartini, 74, 104, 109
Harun, Lukman, 58
Hastings, Peter, 127-8
Hatta, Mohammad, 28, 44, 54, 140, 200, 233
Hawkins, Bob, 153
Hidup Nasakom. See Long Live *Nasakom* organization
Himpunan Mahasiswa Indonesia (HMI). See Indonesian University Students Association
Ho Chi Minh, 206
Holden affair, 76
Hong Kong, 120, 149, 154
Hutapea, Oloan, 96-7, 100-3, 106, 122
Hutton, Geoffrey, 150

1-am-a-Sukarno-Supporter organization, 20, 91
Independence Upholders Party (IPKI), 48, 61, 98, 225
Independent Group, 47-8, 52, 57-8
India, 204
Indian Ocean, 192-4
Indonesian Christian Party, 26, 47, 57, 61

Indonesian Islamic Party, 55, 58-9, 61, 63, 180, 216, 218, 224-5, 237, 241-2
Indonesian National Party (PNI), 14, 19, 20, 23, 28, 35, 38, 47, 49, 59, 61, 70, 73-4, 91, 98, 101, 105, 137, 220-1, 225, 239
Indonesian People's Liberation Army (LPRI), 99, 102
Indonesian People's Liberation Army (TPRI), 92, 96, 98, 101-2, 122
Indonesian People's Republic, 101-2
Indonesian Socialist Party, 20, 47-8, 51, 58, 212, 216-8
Indonesian Student Action Front, 18, 20, 23-4, 26, 32, 38, 47, 60, 62, 66-7, 76, 227
Indonesian Students Movement, 32
Indonesian Tribune, 100, 116, 119
Indonesian University Students Association, 97
Indonesian Women's Movement, 6
Indonesia Raya, 78, 89, 200, 213, 230
industry, 167-8
inflation (See also economic problems), 40, 231
Institute for the Defence of Basic Human Rights, 71-2
Inter-Governmental Group on Indonesia (IGGI), 164-6, 181, 208
Irian Barat. See West New Guinea
Islam, 51, 57, 108, 210, 213, 223
Islamic state concept, 53-4, 57
Ismail, Ahmad, 113
Israel, 210

Japan, 2-3, 84, 149, 165-6, 197, 203-4
Jasin, Mohammad (Army Major-General), 103-4
Jillett, Neill, 114
Jouwe, Nicolaas, 130, 133-4, 147-8

Kabinet Pembangunan. See Development Cabinet
Kala Tjakra, 101
Kamaruzaman. See Sjam
KAMI. See Indonesian Student Action Front
KAP-Gestapu. See Action Front for the Crushing of *Gestapu*
Kartakusumah, R. (Army Lieutenant-General), 87
Kartosuwirjo, 217
Kasiepo, Frans, 147
Kasiepo, Marcus, 133, 147-8, 151
kelompok persatuan. See union group
Kennedy, John F., 4

251

Supardjo, M. S. (Army Brigadier-General), 7, 10, 12, 18, 36
Surabaya's People's Guerilla Movement, 96
Surachman, 49, 98, 103
Sutjipto (Army Brigadier-General), 131
Sutowo, Ibnu, 79, 230
Sydney Morning Herald, The, 144, 150

Tamins, 14
Team Pemberantasan Korupsi (TPK), 76
Tentara Nasional Kalimantan Utara (TNKU). See National Army of North Kalimantan
Tentara Pembebasan Rakjat Indonesia (TPRI). See Indonesian People's Liberation Army
Thailand, 200
Thomas, K. D., 161
three banners, 100, 117
Tianlean, Bakri Abdulgani, 138
Tjugito. See Siam
tjukong, 181, 238
trade unions, 22
transmigration, 178-9
Tricontinental, 9
Trisula, 103-4

unemployment, 176-7, 234
union group, 225
United Indonesian Islamic Party, 47, 57, 59, 140, 214, 217, 225, 237
United Nations, 6-7, 22, 134, 142-3, 146-7, 152, 184, 186, 209-10
United States, 18, 65, 122, 141, 165-6, 195, 204, 207-8, 211
US Defence Liaison Group, 196
United States Information Service, 5

Universitas Rakjat. See People's University
Untung (Army Lieutenant-Colonel), 8-12, 19
Usman, K. H. Fakih, 54
USSR, 115-9, 165-7, 190, 192, 211
U Thant, 136, 142-3
Utomo, Kusno (Army Major-General), 109
Utomo Ramelan, 8
Utrecht, E., 175

veterans, 62
Viet Cong, 96-7, 103, 198
Vietnam, Democratic Republic of, 182, 198, 206-8, 209, 211
Vietnam, Republic of, 206-8
Vietnam war, 197, 199, 206

Walujo. See Muljono
Wardhana, Ali, 82
Warta Harian, 136, 181, 205, 238
West Germany, 141, 165
West New Guinea (Irian, West Irian Irian Barat), 3-4, 45, 108, 125-55, 200
West Papua Liberation Front, 141
Widjajasastra, Ruslan, 95
Wilopo, 78, 233
Wilson, Harold, 130
Wirjomartono, 120, 190
Witono, A. J. (Army Major-General), 112-3, 221
World Marxist Review, 9, 95, 116
World War II, 2-3

Yani, Ahmad (Army Lieutenant-General), 11-2, 15
Yap Thiam Hien, 70-1
Yugoslavia, 191

Zambia, 209